I0105220

Light Garden

a handbook for planetary rejuvenation

by Anne Whittingham

Dedication: This book is dedicated to the living creatures of planet Earth who are born in the 21st century, plus my own wonderful family and friends, past and present. It is intended for readers interested in making the changes that are needed to rejuvenate Life in the 21st century. The book presents a new *Light Garden* model that draws upon the subjects of light, the beauty of nature, quantum biophysics and the interaction between the spiritual and practical dimensions of Life. It considers how humanity may best manage natural resources, society and climate change in the 21st century. The potential of cooperative collaboration in those fields to make a positive contribution to Life in the 21st century inspired me to write this book.

Acknowledgements
Dr John Tyman, Aysha Sun, Irene Brown, Professor Robert Pope,
Sandra van Woesik, John Whittingham, Manna Hart, Jude Fanton,
Dede Callichy, Jain, Helena Norberg-Hodge, George Williams, Neil Howe,
Dr Liz Elliott, Dr Jacqueline Christensen, Helena den Exter, Melanie Saunders.

Third edition, paperback, July 2021. Reprinted March 2022.
Copyright Anne Whittingham

ISBN: 978-0-6487308-3-5

All rights reserved. The material contained within this book is protected by copyright law. No part may be copied, reproduced, presented, stored, communicated or transmitted in any form by any means without prior written permission. All enquiries should be directed to the author.

This book is also available in ebook format: ISBN 978-0-6487308-4-2

Self-published by Anne Whittingham,
PO Box 349, Billinudgel, NSW 2483, Australia.

Email: annewhit@internode.on.net

Printed in Australia

For further information about orders:

https://amazon.com or email to annewhit@internode.on.net

A catalogue record for this book is available from the National Library of Australia

Some of the content of this book was first published in full colour paperback and ebook formats in December 2019 as "Light and Quantum Biophysics in the 21st century: Globalisation, Extinction and Cultures that revere and sustainably harvest sunlight," by Anne Whittingham. That book was re-titled, updated and published April 2020 as "Cultures that revere and sustainably harvest sunlight – a 21st century perspective: ten principles and a model for rejuvenation the living systems of Earth.

Disclaimer: The material in this publication is of the nature of general comment only, and does not represent professional advice. It is not intended to provide specific guidance for particular circumstances and it should not be relied on as the basis for any decision to take action or not take action on any matter which it covers. Readers should obtain professional advice where appropriate, before making any such decision. To the maximum extent permitted by law, the author and publisher disclaim all responsibility and liability to any person, arising directly or indirectly from any person taking or not taking action based on the information in this publication.

Contents

Preface

In early 2017 I was living in Australia and working on a book and a website about common principles that underlie the design of beautiful gardens the world over. The beauty of nature had long fascinated me, beginning well before I decided to build a career as a Landscape Architect and Planner. Now, after several decades of working in professional and volunteer community group roles, I felt the time was right to share what I had learned and discovered with others.

Having written that first book, I continued to research how beauty manifests in nature. The world of nature is vast and the innate human response to natural beauty transcends culture. As part of my research, I discovered the world of quantum biophysics, which describes how living organisms organise the repair, reproduction and growth of living cells.

That subject took me back to my interests as a teenager when I studied various arts and sciences. I understood how sunlight powers the process of photosynthesis in plants and thus supports the growth of many living organisms. Since those early years, I had also known that humanity was not managing the Earth's natural resources in a sustainable way. We needed to make some radical changes to avoid resource depletion, adverse impacts on human health and climate disaster. Hence it was important to study and write about the cultural, political, health and economic dimensions to this scenario, as well as the scientific ones.

By 2017 I had added another dimension to these concerns. Having gone back to university and developed a second career as a Low Vision Specialist, I had learnt much about how our eyes respond to and process light. Light entering our eyes passes to the retina at the back of the eye. In the retina, special cells called photoreceptors initiate a series of impulses that lead to visual information being transmitted via the brain. I could see an exciting interface between light and the messages sent through living cells. This interface exists in the human body and the leaves of plants.

Light travels in discrete parcels called *photons*. Albert Einstein was the first to use that term *photons* in a paper that he published in 1905. We now know that living organisms emit what are called biophotons. They also a communicate through biophotons. Biophotons are photons emitted by living organisms. Reading more about this, I soon discovered the world of photonics and learned how with nanoscale-sized wires, photons, rather than electrons, are transmitted in a range of hi-tech 21st century devices. For example, the application of this technology through the Optical Coherence Tomography imaging technique allows the ten different layers of cells found in the retina of the human eye to be seen quite clearly.

This technique was familiar to me through my work in eye specialist clinics. However, there were still questions remaining. What were the basic principles of quantum biophysics and how did these relate to light? Were there some unique dimensions to this interface in living organisms that might also provide keys to developing better ways to manage natural resources and climate at the larger scale? The answers to these questions led me to create the *Light Garden* model.

I found that quantum biophysics has a strong foundation of synergistic, multiplication effects that arise because of the way in which living organisms align with the magnetic and gravitational fields of the Earth and harvest plasma energy from the Sun. The *Light Garden* model is a logical extension of this.

It makes *living* systems the focus and priority of our activities, rather than allowing abstract concepts such as "economic" growth to continue to deplete these natural resources and climate. When we choose to make decisions based on criteria that align with how living systems operate, we can expect quantum biophysics multiplication effects to arise. In turn, we can expect these to give us the boost we need to rapidly address the natural resource and climate management issues that have so far eluded effective management.

To test the *Light Garden* model for its usefulness in a range of cultures around the globe, over the next three years I researched and wrote about historical and contemporary roles of light in cultures from each continent. This process validated the usefulness and relevance of the model across a range of different cultures. The model was also found to apply to varying scales from the local to the global. I discovered some excellent examples of where *Light Gardens* already existed. I also found many more opportunities to integrate the *Light Garden* concept, as part of the rejuvenation of employment, local cultures, natural resources and climate in the 21st century. To make the *Light Garden* model and the fundamental quantum biophysics principles that it is derived from more easily understood, I also developed some illustrations and the mnemonic that is described in Chapter 2.

Introduction

Sweeping across the globe that is planet Earth, each day a wave of sunlight calls forth Life. The light comes not from a tiny source, but in great abundance. This book aims to promote an expanded awareness of light, as part of humanity's efforts to rejuvenate the living systems on this planet that we call home.

Towards the end of his life, Albert Einstein, the Noble Prize winning Physicist, was still speculating about the nature of light. Many other scientists have continued working in related fields since then. They have developed more comprehensive understandings about physics, light and other associated phenomena. The fields of quantum biophysics and photonics have also evolved. A summary of the history of these developments is given in the next chapter, in addition to a discussion of some related concepts.

Based around the *Light Garden* model that is developed, this book aims to articulate and promote an expanded consciousness of light at two scales. The first scale can be usefully applied in both the theory and the practice of farming and gardening. The second scale is global in extent. It addresses regeneration of Earth's natural living systems during our current era, which has been described as the Anthropocene. The Anthropocene is a term used by many scientists to describe the current geological age, where human influence has impacted the geochemistry of the Earth, the atmosphere, the oceans and terrestrial ecosystems. Although there is much debate about when the Anthropocene started, the time of the Industrial Revolution may be taken as a guide.[1]

The book's *Light Garden theme* is illustrated by examples of cultural movements for self-reliant communities living in harmony with nature, light, and beauty. These movements are quite diverse and include coalitions of indigenous peoples; organic farmers; traditional cultures and various city-based communities and groups in the 21st century. Many of these groups use state of the art, innovative technology to foster effective action for group decision making, meaningful employment for all, access to natural resources, management of climate change and related subjects. For example, in North America, many urban communities have generated employment that is based around community agriculture and gardens. In rural areas, Amish communities continue to use centuries-old techniques of organic agriculture. At the same time, they also embrace appropriate new technology, where their members agree that it is compatible with and supportive of their traditional values.

Why is the *Light Garden* theme linked with communities seeking to live in harmony with nature, light and beauty? Why is beauty relevant? Beauty is not restricted to the eye of the beholder. There is a high degree of consensus about natural beauty and the life-sustaining principles that it embodies. It is time to re-examine old notions, such as *beauty is in the eye of the beholder.* Natural beauty naturally evolves when the Life force is allowed to unfold. Many of us in the modern world have been trained *not* to expect beauty to be part of the attainable, essential and cooperative mosaic of the social, economic and environmental justice that is needed for Life as we move through the 21st century.

As described in Chapter Two, our perception of beauty is linked to how fractal patterns form in nature. Human perception of beauty is intrinsically woven into the processes that create natural Life on Earth.

It both *transcends* culture and is a common language *between* cultures. This process of perception and subsequent communication is reflected in the *Light Garden* model developed in this book. For example, the *Light Garden* model includes the principles of *"Storage and Sharing of Information"*, *"Perception and Measurement"*, and *"Human Use"*. These principles provide specific tools to help benchmark and evaluate the effectiveness of proposed action in the context of managing natural and human resources on a *Light Garden* planet.

Encompassing beauty, harmony, order and balance is the essence of the Navaho philosophy.[2] That essence is included within the philosophies of other cultures, such as some contemporary African cultures and the ancient Greek and Chinese cultures. As modern men and women, born to travel on our endless journeys through space as planet Earth rotates, we too can embody that essence of beauty. It is my hope that this book may help humanity work collectively towards that goal and be part of the rejuvenation of the living ecosystems of the Earth.

Each chapter of the book focuses on different aspects of the *Light Garden* concept. For example, light as a form of plasma is introduced in Chapter Two, while subsequent chapters consider *Light Gardens* in different cultures around the globe. Different cultures can be compared in terms of Sun worship traditions but there is space in this book for only a few comparisons of that nature. Other texts, such as *"Ancient Religion of the Sun"* by Lara Atwood, have described that history of sun worship in far more detail.[3]

Plasma science, photonics and quantum biophysics are some of the disciplines that now influence the human understanding of light. So far, these concepts are largely unknown to the general public. As described in this book, they are compatible with many traditional religious and cultural practices. It is only a matter of time before they are more widely known. Once comprehended, the concepts expand our knowledge of the conditions that support life and how we may work towards rejuvenating Earth's living systems.

In Chapter 3, the fascinating history of Feng Shui as a form of energy in North Asian cultures is considered. The fourth chapter describes how *Light Garden* principles are reflected in historic Islamic paradise gardens. Contemporary 21st century innovations in the Islamic city of Dubai are then discussed. There is the potential for this type of innovative settlements in arid environments to be established as viable new homes for millions of refugees. These global citizens seek identity, shelter, long term sustainable settlements, meaningful employment and happy communities. This concept is described further with an example from Bangladesh in Chapter 6.

As described in Chapter 5, Africa too has millions of refugees who have been forcibly displaced from their traditional homes, as governments and corporations engage in grabs for power, land, resources, sunlight and water. These conditions create a challenging environment in which to consider the viability of the *Light Garden* concept. Once again, by comparing some traditional villages to 21st century alternatives, the validity of the basic underlying principles of the *Light Garden* model can be seen to unfold as a means to support human rights, plus equitable management of climate and other natural resources.

Moving from Africa to India, the radiance of light that has underpinned Indian culture for millennia is gradually revealed in Chapter 6. This is done through a series of vignettes on biodiversity civilisation, ancient groves, traditional villages, temple gardens and contemporary developments. As described in Chapter 7, the biodiversity and use of light in Europe have been different from in India. India has a rich scientific tradition but Europe was the birthplace of the 20th century scientists who developed the principles of quantum physics. In the 21st century, that work, in turn, blossomed into the international field of quantum biophysics.

European culture started impacting on South American cultures in the 15th century. Machu Pichu was one of the most famous settlements that eluded capture by the conquistadors. It is one of several South American sites and discussed in relation to the *Light Garden* model described in Chapter 8.

North American culture has included many frontiers and milestones in the ongoing development of farming practices, settlements, technology and the use of light. Chapter 9 begins with a description of a number of these. They are then considered in terms of how well these sites rate as *Light Gardens*. Some, such as the farming communities of the Amish, rate well as *Light Gardens*. Others operate in a more constrained context. For example, the famous floral displays of Butchart Gardens on Vancouver Island are considered beautiful by many visitors. However, the site as a whole achieves a moderate rating in terms of *Light Garden* principles.

Moving to a broader scale, in Chapter 10 the management of the forests of South East Asia is considered in relation to *Light Garden* principles. Management of these forests could make a huge and immediate difference to humanity's capacity to manage climate change at the global scale. This discussion is supplemented in Chapter 11 with practical examples of smaller scale *Light Garden* innovations and trends in the 21st century. These examples are followed by a review of several examples of *Light Garden* trends in the 21st century. The book concludes with a summary of the *Light Garden* decision making criteria and their usefulness for establishing more effective means of managing climate change, natural resources, economies and society. When we focus on rejuvenating Earth's living systems, there are livelihoods and meaningful roles for all!

Light Garden

1

An expanded consciousness of light

Image 1. *Young Men pause and reflect in the light of late afternoon*

Why would you read a book about *Light Gardens*? Perhaps you are aware that human health depends upon the Life-giving energy of the Sun and you would like to know more about how to harness it skillfully for food production. Perhaps climate change concerns you, as you seek to create a joyful, sustainable future for your family, your community and all the creatures who share the biosphere with us. The new technology of quantum biophysics and photonics that is emerging in the 21st century might fascinate you, with its potential for so many ways of harnessing the energy of light. Or perhaps it is the beauty of the sunrise and sunset that fascinates you and bringing more of that beauty into your life each day is important to you.

We need a way of drawing together these dimensions and them making accessible for the common good. Whether one lives in a high rise city tower, in the shadow of a tall city tower, in the countryside, or a forest, the same question arises. How can we better support and understand these processes?

Light and trees are common symbols in the traditions and religions of many cultures, so we know the answers to that question have ancient origins. The Tree of Life symbol, for example. Light is so closely aligned with beauty in the natural world and in the configuration of our minds that we cannot escape it. The light, space and patterns of leaves create the beauty of a tree in autumn. As we see the shafts of light pass through the spaces between the leaves, our minds are drawn in. We stop, pause and recognise beauty.

Only weeks before, those same leaves were reflecting green light and turning the energy of sunlight into food energy. They were releasing oxygen to sustain Life and drawing up moisture from the soil, so that once more it could gather in clouds and fall upon us, with the blessings of life-giving rain.

As Galileo said about planet Earth: *"It moves."* We live on a continually spinning, orbiting, moving globe and as it moves, the light also moves. Each day is defined by the movement of light from dawn to dusk, as the Earth spins on its axis. Our eyes move, absorbing electrons[4] and following the light. Plants move. People move. The moon, sun, stars and galaxies all spin, rotate and spiral.

Our eyes are in continual motion, from the perception of what is close to us, to what is far away, or vice versa. We have specialised cells for detecting fast moving patterns of light at the periphery of our vision. We have different retinal cells in our eyes for detecting light and colour in more detail at close range. Over seventy percent of the human brain is involved in receiving and processing light messages received from our eyes.

Utilising these dual capacities to see light with the vision system and realise meaning with the brain, humans often find delight when there is a happy combination of what is near and what is distant. Things that are near may offer refuge or safety. Those that are distant may offer prospect, adventure or inspiration. People in many cultures have worked to enhance the meaning and purpose of their stewardship of natural resources, spiritual practices and everyday activities through utilising these dual human capacities.

For example, in Bali, delightful thatched shrines are found throughout the island's farms, gardens, and villages. They are aligned to face towards Mt Agung. This mountain has great spiritual significance for the people. From a practical perspective, it is the source of the rich volcanic soils and rainfall upon which the island's food supply and ecology depend. The visual link between what is near, (the thatched shrines) and what is far (the similarly shaped from of Mount Agung) can be seen in the photograph at right.

Image 2. *Thatched shrines mirror the shape of Mt Agung in the distance*

In Chinese gardens, moon gates are designed to highlight the psychological transition between what is near and what is further away, on the other side of the gate. A moon gate is not usually a solid gate, but rather it is a patch of light. Moon gates are circular openings in garden walls, through which one steps, as if stepping into the light through a large round window at ground level.

Being round and reminiscent of the moon, moon gates can symbolise birth and renewal of Life. The round vertical shape is somewhat like a full moon rising above the ocean. Moon gates can also be interpreted as symbolic of the joy a family experiences when being together. Their feelings of fullness and cohesiveness are symbolised by the circle. Another meaning attributed to moon gates is the symbolic connection they inspire between the Earth, the moon, other planets and the cosmos.

Image 3. *View through a moon gate.*

Why a Global Light Garden?

Suppose we are to expand from considering the principles that apply to just one moon gate experience, to considering many other broader scale scenarios. We will need to work with a set of principles designed to *act in unison* to address natural resource management opportunities and problems that coexist around the globe.

Today, a set of four moral crises - social, environmental, economic and governance - is recognised by many people.[5] This book focuses on natural resource management within the environmental sphere but all the crises are related. Dr Vandana Shiva is one of many people who have devoted their lives to addressing these related crises. She is recognised as a physicist, an internationally renowned speaker, an organic farmer, a supporter of women's rights and an award-winning writer and activist. Speaking in 2019 at the United Nations Office in Geneva, she said:

> *"...I started this journey with seeds - with biotechnology. Now there's this new convergence of the bio technologies, the digital technologies and the financial technologies and this new convergence means that the ordinary ways we used to organise...those silos, they're already broken."* [6]

Dr Shiva highlights that citizens and the United Nations cannot expect to be effective against the powerful convergence that she describes if they confine their actions to old, broken silos that hold separate ideas. For example, this convergent coalition of business interests often runs contrary to the interests of self-sufficient organic farmers growing their own seeds. The farmers do not want to be forced to buy patented seeds from a biotech company. Similarly, local merchants do not want prices to be controlled by forces emanating from trading in derivatives and options on faraway financial markets. Dr Shiva is calling for citizens to unite and build their advocacy. To be strong enough to identify and counter the synergistic power of the biotech, digital and financial technologies they need to do this. How is it to be done?

The *Light Garden* set of decision-making principles described in this book is one tool that can be used as part of the process. In addition, the *Light Garden* principles provide some common ground between the individual citizen and the huge global corporations and elite entities of the global financial system. This is because the *Light Garden* principles encompass both the local and the global scales.

Also, because the *Light Garden* principles are derived from the principles of quantum biophysics that order life processes, they are inherently supportive of people living in harmony with natural resources. This concept applies, regardless of whether *Light Garden* principles are used at the local or the global scale. The connections between people's lives, diverse cultures and diverse ecosystems are valued in the *Light Garden* model. Life is not to be broken into silos, devalued, separated from place and context, then herded as fodder for profit and power.

Hi-tech industries are already using the synergy of the digital, bio and financial technologies to their advantage. However, although almost every culture wants the benefits of hi-tech industries, many of these industries are not harnessed to support Life. They are actually destroying Life, biodiversity, a stable climate and human health. If citizens are to create governments that respond to their needs, we need to harness the synergies of the living world. Biophysics describes what these synergies are. The *Light Garden* model provides a way of applying them. What is needed is a survival package to avoid catastrophe; rejuvenate the Earth's living systems and support human livelihoods and psychological wellbeing. This survival package is not another bailout package based on a disjoint between the planet's living systems and destructive concepts of mismanaged economic growth.

The global Covid pandemic of 2020 highlighted how relevant it is to call this a survival package. Modelling showed that under economic conditions in 2020, a twenty-five per cent increase in suicides was expected. This increase was expected as people sensed they had been cast aside and had little hope of personal economic recovery in the coming years. Modeling predicted that people would experience the personal mental health flow-on effects from participating in an economic system that did not need or want them as valued, paid contributors.

Eminent researchers estimated that about thirty per cent of the lives lost were expected to be among young people. This death rate was expected to overshadow the number of deaths directly attributable to covid virus infection among all age groups.[7] Although these figures pertain to Australia, they are likely to be similar in other Western globalised economies. They were released in May 2020 through a joint public statement by the President of the Australian Medical Association; the Co-Director of Health and Policy at the University of Sydney Central Clinical School, Brain and Mind Centre and the Executive Director of the Orygen Centre for Youth Mental Health at the University of Melbourne.

A radical change is needed so that young people perceive they are wanted and valued as members of society. Society must be willing to prioritise resources around two important factors, rather than around abstract economic models. The first of these factors is the wellbeing of young people. The second is the inextricably interconnected wellbeing of the planet's living systems. It is not a coincidence that young people also have been prominent in calling for government action to address climate change during 2020 – 2021. They know their lives and livelihoods are at stake and mostly due to social media, they know their governments have failed them. Once upon a time, young people grew up thinking the role of government was to create a just and safe society. People still want that but they know that radical change is needed so that governments can be freed from the pervasive influence of the elite groups that fund and lobby them.

Addressing this need, the *Light Garden* model is based on quantum biophysics principles. These are explained in more detail in the following chapter. Biophysics offers us a holistic understanding of how

Life happens. Life grows, repairs and reproduces to produce the myriad of diverse forms in the plants, animals and microorganisms that are all around us. By applying the principles of the life sciences to how society is governed, a sustainable future can be achieved. This is a future dedicated to the young and future generations. It is a future where the lives of small farmers who save seeds and grow organic food are championed, not locked into silos. It is a future where there is a role for everyone who lives in the cities and everyone who lives in the country - tending their *Light Gardens* and rejuvenating the Life that is all around and within.

Image 4. *A future with a role for everyone, tending their Light Gardens.*

Biophysics

Quantum biophysics has been found to be better than earlier schools of thought in explaining the behaviour of light, energy fields, waves, electromagnetism and the way in which living organisms regulate their growth, repair, reproduction and collaborative existence on planet Earth. It is in this context that the need for the Earth as a *Light Garden* model has arisen.

Fields such as human settlements, medicine, ecology, natural resource management and climate change have lagged some one hundred years behind in implementing quantum physics principles and our understanding of the nature of light, as both a particle and a wave. The *Light Garden* model provides one way of quickly stepping forward to redress that lag.

At a practical level, application of the *Light Garden* principles and priorities makes it feasible for humanity to become self-sufficient in healthy organic food, water and medicine. Many smaller communities have done this in times past. In the 21st century, it also means that slowing climate change becomes feasible as we reorder our priorities for natural resource management and human cultures. Even the long, slow, dedicated and loving processes of disentangling from unspeakable intergenerational psychological trauma, alienation, hopelessness and loneliness can take shape with more hope when applying these principles.

Biophysics, as defined in Encyclopaedia Britannica, is:

> "concerned with the application of the principles and methods of physics and the other physical sciences to the solution of biological problems. The relatively recent emergence of biophysics as a scientific discipline may be attributed, in particular, to the spectacular success of biophysical tools in unravelling the molecular structure of deoxyribonucleic acid (DNA), the fundamental hereditary material, and in establishing the precisely detailed structure of proteins such as haemoglobin in order that the position of each atom may be known." [8]

Given this broad description of biophysics, the reasons why some simply stated principles were derived from quantum biophysics as the basis for creating and testing the *Light Garden* model in this book may be sequentially outlined as follows:

1. Start with the goal of regenerating of the living systems of the planet. Currently, there is a problem that humanity is not moving rapidly or effectively enough to do this and to avoid further degradation of these systems. Consequently, the survival of humans and multiple other species are threatened.

2. Biophysics is concerned with the solution of biological problems. It has identified the precisely detailed structure and functioning of living creatures, down to the scale of each atom.

3. Quantum biophysics places emphasis on understanding the discrete parcels of energy found in living creatures, in the atomic structure of crystals and in the plasma of light.

4. One could say that Life on Earth has evolved in a great diversity of forms which align with electromagnetic and gravitational fields; harvest light plasma, and transform light into living matter.

5. The behaviour of light, when described in terms of quantum principles, started the ball rolling to develop the set of *Light Garden* principles. When acting in unison, these principles generate positive multiplication effects and operate with synchronicity across the boundaries between biophysics, plasma science and living organisms.

6. By articulating, supporting and applying these principles at the local and the global scales, *the Light Garden* model is inherently focused on supporting living systems, rather than on mechanised, or non-living systems.

7. Application of the synchronistic quantum principles embedded in the *Light Garden* principles allows multiple benefits to accrue simultaneously. This process gives humanity opportunities to make changes at a scale and pace that can effectively regenerate the living systems of the planet. The evidence is already apparent about the dire consequences of not making changes at a scale and pace that is effective. These consequences have impacted millions of lives around the globe, while priorities have been focused elsewhere in the digital, artificial intelligence, military and financial technologies.

8. Identifying the set of *Light Garden* principles through a simple ten-word mnemonic, (Every Summer We Love Mother Eating Perfect, Crimson, Heavenly Strawberries), makes the concept one that most people can recall by counting on ten fingers. It is suitable for children and adults. The same concept can be translated into other languages. People can then apply it and call upon their governments to implement it as public policy.

Having thus far introduced briefly some basic concepts of quantum biophysics which are discussed by scientists working in the field, let us now consider a simplified summary of them. The ten concepts listed below are proposed as the contributing factors that act in unison to create the *Light Garden* model for natural resource management.

1. Energy
2. Space and Time
3. Waves and Particles
4. Lines, patterns and probabilities
5. Multiplication and coherence effects
6. Entanglement and focal points
7. Perception and measurement
8. Context and Environment
9. Human Use
10. Storage and Sharing of Information

Bearing in mind these ten factors as we imagine stepping once more through a moon gate, let us explore and consider how each of them contributes and adds meaning to the overall experience.

As you read through the following table, perhaps you might describe your experience differently, or perhaps you will find there is much in common with what is described.

Light Garden Model to Describe Moving Through a Moon Gate

General category	A set of ten factors that act in unison when walking through a moon gate
1. Energy	We need the **energy** of light to illuminate the moon gate so that we can see the gate and see through it.
2. Space & Time	We need adequate **space and the time** to move through a moon gate.
3. Waves & Particles	A group of people may move through a moon gate as a **wave,** but each person is also an individual **"particle"** or person unto themselves.
4. Lines, patterns & probabilities	The **probability** of finding a moon gate in a classic Chinese garden is relatively high but the probability of finding one in an African garden is relatively low. The likelihood is reasonably high that a moon gate will be located where the lines and paths of a particular garden lead through it.
5. Multiplication effects	As shown in Image 3 of a moon gate, the presence of a moon gate acts in conjunction with other nearby features to **multiply** the impact of the view through the gate towards the lake.
6. Entanglement & Focal Points	Moon gates are often located to direct people's attention towards focal points of interest or frame attractive views.
7. Perception & measurement	The experience of the moon gate is dependent upon the **human perception** of it and upon careful measurements to build it at an appropriate size and scale.
8. Context & Environment	Moon gates do not exist in isolation but inevitably require there to be an **environmental context** on either side of the gate.
9. Human use	Moon gates are designed for **human use** but in a restrained, thoughtful and contextual manner. They add layers of meaning to the basic function of gates.
10. Storage + Sharing of Information	**Storage and sharing of information** are needed to communicate and pass on the symbolic meanings of moon gates and the skills to build them.

Image 5. *Applying the Light Garden model to describe moving through a moon gate*

Can this set of ten *Light Garden* principles also work at a broader scale beyond a particular place? Can they help to strengthen communities and the sustainable connections between people and nature? Many cultures around the world would send forth a resounding Yes, in answer to that question – and later chapters of this book consider some of their brilliant creations in more detail.

Light Gardens in the context of Globalization and Localisation

The great diversity of cultures in the world may be broadly grouped according to the degree to which they are part of the globalised and localised economies. Amidst the many *Light Garden* global cultures, there is the widespread influence of Globalization. What is a globalised economy and why is it relevant here? Globalisation in the 21st century tends to focus on economic principles that conceive of Life in abstract concepts such as consumers, products, supply chains and profits. There are multiple definitions of Globalisation but the relatively simple one from Wikipedia states that it is:

> *"…the process of interaction and integration among people, companies, and governments worldwide. As a complex and multifaceted phenomenon, Globalisation is considered by some as a form of capitalist expansion which entails the integration of local and national economies into a global, unregulated market economy."* [9]

Globalisation is often seen as inevitable. Historians would take another view. They have charted the design of this system going back for centuries. In particular, they have chronicled how during the fifty years preceding 2020, deregulation of big business occurred through a suite of measures such as treaties, regulations, taxes, central bank edicts, debt systems, international conferences, media campaigns and research strategies.

In response to this long term process, the International Alliance for Localisation (IAL) was formed.[10] In 2014, activists from around the world came together to explore and spread the word about alternative visions of development and progress. They knew happy, sustainable lives and communities were possible, without being dependent upon the growth paradigm of Globalisation. The IAL takes the view that Globalisation entails more than what is implied in the Wikipedia definition. The IAL describes how

> *"Across the world, people are coming to realise that today's crises — ecological collapse, economic instability, social disintegration, even terrorism — are inextricably linked to a global economy dependent on rampant consumerism, financial speculation and "free" trade…"* [11]

Local Futures is one, not for profit, member organisation of the IAL. They have been working since 1978 to advocate for Localisation as a big picture, systemic alternative to Globalization. Localisation is not about reducing all economic activity to the village scale, or about eradicating international trade.

Image 6. *Public Banking by Liz Elliott.*

14

"Localisation simply means shortening the distance between producers and consumers wherever possible. It is about ensuring that business conforms to the needs of democracy and genuine sustainability." [12]

Advocates of Localisation demand that big banks and corporations be subject to democratic control and regulations. Similarly, corporations should stop receiving vast subsidies and bailouts from governments. The sustainable localisation agenda also includes a more level playing field, where taxes, subsidies and regulations are redirected from big business to support small to medium-sized business and gainful roles for all citizens. Public banking is a crucial ingredient in the Localisation strategy. It aims to support local communities, not drain them of funds and resources.

In addition, there are those who say that the future for humanity does not lie in cities, although over half the world's population now lives in cities or urban areas. Regardless of whether people live in cities or not, the goals of the Localisation and decentralisation movements include but are not limited to:

- Building meaningful, inclusive, place-based communities that have a reasonable level of self-government, within a network of larger scale governments
- Supporting healthy food and lifestyles of happy restraint
- Prioritising carbon sequestration and avoiding the use of fossil fuels
- Rejuvenating the natural environment and biodiversity, (including reafforestation and biodiversity conservation).
- Restructuring social support systems through a much greater emphasis on well paid, meaningful careers based around labour - intensive stewardship of land, light, air and water resources. This restructuring includes supporting and spreading the knowledge and practices of traditional indigenous people. It also includes acknowledging that local businesses and small, biodiverse farms have been shown in a number of well-documented research studies to provide more local employment and produce more food than is obtained through large, industrial-scale farms.
- Supporting public banking and small to medium scale business economies where tax is paid. This type of financial structure is an alternative to the pervasive presence of those multinational companies and financial entities that seek to maximise their profits and wherever possible, avoid paying tax and being accountable for the welfare of local communities. During the first quarter of the 21st century, the FAANGS groups of companies came to be known for such activities: Facebook, Apple, Amazon, Netflix and Google.

  These companies operate through digital technology and have been wildly profitable. Some of these companies have been involved in various lawsuits, as governments try to garner tax from them and make them more accountable for the social consequences of their social media services. Companies and the general public have widely taken up the services these companies offer. Many other businesses, such as face to face local retailers, have suffered a loss of trading revenue and former customers as a result.

Locally grown food, local currency, local media and locally owned electricity companies are examples of activities that the Localisation movement has supported. Many of these activities are consistent with the *Light Garden* model as well. For example, many traditional cultures rely upon the sun as the energy source that powers their food production. They do not require outside input from activities organised at the global scale. Many globalised corporations also use advanced technologies that harvest the energy of the Sun.

The Strong Towns group that operates in the USA and Canada is interesting. Contrary to the Hollywood image of an affluent lifestyle in the USA, its focus is on supporting people to become informed, "strong citizens" who can advocate for urban renewal in the face of debilitating urban decay. Using his articulate internet blog, Clay Space has described how the whole image of self-reliant American men and women has changed since the pioneering days when it was forged. Pioneers could feed their families by hunting and growing vegetables; they could build their own homes; make their own clothes; raise their children and defend their back yards. Clay describes how this ability has disintegrated, alongside the urban fabric of many American towns:

> *"By letting globalisation knock down the fence of localism and tradition, vast portions of the first world are completely reliant on faceless corporations and government entities to survive…"* [13]

Speaking in the context of the covid 19 global pandemic event of 2020, Clay Space added:

> *"All it takes is a single chaotic event that leaves a government inept — or those huge corporations immobile — and enormous swaths of the American public could perish."* [14]

Writing from southern India in May 2020, Suprabha Seshan described a similar process. She was acutely aware of the privations suffered by the millions of Indian workers forced from their villages in past years. These people had later found sources of income and sustenance, working in city sweatshops and construction sites.

> *"When the oil-guzzling machines give way and the monoliths, monuments, highways, terminals, pipelines and cables freeze, decay, crumble, crash or powder and become dust, each particle will go home to the elements…* [15]

Harking to what she saw as the impending collapse of this way of life, she wondered how many of these workers would make the same choice that she made some years ago: *"So I am done with this way of life."* [16]

Everywhere, people are building alternatives. In her 2017 book *"New Way Now"* [17], Dr Liz Elliott describes a quiet, cumulative process where a new form of decentralised and localised society is gradually taking shape. It is based on a combination of the principles of capitalism and socialism. It is composed of movements such as Ubuntu in Africa, Indian village trading schemes, African trading clusters, Strong Towns in the USA and Canada, La Via Campesina, Transition Towns, ecovillages, cooperatives, credit unions, farmers' markets, organic farms, Christian outreach programmes, some not for profit organisations and many more groups.

None of these groups has the power to tackle global issues such as climate change in one hit. However, the collective actions of all these groups are effectively creating an alternative reality into which many people are choosing to step. Taking this step is like choosing to move as both a particle and a wave through the moon gate of the *Light Garden.* This analogy was described in more detail on page 13.

Although it might sound ambitious, this process has already dawned in a range of communities around the globe. For example, in 2017, the Himalayan state of Sikkim was recognised as the world's first entirely organic farming state. [18] This north Indian state has enacted legislation to support organic agriculture and ban the use of commercial pesticides and fertilisers. In North America, when Amish settlers started moving there from Europe in the 1730s, they brought their traditional culture. This culture included self-sufficient, organic agriculture, religion, health care, energy, transportation and child-raising practices that had been developed in Europe over the preceding centuries. The Amish still follow this lifestyle today and their numbers are reported to be growing. More detail about some Himalayan and Amish communities is provided in chapters six and nine.

The worldwide Transition Towns movement is another initiative. It began in Ireland and the United Kingdom during the period 2005 – 2006. The Transition Towns movement is based on a set of values and principles that are applied by a diverse range of participating groups in different cultures all around the world. The movement has a comprehensive set of resources that guide the formation and operation of groups. These resources help the groups develop skills to happily and effectively work together; to engage in participatory decision-making and celebrate successes! In large cities, populations generally subdivide into the small and medium-sized communities for which the movement was designed. It seeks to

"…to nurture a caring culture, one focused on connection with self, others and nature. They are reclaiming the economy, sparking entrepreneurship, reimagining work, reskilling themselves and weaving webs of connection and support." [19]

The common ground between the Transition Town movement principles and the *Light Garden* principles is summarised in the table on the following page. Although the *Light Garden* principles are focused on the management of living systems, (instead of the economy and society per se), the subjects do overlap. Not all people are altruistic and interested in change to nurture a more caring culture. Those who are not interested tend to be motivated to change if they perceive that more egocentric, short term benefits are available. For example, they might make a change to refrain from law-breaking behaviour, if they perceive they will thus avoid paying expensive fines.

Concepts of altruistic behaviour for the benefit of all living creatures are deeply embedded in many religious traditions. For example, Buddhists receive teaching in the practice of Bodhicheeta. This teaching is adapted according to the intelligence and predisposition of each person, so although a person who is not gifted with a high intelligence may not be altruistic by nature, they are none the less educated about the benefits of thinking and acting in that way. They learn to live within the norms of their society.

Similarly, people who grow up within the traditional culture of Bali are immersed in an effective system of governance and social organisation where everyone has a role and a landscape scale approach to natural resource management is adopted. This system is based on the Tri Hita Karana philosophy, which is described in more detail in Chapter 10. It has led to a society where a diverse range of arts and ceremonies are woven into the fabric of everyday life.

People are often sceptical about humanity's ability to work cooperatively at a large scale to create a more humane, nurturing society and change an economic system so that it supports such a society. Reasons cited for this are often related to human attributes such as greed, ignorance, distrust, lust for power, lust for domination, trauma, impatience, sloth, selfishness, addiction, poor health and limited resources. Fortunately, many people strive to overcome these afflictions and find a better path. The set of Transition Town principles described below[20] are one example of how a movement has sought to overcome scepticism and proactively encourage people to imagine and shape a positive future.

Comparison between Transition Towns and Light Garden

Light Garden Principles	The Eight Transition Town Principles [with notes in brackets comparing them to some of the *Light Garden* principles]
1: Energy **10: Storing & Sharing of Information**	**We foster positive visioning and creativity** – Out primary focus is not on being against things, but on developing and promoting positive possibilities. We believe in using creative ways to engage and involve people, encouraging them to imagine the future they want to inhabit. The generation of new stories is central to this visioning work, as well as having fun and celebrating success. [Several Light Garden principles are relevant to this concept, such as "Energy." This includes the energy and creativity to develop positive possibilities.]
2: Allowing Space & Time	**We pay attention to balance** – In responding to urgent, global challenges, individuals and groups can end up feeling stressed, closed or driven rather than open, connected and creative. We **create space** for reflection, celebration and rest to **balance the times** when we're busily getting things done. We explore different ways of working which engage our heads, hands and hearts and enable us to develop collaborative and trusting relationships.
3: Waves & Particles **7: Perception & Measurement**	**We are part of an experimental, learning network** – Transition is a real-life, real-time global social experiment. **Being part of a network** [the network is like a wave and the individual person is like a particle,] means we can create change more quickly and more effectively, drawing on each other's experiences and insights. We want to acknowledge and learn from failure as well as success [conscious perception] - if we're going to be bold and find new ways of living and working, we won't always get it right the first time. We will be open about our processes and will actively seek and respond positively to feedback.
4: Lines, patterns & probabilities	**We promote inclusivity and social justice** – The most disadvantaged and powerless people in our societies are **likely to be** ["likely to be" is a statement that includes the *Light Garden* concept of probability] worst affected by rising fuel and food prices, resource shortages and extreme weather events. We want to **increase the chances** ["increase the chances" is another concept aligned with probability], of all groups in society to live well, healthily and with sustainable livelihoods.
5: Multiplication **6: Entanglement & Focal Points**	**We collaborate and look for synergies** – The Transition approach is to work together as a community, unleashing our collective genius to have a greater impact together than we can as individuals. [a "multiplication effect"] We will look for opportunities to build creative and powerful partnerships across and beyond the Transition movement and develop a collaborative culture, finding links between projects, creating open decision-making processes and designing events and activities that help people make connections. [Such events act as "focal points" which are part of *Light Garden* principles].
8: Context & Environment	**We freely share ideas and power** – Transition is a grassroots movement, where ideas can be taken up rapidly, widely and effectively because each community takes ownership of the process themselves. [Transition principles incorporate "context & environment."]
9: Human Use (restrained)	**We respect resource limits and create resilience** – The urgent need to reduce carbon dioxide emissions, greatly reduce our reliance on fossil fuels and make wise use of precious resources is at the forefront of everything we do. ["Restrained human use" is a Transition Towns principle.]
10: Storage & Sharing of Information	**We adopt subsidiarity** (self-organisation and decision making at the appropriate level) – The intention of the Transition model is not to centralise or control decision making, but rather to work with everyone so that it is practised at the most appropriate, practical and empowering level. [This Transition Town principle incorporates "storage and sharing of information".]

Image 7. *Comparison between Transition Towns and Light Garden*

Continuing with another example, Dr Liz Elliott also presents a series of counter-arguments to scepticism and doubts about people's ability to work cooperatively. These are included in her book "New Way Now."[21] A summary of these counter-arguments is presented below, under a set of simplified headings.

1. **Scale.** Lack of lived experience with successful cooperation leads people to doubt cooperation and Localisation could work on a large scale.

2. **Enough food.** Fear that Localisation would lead to there not being enough food (without broadacre farming and supermarkets).

3. **Repression.** Fear that small-town life will have limited opportunities for stimulating social interaction, travel and education.

4. **Defence.** Fear that Localisation of the economy would not be accompanied by the security of having a national defence force.

5. **Technology.** The concept that there is no need to change to a localised economy because technology will fix things under the existing system.

6. **Market forces.** Adherence to the idea that market forces will solve all problems, despite evidence arising from the 2008 Global Financial Crisis and other events.

7. **Socialism.** Lack of understanding that appropriate principles of socialism can be intelligently mixed with capitalism in a democratic system.

8. **Mass media.** Opposition to localised economies, (which tend not be very interested in large scale, mass media, paid advertisements).

9. **Police & army.** Lack of expertise and bravery to work with the police and military creatively, so they support, rather than crush localisation processes.

10. **Inertia.** Lack of willpower to overcome inertia and act as citizens working for the common good.

Reviewing these ten doubts in relation to the *Light Garden* principles leads to some interesting insights:

1. **Scale:** The viability of cooperation and Localisation on a large scale is doubted. However, it is supported by the *Light Garden* principle of *Multiplication effects*. This principle is based on the positive multiplication benefits that accrue in living systems, as actions move from the small and local to a larger scale. Rather than doubting that a larger scale will be feasible, the *Light Garden* principles build confidence that the larger scale will occur as an outcome of many smaller actions.

2. **Enough food:** Fear there won't be enough food. Multiple well-documented research studies have shown that small scale, diversified agriculture produces more food per hectare than large scale broadacre farming. This is consistent with the *Light Garden* principle of *Entanglement* and the positive interaction effects between different entities in biodiverse agriculture.

3. **Repression:** Fear that small town life will have limited opportunities for stimulating social interaction, travel and education. The *Light Garden* principles act in unison. *Light Garden* principles such as *energy, space and time, waves and particles*, and *restrained human use* are not dependent upon the size of a population.

4. **Defence:** Fear that Localisation of the economy would not be accompanied by the security of having a national defence force. The *Light Garden* principle of *waves and particles* applies here. The national defence force is analogous to a wave, whilst individual local economies can coexist with that. The two entities are not mutually exclusive.

5. **Technology:** The concept that there is no need to change to a localised economy because technology will fix things. The *Light Garden* principles are derived from the behaviour of living creatures and act in unison to support Life processes. Technology that is not based on principles that support living systems will not fix problems involving living systems. This phenomenon includes the current set of multiple, related, global environmental, social, economic and governance issues.

6. **Market forces:** Adherence to the idea that market forces will solve all problems, despite evidence arising from the 2008 GFC and other events. *Light Garden* comment as for item five above.

7. **Socialism:** Lack of understanding that appropriate principles of socialism can be intelligently mixed with capitalism in a democratic system. Virtually all the *Light Garden* principles are relevant here and support the concept that two valid ideas acting in unison are not mutually exclusive but when intelligently applied, lead to better outcomes.

8. **Mass media:** opposition to localised economies: Localised economies tend to be not very interested in large scale advertising in mass media. Although they do not comment on this particular subject, the *Light Garden* principles of *Perception and Measurement*, plus *Storage and Sharing of Information* are relevant here.

9. **Army and police:** Lack of expertise, good health, inspiring examples and bravery to creatively work with the police and army, so they support, rather than crush localisation processes. Comment as for item eight above.

10. **Inertia:** Lack of willpower or sufficiently good health to overcome inertia and get active as citizens working for the common good. *Light Garden* comments are the same as for eight above. In addition, the *Light Garden* principle of allowing *Space and Time* for results to be achieved also applies. The *Multiplication effects* principle and the *Waves and Particles* principle also apply, as they reinforce the cumulative effect of many citizens acting together to create a wave that is far greater than any one of them might initially imagine.

Image 8. *The Hindu Temple of Konark, devoted to Surya, the God of Sun and light in India*

In summary, the *Light Garden* principles generally support the validity of the counter-arguments put forward by Liz Elliott to assuage the *Ten Doubts* other people often have about the feasibility of working cooperatively. Given an appropriate framework, people can work cooperatively to create a decentralised economy and society. For example, in India, the Hindu Temple of Konark is devoted to Surya, the God of Sun and light. As illustrated in Image 8, a great deal of effort, cooperation and expertise went into constructing this temple. It continues to be well patronised by crowds of visitors.

Having begun to explore how the ten *Light Garden* principles can act in unison when applied as part of the movement towards decentralised economies and societies, let us now consider how well they are received when like a band of musicians, they play in different cultures.

Light Garden principles applied in different cultures, with examples of Regenerative Agriculture, Net Positive Design and Community Groups

Regenerative agricultural practices operate on principles that run as a common thread across many place-based cultures. Traditional regenerative farming in Kenya, Africa, is discussed in Chapter 5 as an example of this. Photographs taken in the field during the 1980s illustrate this way of life.[22] In the 21st century, regenerative agricultural practices are becoming more prevalent in contemporary Western culture. As described in Chapter 11, the *Light Garden* model includes an expanded role for regenerative agriculture and agroecology.

At present, regenerative agriculture aims to strengthen the health of farm soil, improve the broad scale water cycle, support bio-sequestration of carbon from the atmosphere and enhance biodiversity and ecosystem services that contribute to the general health and functioning of the environment and people. Any 'waste' material produced on a farm is composted or recycled. Composted material from off-farm sources may be added as well. The potential is apparent for regenerative agriculture to operate at the bioregional scale, as well as on individual properties. As an idea, it sits beside associated activities such as localisation, permaculture, agroforestry, ago-ecology, keyline design, minimum till and reduced till.

The 21st century regenerative agriculture movement has adopted an agenda that is more consciously global in scale than what generations of regenerative farmers have been practising in Kenya and many other regions of the Earth. For example, the mission statement of the Regeneration International organisation is

> *"to promote, facilitate and accelerate the global transition to regenerative food, farming and land management for the purpose of restoring climate stability, ending world hunger and rebuilding deteriorated social, ecological and economic systems."* [23]

Bearing in mind this wide-ranging mission, Professor Janis Birkeland has none the less described how in the 21st century, we need to do more. She advocates for sustainable design paradigms where we *over-compensate* for the net embodied waste, energy and resources that are consumed by human societies at large. This includes both urban and rural areas. Unless this over-compensation is achieved, little is gained to address the existing, (and ever burgeoning) levels of natural resource depletion, climate change, and inequitable wealth distribution inherited by the countless generations of living creatures born in this century.[24]

In her 2019 book, *"Net-Positive Design and Sustainable Urban Development"*[25], Janis describes what net positive design means. She also gives a detailed historical account that provides the context for why it is needed in the 21st century. Over several decades Janis has developed and refined the net positive concept and a set of associated tools to implement it. Her work documents how sustainable design can over-compensate and reverse the processes that have led to resource depletion, nature degradation and inequitable wealth distribution in the past.

In many ways, the *Light Garden* model was motived by a similar concept but it approaches the subject from a different perspective. The *Light Garden* model and analysis are based on applying the positive *multiplier effects* and other quantum biophysics principles to managing living systems, including human ones.

The benefits of the *Light Garden* model accrue when all the principles are applied in unison. This is similar to how a living creature needs to have all its life support systems operating in unison to maintain a healthy life – the circulation system, the nervous system, the waste disposal system and so on. The *Light Garden* model proposes that by applying quantum biophysics principles, humanity can make the substantial, net positive leaps forward needed to redress systemic problems at the global and local scales.

Interestingly, *"Human use"* is only one of the ten principles that need to be implemented together in a successful *Light Garden* model. Climate change is one phenomenon that can be considered in that context.

Naomi Klein elegantly described the dilemma in her 2014 book *"This Changes Everything: Capitalism vs. The Climate"*:

> *"our economic system and our planetary system are now at war. Or, more accurately, our economy is at war with many forms of Life on Earth, including human Life. What the climate needs to avoid collapse is a contraction in humanity's use of resources; what our economic model demands to avoid collapse is unfettered expansion. Only one of these sets of rules can be changed, and it's not the laws of nature."* [26]

Light Garden principles are based on the laws of nature and they not about warfare. They are a tool for decision making that calls forth the benefits of cooperative action. In the 21st century, humanity's whole approach to the management of ecology, landscape, urban areas and oceans is predicated by a widely recognised need. That is to simultaneously address multiple global scale environmental, humanitarian and economic crises. These crises are interrelated, just like the quantum field innerspring mattress analogy illustrated later in this chapter.

One of the prime causes of these related crises is not making decisions based on the laws on nature. This book seeks to address that problem by going back to basics and identifying the principles that underpin the growth of living organisms. These principles are then applied to develop a new set of criteria for making decisions that *are* based on the laws of nature, not on abstract economic concepts that have appropriated the original meaning of the word "growth". Once free from these abstract growth concepts, the way forward is much clearer towards meaningful employment and humanity's coexistence with nature.

Ironically during the last century, humanity and scientists gained a far greater capacity to understand the laws at the galactic, global and sub-atomic scales. However, on the global scale, we were, (and continue to be), sadly remiss in applying the laws of nature to maintain ecosystem and human health.

For example, Naomi Klein has said that what the climate needs to avoid collapse is a contraction in humanity's use of resources. However, Janis Birkeland has said that what the climate needs to avoid collapse is not only a contraction in humanity's use of resources but also *net positive* design and sustainable urban development. That means humanity needs to over-compensate for the past overuse of resources that has led to depletion and degradation of natural resources and inequitable wealth distribution.

One way this depletion and degradation has occurred is through the promotion of interest-bearing loans as a means of propelling economic "growth," without a counterweight in the system. The counterweight would apply the laws of nature and ensure natural resources, (including climate), are managed sustainably. We know these resources cannot keep "growing" on a finite planet.

Image 9. *Captain Interest - cartoon by Liz Elliott.*

Economists and others have done a vast body of work to model how economies and natural systems interact. An example of this is Economist Kate Raworth's *'Doughnut Economics'* model published in her 2017 book "Doughnut Economics: Seven Ways to Think Like a 21st Century Economist."[27]

Kate refers to a "regenerative and distributive economy" as a necessary part of the doughnut. The *Light Garden* model of this book is developed in that context. It proposes one more step towards working within the laws of nature, through an expanded consciousness of light and quantum biophysics. Refer overleaf to the conceptual diagrams on pages 24 and 25. Those diagrams show how the Light Garden model does this, by focusing on regenerative and distributive management of natural resources.

In an associated and important call to action, Dr Liz Elliott notes that 50 – 70% of global resource use occurs because of waste, corruption and "needless profit". In her book *"New Way Now"* [28] Liz explains how this undue level of profit accrues in many ways. These include unnecessarily high interest charges, other rentier charges, financial transaction fees and profits, tax evasion and similar means that lead to accumulation of funds for a relatively small number of already wealthy entities. Based on Liz Elliott's quoted calculation of 50 – 70% of global resource use going to "waste, corruption and needless profit", if humanity's use of resources was channelled to avoid this type of consumption, things could be different. Current calls to cut resource use would be more than met, thus avoiding climate chaos and the associated biological disruption and human misery.

However, such a process would take a long time to implement, as it challenges existing power structures that would resist and fight it as long as possible. There is a need for other strategies as well.

In North Eastern India, an unexpected strategy that could be applied more widely to avoid climate chaos and the associated biological disruption evolved rapidly during the 2020 covid lockdown. Forced out of the cities, young people returned to rural villages and began working on family farms. This work transition significantly reduced resource use in urban areas and increased the number of people living on the land. Here they had much lower ecological footprints than in the cities. For example, an estimated 23,000 young people returned to fifty villages within one region of the State of Nagaland.[29]

Seno Tsuhah and Akole Tsuhah described how the women of the North East Network in Nagaland managed during the 2020 covid lockdown. They said they did not know what the future would bring: famine, poverty, war, disease and insecurity. However, they did know that they were pulling together as a community of people in their traditional way. The women emphasised how their culture was framed within the local ecosystem and how that added to their resilience.

Doughnut Economics

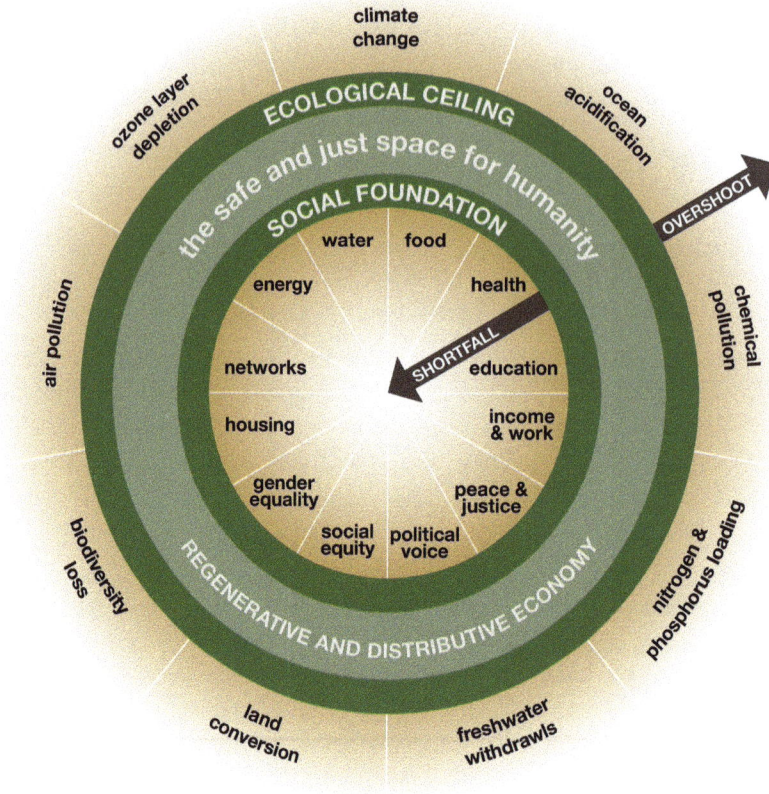

Image 10. *Doughnut Economics by Kate Raworth.*

Some of their initiatives included starting to grow cotton to supply local weavers, instead of buying cotton elsewhere. Weavers started making covid masks. Farmers contributed to local, biodiverse seed banks so that neighbouring people could become more self-sufficient with their food needs. Local food marketing outlets were negotiated with the authorities who were supervising quite strict covid lockdown rules. Prior to that, food vendors had become destitute under strict covid lockdown protocols because the rules forbade people to congregate, or distribute food through local vendors.[30]

In contrast to this, at the scale of the global economy, Naomi Klein refers to a *war* between humanity's economic system and the planet's living systems. The *Light Garden* model provides a structure through which humanity can transition out of this war zone. The *Light Garden* model refers not a war but to the peaceful application of principles to proactively support the management of and alignment

The Planetary Light Garden

New priorities for living systems

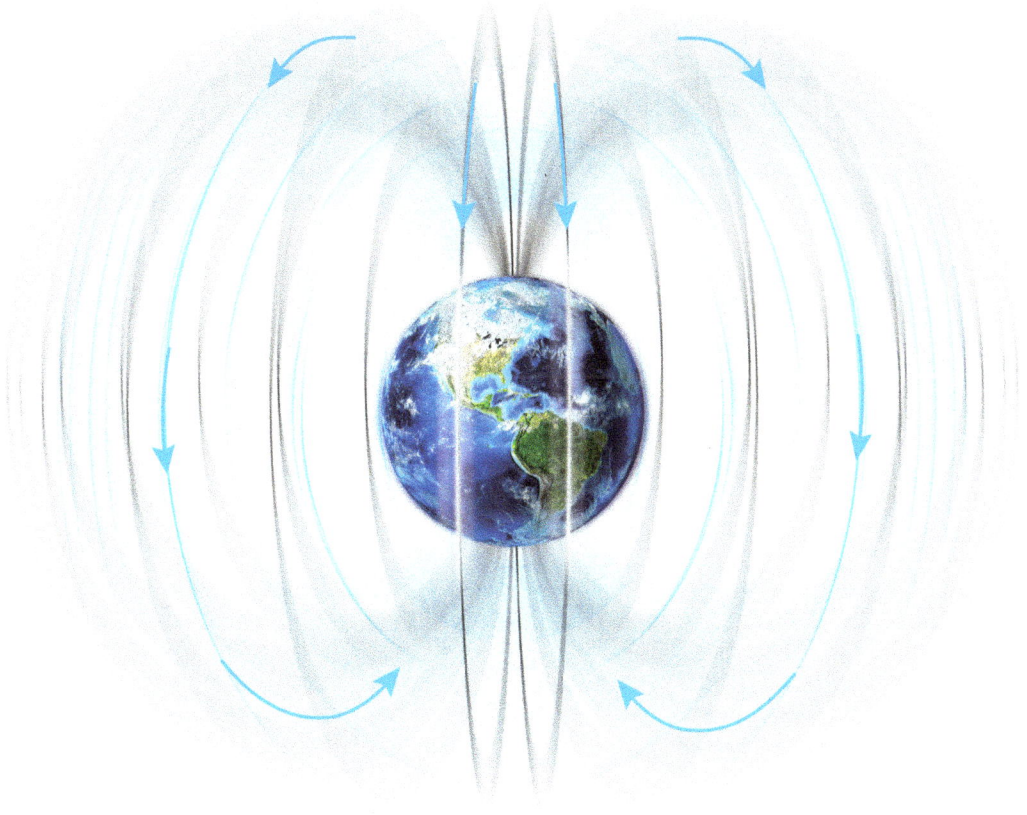

**A welling up of human energy & resources
devoted to regeneration of Life.**

Image 11. *The planetary Light Garden with a focus on regeneration. This leads to new jobs, a new role for agriculture, cultural renewal and a new, integrated focus for the economy, society and government.*

- All people contribute labour or resources to care for the land, society, water and natural resources. All people have valued, meaningful roles as part of this.

- The economy, machines, artifical intelligence and the like are focused towards regeneration of living systems and not as ends unto themselves.

with living systems. For certain, this requires a major realignment of priorities - as Naomi would advocate and the people of Nagaland have demonstrated is possible.

The structure of the *Light Garden* model is based on the principles that underpin the growth of *living systems*, rather than those that underpin many existing *economic systems*. It is inherently peaceful and abundant, rather than adversarial. It incorporates a new concept for the role of economic systems within a broader framework.

The regenerative *Light Garden* model illustrated in Image 11 may be compared to the *Doughnut Economics* model in Image 10. In the *Doughnut Economics* model, the inner space is a zone of "shortfall" in life's necessities such as food, shelter, and income. In the *Light Garden* model, the inner core is formed by the contribution of human labour and resources towards the regeneration of Earth's living systems. As in the *Doughnut Economics* model, the "safe and just space for humanity" lies in a ring surrounding the core of the *Light Garden*.

The need for the traditional virtues, such as wisdom, justice, moderation, courage, cooperation, peace, patience and love to be applied in this process is apparent. The Transition Towns movement, Dr Liz Elliott, and countless others have emphasised this. As interfaith dialogues have shown in the past, there will be many common interests between different cultures when applying such virtues. For example, the Buddhist perspective on this particular set of virtues would probably identify different priorities from those that are otherwise implied to the Western mind. The Buddhist concept of bodhicitta may be achieved in a range of ways, including practicing the six virtues of generosity, morality, patience, diligence, meditation and wisdom.[31]

More exploration of that subject occurs in later chapters, where some Asian Buddhist cultures and *Light Garden* examples are reviewed.

As the second decade of the 21st century drew to a close, more and more people were calling for transformative change in the way decisions are made about resource management at the global and local scales. For example, as noted by the United Nations Intergovernmental Science-Policy Platform on Biodiversity and Ecosystem Services (IPBES):

> *"By transformative change, we mean a fundamental, system-wide reorganisation across technological, economic and social factors, including paradigms, goals and values."* [32]

The *Light Garden* model developed in this book is framed in this context. It encompasses current work in society, industry, information technology, science, medicine, food production, sustainability, and a host of other areas. Regeneration of healthy living systems is placed as the central motiving force for collective human activity in the *Light Garden* model. This priority is a point of difference between the *Light Garden* model and other models that seek the integration of society, economy, environment and governance.

The *Light Garden* model includes the multiplier effects generated once we chose to increase awareness of the quantum biophysics principles underpinning how living organisms regulate their growth. It also helps us realise the limitations of our existing approaches for the management of the planet's natural resources.

> *"When projected upon reality, a model shapes one's understanding but, more importantly, what one does not see."* [33]

Any model for transformative change will have its limitations. As Professor Janis Birkeland has explained, circular and "closed loop" sustainability models have limitations. For example, limitations occur when a model is supported by allusions to nature, such as ecosystem recycling processes. Limitations also happen when a model is supported by analogies with a living organism's metabolic system, or to a meta-organism, such as GAIA. In this context, GAIA may be defined as all Life on the mother planet Earth existing as one, interconnected, large, wise, meta-organism.[34]

Although the scale of these closed loop metaphors and sustainability models is huge, we need to do more. That is because these models are not framed to comprehensively curtail and *reduce* large scale flows of energy and materials, plus the associated ecological impacts. Trends to Localisation rather than Globalisation of the economy *do reduce* some overall scale flows of energy and materials. For example, they reduce the energy and materials involved in unnecessary international trade, as people meet more of their needs through locally available goods and services. They also reduce the adverse ecological and social impacts that arise in small communities when such communities are displaced by broad scale agribusiness farming as part of the Globalisation of the economy.

The "open system," net positive models that Janis Birkeland and others have developed can reduce these flows and impacts too. That is because they conceptualise human activity as occurring in landscapes that go beyond maintaining sustainable cycles. The aim is to

- Generate more energy than is consumed
- Improve air and water quality
- Increase biological and agricultural diversity (which also sometimes happens with Localisation of the economy)
- Increase social capital in terms of inclusion, purpose, meaning and connection, (which also often happens as part of Localisation of the economy)

These landscapes - be they urban or rural, land or water, degraded or regenerating - can be managed to make net positive contributions to the management of global natural resources, including climate. An exciting application of this concept for transformative change and climate management could be used in conjunction with the *Light Garden* model in refugee camps. As discussed in more detail later in the book, refugee camps offer opportunities for investing in cost-effective modern technology to support the necessary activities of human life. These include generating energy from waste materials; growing organic food in limited spaces, establishing biodiverse vegetation on barren land plus harvesting and storing water.

Gradually establishing a society with employment and a participatory decision-making process for all who live in refugee communities is an integral and necessary part of this process. Refugee communities could thus become net positive contributors to managing global climate change. That would be a positive alternative to current scenarios where refugees often are viewed as recipients of outside donor funds; sources of exploitable labour for nearby profit-oriented enterprises or exploitable collateral in the ransom demands of warfare.

Considering how to transition from exploitative community structures to net positive communities leads to a discussion of the general motives for human activity. A general discussion of what motivates people to act is beyond the scope of this book. However, one of the ten *Light Garden* principles is framed to broadly encompass that subject under the banner of "Human Use." Principle number nine refers to human activity as consciously restrained, rather than exploitative.

Unfortunately, public trust in the motives associated with most national government economic programs in the first quarter of the 21st century has been seriously eroded. This erosion of trust has occurred to the extent that a majority of citizens see the need for a *transformative* approach and an alternative to retaining current, more limited motives. For example, Richard Edelman, President of the world's largest public relations firm Edelman, reported in the *2017 Trust Barometer* that there had been an

"implosion of trust" where one in two countries (including Australia) believe the entire system is failing and harbour deep fears of immigration, Globalisation and changing

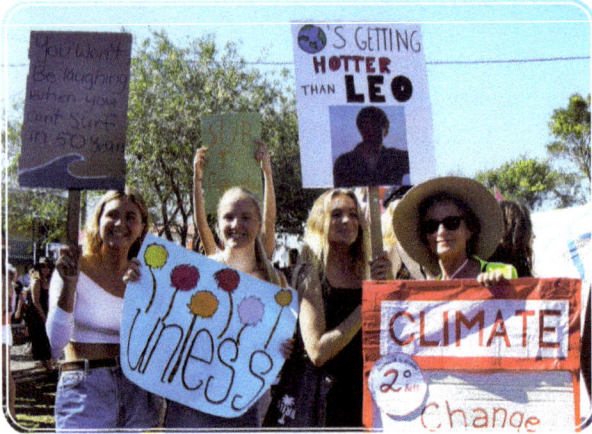

Image 12. *Citizens calling for action on climate change as part of a global movement in 2019.*

values…We're talking about a trust crisis that is causing a systemic meltdown." [35]

As one example of what *transformative change* means in the environmental context, in 2016 Biologist Edward O. Wilson proposed that half the planet's land and water areas be set aside as nature reserves. Supporting this proposal, he set out the scientific basis for calculations that 80% of existing living species could be preserved by such action.[36]

As another example of transformative change, the word *disentanglement* has come into parlance during the 21st century. It describes the multi-faceted, conscious process of stepping away from what is not needed, whilst rejuvenating local communities and the planet's natural living systems. In this context, the *Light Garden* model proposed in this book gains significance. It points to a future in which the growth of living organisms - and Life processes themselves - are at the centre of the next wave of local and international cooperative efforts. This wave is an alternative to allowing non-living concepts such as "economic" growth to prevail.

By the year 2019, record temperatures, droughts, floods, bushfires, rising sea levels, loss of biodiversity and human immune system diseases were consistently making headlines. The word "unprecedented" was upon the lips of English speaking peoples all around the globe. They grew ever more incredulous at the transformative changes occurring before their eyes in the world of nature.

Sunlight is a resource to be managed equitably. Sunlight may be valued primarily for the heat it transmits, the light it transmits, the energy it transmits, or its vital role in maintaining global climate patterns and ecosystems, (including the health and welfare of human beings). Recognition is growing about the role of sunlight as a global natural resource. It is not to be taken for granted, or corralled into the grip of the rich and powerful. In 2011 Sir David Attenborough described high-tech "geo-engineering" solutions to climate change as *"fascist"* because they put too much power into the hands of advanced nations.[37] Such studies have investigated the effects of spraying particles into clouds, the atmosphere, or onto the surface of oceans. Findings to date indicate that particular projects could lead to approximately four billion people being adversely and directly affected, such as through the failure of life-giving rains.

This book proposes a more equitable approach: applying the principles of quantum biophysics to manage the Earth as a *Light Garden*.

2

Light, Biophysics and Growth

Life as we know it would not exist without the biofield.

This book is about living, designing and working with light and the Earth's natural living systems. How are these created – and how we can synchronise our activities with them?

By understanding the electromagnetic and gravitational fields that make the tiny mandalas underlying all natural living beauty, we can then apply that knowledge to designing and living in harmony with the life force - rather than designing an inherently non-living, unsustainable system.

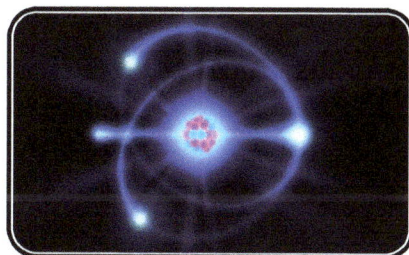

Image 1. *An artist's image of electrons in an atom.*

In Western culture, at least as far back as the Greek philosophers, there have been two schools of thought about how matter is formed. One school, attributed to Democritus, is based around the concept that particles are the building blocks of life – and that life can be scientifically understood by examining each building block, plus the sum that they make.

The second school of thought is attributed to Aristotle. He stated that the life process is wholistic, autonomous, self-regulating and evolving in a way that cannot be broken down, understood and reassembled in the manner of building blocks.[38] This school of thought is more closely aligned with tribal cultures, Eastern cultures and some concepts found in Hinduism, Buddhism and Taoism.

Since the early 20th century and the work of Albert Einstein, Max Plank and their contemporaries, quantum physics has come to be the accepted springboard upon which further scientific study in the realms of physics is based. Quantum physics does not focus on either of the schools of thought associated with Democritus or Aristotle: it provides a third one.

Quantum physics incorporates principles such as uncertainty, probability, quantum entanglement, non-locality, coherence and the so-called vacuum in space. This set of principles is more comprehensive than either of the earlier schools of thought in explaining the behaviour of light, energy fields, waves, electromagnetism, and how living organisms on Earth regulate their growth, repair, reproduction and collaborative existence. It is in this context that the need for this book arose.

This book addresses fields that deal with living organisms on Earth. These fields, such as biology, ecology, engineering, landscape design, landscape management, human settlement and medicine, have lagged some one hundred years behind the work of the scientists in applying the principles of quantum mechanics, quantum biophysics, and plasma science to a broader range of natural resource management endeavours.

Summary of the Development of Quantum Biophysics

Conventional physics & biology

Since ancient times, concepts of waves have existed. Waves may be in the form of energy, light or sound. They are measured in terms of their amplitude, velocity and power.

Photosynthesis: Scientific understanding of the process of photosynthesis developed in stages. Jan Baptista van Helmont (1580-1644) proved that plants do not increase their biomass from the soil, as had been theorised by ancient Greeks. Joseph Priestley (1733 - 1804) showed that plants produce oxygen. Jan Ingenhousz (1730-1799) showed that light is essential for photosynthesis. [39]

Since the late 19th century: Particles found in matter are called protons, electrons and neutrons (plus other smaller particles that are less well known outside specialist scientific circles).

19 - 20th century - plasma

Late 19th century: Plasma is identified as a fourth state of matter, in addition to solids, liquids and gases. It is composed of ionised gas. It is emitted by many sources, including the sun and by lighting bolts. The solar wind carries ionised plasma past planet Earth.

Plasma and its associated electromagnetic energy interacts with the biochemistry of living organisms on Earth in various ways. For example, the human body interacts with the Schumann Resonance. This is a wave of a constant frequency around the Earth.

20th century - the behaviour of Light

1938 Einstein and Infeld publish a paper describing how light behaves as both a particle, which has mass and as a wave, which does not. This concept remains as part of quantum physics.

1905 Photons: Albert Einstein first used this term when describing the photoelectric effect, in which he proposed the existence of discrete energy packets during the transmission of light. Quantum physics helps describe the behaviour of light and energy better than classical physics can. Classical physics can explain the motion of objects that have mass and move in smooth trajectories, such as a ball rolling down a slope but it cannot explain the growth of living organisms.

21st century

Plasma science, quantum biophysics and photonics add to knowledge of how the growth, repair and reproduction of living organisms occurs through electromagnetic and gravitational fields, biofields and light-emitting biophotons.

Living matter is formed by standing waves of energy or magnetic and gravitational fields, plus the concept of quantum entanglement beyond space and time. This is in addition to the biochemistry and DNA of living organisms. Interactions between photons, plasma and cells can be complex.

Image 2. *One page summary of the development of quantum biophysics.*

The basic principles of quantum science include that large and small scale phenomena are inter-related. These principles were initially developed by scientists such as Albert Einstein and Max Plank while studying large-scale phenomena, including galaxies. The same electromagnetic and gravitational forces act at the small and large scales on living and non-living entities. The *Light Garden* model is based on that premise.

Trees are wonderful light powerhouses on planet Earth in so many ways. Their dozens of attributes include the production of oxygen, water, cool air and soil erosion control. We know that through the process we call photosynthesis, light energy, (or plasma from our Sun), is absorbed by plants and converted into matter, such as amino acids and starches. Once captured in this way, energy and matter can form food for other creatures as well.

Have you ever thought of a garden as a food factory or an energy factory, taking in light and producing food and energy packages? I am using the word "packages" quite deliberately here, because light, (like all other forms of electromagnetic energy), comes in discrete packages, as well as in waves. This is one of the concepts described in the summary of the development of quantum biophysics on the previous page.

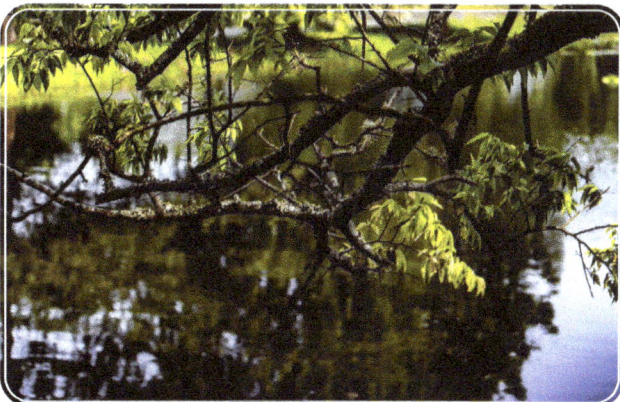

Image 3.

(Above left) *Photons strike millions of sand particles, but there are no trees and few signs of life.*

(Above right) *Millions of photons strike a leaf as photosynthesis uses light energy to make plant tissue.*

(Left) *Trees grow with the energy of millions of biophotons.*

Understanding the process of transition between energy, light, and matter can be applied to how we address the challenge of creating new causes and effects that will regenerate the Earth's natural living systems - rather than continue to deplete them. More details of how that process of transition occurs are given on the following pages.

This transition process is highly relevant to developing new, feasible, 21st century solutions to climate and natural resource management. For example, as described earlier, in 2019, the scientific journals *"Nature"* and *"Science"* published the research of Thomas Crowther's team at their Swiss laboratory. They calculated that although there are many options, planting 1.2 trillion trees is the most feasible solution to climate change. Their work also indicates the scale of reorganisation needed in our employment, social and economic systems. Further detail about particular projects and cultures that contribute to this overall process is provided in succeeding chapters.

In addition to photosynthesis in trees, there are other interesting biological processes at play here too. Let's look at some of them: photons, biophotons, spirals, fractals, biofields and quantum biophysics. A quanta of light is the smallest discrete package of light that is known to exist. A *quanta* of light is also referred to as a photon. When an electron is accelerated, a photon can be produced.

Biophotons are photons emitted by living organisms. They are discussed in further detail below. Our basic genetic code is stored in DNA. It doesn't engage in photosynthesis, but DNA does absorb and emit biophotons.

Biophotons

> *"Biological organisms continuously emit weak light. This light has been referred to as biophotons and is now currently referred to as ultraweak photon emission (UPE). This phenomenon is different from bioluminescence."* [40]

Biophotons, or ultra-weak photon emission, (UPE), are the discretely sized packages in which electromagnetic radiation occurs within living organisms. Biophotons are emitted and absorbed by DNA and other living material. Photons are emitted within the light spectrum at a range of 350 to 1270 nanometres. A billionth of a meter is called a nanometre, or nm.[41]

The human eye can detect light within the range of 400 to 700 nm. So the human eye is able to see some of the photons emitted by living material. The mechanism by which ultra-weak photon emission (UPE) regulates the activity of living organisms is the subject of much research. One theory states that

> *"...neurons contain various light-sensitive neurotransmitters (tryptophan, phenylalanine, tyrosine, and other molecules), and it is difficult to imagine that the nervous system is not affected by the phenomenon of UPE and that such conduction of photons does not transport encoded information."* [42]

Other theories refer to biochemical interaction with biophotons at the cellular level. Blood also carries biophotons. UPE is detected, photographed, recorded and measured with low-noise photomultiplier tubes and imaging using highly sensitive charge-coupled device cameras.[43] The optical coherence tomography (OCT) imaging technique commonly used by Ophthalmologists is one example of the use of this technology in the field of medicine. High resolution, cross-section images of the layers of cells in the retina of the eye are obtained and used to diagnose and monitor retinal conditions such as macular degeneration.

The general term given to the technology of generating, manipulating and detecting photons is Photonics. Photons and photonics also play important roles in information technologies such as fibre optics. Photons are to fibre optics what electrons are to electronics.[44]

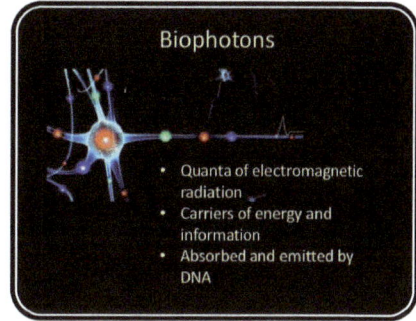

To place these concepts within the context of the historical development of relevant aspects of Western philosophy, a very brief summary was given at the start of this chapter. As we move forward into the 21st century, the words of philosopher Bertrand Russell, (1872 – 1970), are relevant. He was awarded the Noble Prize for Literature in 1950. He was prescient about the need to place human activities within a broader context, as advocated through *Light Garden* Principle Number 9: *Human use* that is restrained:

Image 4. *A graphic image of a biophoton*

> *"Democritus is the last of the Greek philosophers to be free from a certain fault which vitiated all later ancient and medieval thought...What is amiss, even in the best philosophy after Democritus, is an undue emphasis on man as compared with the universe."* [45]

Spirals, plans and movement in living creatures

The world of Nature is not full of rectangles and plans on paper. It is a big step to move from drawing concepts and diagrams on paper, to working in harmony with Nature. The generation of ecologically sound and beautiful creations that fit into the moving, multidimensional world of Nature needs much more than diagrams.

Whether we are planning particular places or managing an ecosystem, we need a means of communicating what it is intended to construct, do, or change. Drawing a plan or diagram is often the first human impulse. For example, the Australian Aboriginals are known for their bark paintings. Some of these paintings depict pathways, waterholes and other landmarks that help identify a route to be taken across a tract of land. Often there will be symbolic meanings woven into the paintings as well, highlighting the significance of *Light Garden* principles such as *'Perception and Measurement'*, *'Context and Environment'* and *'Human Use'*.

With access to computers and digital technology, for many people living in the 21st century, the process of drawing and communicating images can be quite different. As soon as one enters the digital, software aligned mindset, it's easy to overlook interaction with living creatures and living systems. However, more advanced computer software than is available to the public has enabled much scientific understanding of the biophysical world to progress.

As citizens, our conscious design thoughts need to expand to encompass more than static shapes - such as rectangles on a plan. We also need to be comfortable working with moving entities such as electromagnetic radiation and moving globes. Our unconscious thought patterns have already evolved to do that long ago. For example, many artists utilise their unconscious thought patterns, programed by DNA, to intuitively make artefacts that exhibit the same proportions as those found in the shapes created by Nature. For example, refer to the seashell depicted below. Just as we admire a spiral-shaped shell's natural beauty, we also consider some human-made spiral shapes to be beautiful.

In addition to seashells, many other spirals are found in Nature. For example, our DNA is a spiral axis in three-dimensional space. It emits biophotons. The physical arrangement of genes in the DNA spiral is finely tuned. DNA provides codes to guide our growth. It functions in conjunction with the electromagnetic and gravitational fields that underlie the physical, mechanical and chemical manifestations of our bodies. These fields also underlie the physical, mechanical and chemical structures of all life forms and our galaxy.

While light is being emitted and absorbed from the spiral of our DNA, it is also being emitted and absorbed from the spiral of our galaxy. That light is what we are designing with in a *Light Garden.* It is also what we are seeking to manage intelligently at all scales of living ecosystems.

Image 5. *A shell grows as a moving spiral*

Fractals

As described above, the design of living systems entails far more than plans and diagrams. Fractal patterns give us some more clues. Nature is full of fractal patterns. They may be seen in the spiral shapes of shells. They also can be readily observed in fern fronds, tree branches, rivers, coastlines, mountains, clouds, lightning strikes and hurricanes. Fractals can be described in mathematical equations. They exist beside our more familiar dimensions and systems of measurement.

> *"Driven by recursion, fractals are images of dynamic systems."* [46]

Recursion means self-similar patterns that repeat at all scales. These dynamic systems may be found in non-living plasma and light, such as lightning. They also may be living material, such as the fern frond illustrated on the following page.

Fractals are infinite, never-ending patterns. Their characteristics sound remarkably similar to some of the quantum biophysics principles behind the *Light Garden* model. For example, fractal patterns are self-similar, (or recursive), across different scales. This property of recursiveness relates to the *Light Garden* principle of *"Multiplication effects and Scale."* It also relates to the *Light Garden* *"Entanglement"* principle. Fractal patterns are created by repeating a process in an ongoing feedback loop.

Although it was not the first fractal to be discovered, the Mandelbrot set is the most famous fractal. Benoit Mandelbrot was born in Poland and obtained his PhD degree in Mathematical Sciences at the University of Paris in 1952. In 1980 he discovered the Mandelbrot fractal while working at IBM's Thomas J. Watson's Research Centre in upstate New York.[47] His international career illustrates the ongoing international collaboration and background of people working in this field.

Scientific research has continued in the decades since 1980, and more links between fractals, biophysics, and the properties of quantum materials have been found. In 2010, the journal Science published the work of scientists Richardella et al., where they described how they had found fractal patterns occurring in their images of quantum materials.[48] Since then, other researchers have found additional evidence of this phenomenon. For example, in 2018, the journal Nature published an article by Berciux and Iniguez entitled "Quantum Fractals". Dario Berciux works at the Donostia International Physics Center, at Donostia–San Sebastian, Spain.[49]

Fractal patterns are also being used in cardiology, as described by Gabriella Captur et al., in their 2017 publication "The fractal heart - embracing mathematics in the cardiology clinic."[50]

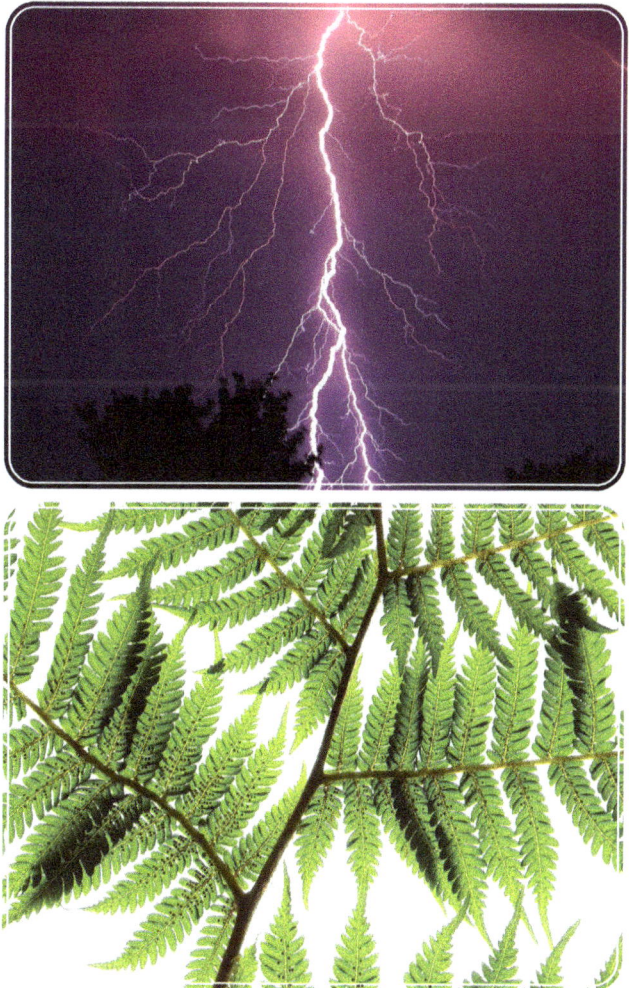

Image 6. *Fractals.*
(Top) *The fractal pattern of lighting, which is a form of non-living plasma and light.*
(Bottom) *The fractal pattern of a fern. The living plant reaches for sunlight and the non-living fractal of lightning reaches for the Earth.*

Energy flows

To encompass a broader view of the laws of natural systems, in addition to fractals, we need to talk about light in terms that reach beyond trees, photosynthesis and renewable solar energy.

In the previous chapter, ten principles involved in living with the Earth as a *Light Garden* were outlined to set the scene for understanding how to create gardens and places that embody Nature's energy flows. Let us now consider these energy flows of Nature in more detail, as they direct movement and determine the optimal relative placement of particles and waves in living creatures. The next questions to consider are: What are these energy flows? How are they created and how are particles created?

Plasma science encompasses the Unified Field Theory. It identifies the neutron as the fundamental plasmatic particle. The neutron consists of a dynamic mix of matter, anti-matter and dark matter.[51]

> *"From the smallest particle to the largest galactic formation, a web of electrical circuitry connects and unifies all of Nature, organising galaxies, energising stars, giving birth to planets and, on our own world, controlling weather and animating biological organisms. There are no isolated islands in an electric universe."* [52]

Prior to recent scientific work, the earlier work of Hubacher and other researchers revealed photographic clues about how biological organisms are animated. For example, a leaf's electron flux continues unabated above where it is cut away, as shown in the following photograph. No physical leaf tissue remained above the cut line, but the photon emission and electrical circuitry remained in place after the cut. [53]

This work is not to be confused with earlier work by the British mathematician biologist D' Arcy Thompson in his 1927 book "On Growth and Form". That covers a different topic, as he relates mathematical formula to the gradual evolution of form in organisms, through examples comparing the shape of different skulls. He does not focus on energy. Researchers have applied the ancient principles of sacred geometry in the 21st century to continue to develop our conceptual and intuitive understanding of the geometry, fractals and energy flows that underlie the growth of living organisms and our galaxy.[54] Biofields are interesting to consider in that context.

Biofields

The term "biofields" was coined by a panel convened in the United States of American at the National Institute of Health, (NIH). The panel was convened in 1994 to discuss complementary and alternative medicine (CAM).[55]

Biofields may be defined as an organising principle or information flow that regulates the biological functions and homeostasis of organisms. Biofields operate across a hierarchy of levels from the subatomic scale to the molecular, cellular, organismic, interpersonal and cosmic scale. They are recognised in several professional disciplines, including medicine, biology and physics.[56]

Many of the founders of quantum physics, including Max Plank, understood and advocated for "wholeness" in physics and biology. However, biochemists traditionally did not accept the relevance of biophysics to the study of molecular biology and living organisms.[57]

Niels Bohr was a Danish physicist who received the Nobel Prize in 1922. He understood the principle of *complementarity* in quantum physics, which holds that objects have certain pairs of characteristics which cannot be measured simultaneously. He also understood that complementarity is an essential part of understanding biophysics and the complex organisation and synchronisation of activity that occurs in living organisms. These factors cannot be explained by biochemistry alone.[58]

Although biofields exhibit electromagnetic properties, (such as with the phantom leaf effect), they do so within the context of bio-information and quantum field theories. These theories help explain additional properties of living organisms, such as biophotons, interaction with the quantum vacuum, coherence, non-locality and entanglement. Many of these properties are discussed in relation to specific examples of *Light Gardens* found in later chapters of this book.

> *"Without the biofield life would not exist and there would be only an inner biochemical mix."* [59]

Since Nicholas Tesla, Albert Einstein and others released their research findings from 1899 onwards, scientific work has continued in this field. Awareness of all forms of electromagnetic radiation and electromagnetic frequencies (EMF) has grown. EMF naturally occur throughout Nature and the human body. Many people who are concerned about the adverse health effects on living organisms of the spread of the 5 G network in the 21st century are aware that:

> *"Electricity and Wi-Fi etc. signals are stronger and foreign EMF, overriding the inherent Human, Nature and essential Human-Nature connection. Undesirable EMF alters the body's electrical system which directs the chemical messaging system in the brain."* [60]

Many studies have now documented the need for protection against harmful EMF. The insurance underwriters *Lloyd's of London* and *Swiss Re* refuse to include health cover against EMF in their policies, due to the high risk to life forms.[61] Under new work from home arrangements initiated during the covid pandemic of 2020, the risks of worker exposure to all forms of EMF have been mainly transferred from the workplace to the home, for the many people who now work from home.

Meanwhile, debate continues among those who monitor the research as to whether 5G EMF is harmless, or whether it increases the risks of cancer, oxidative stress in living organisms and other adverse health events. Further discussion of that research is beyond the scope of this book.

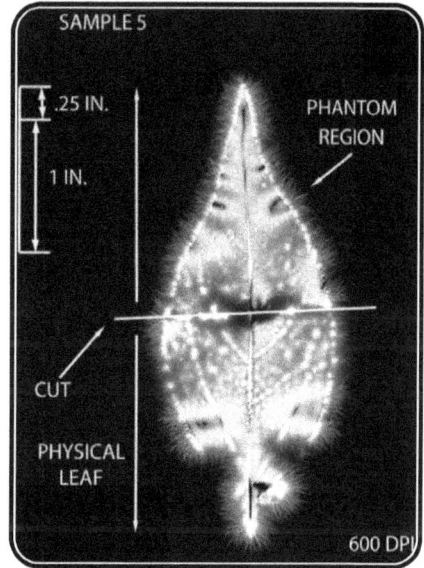

Image 7. *When a leaf is cut, the electron flux, (or biofield), continues for the full leaf*

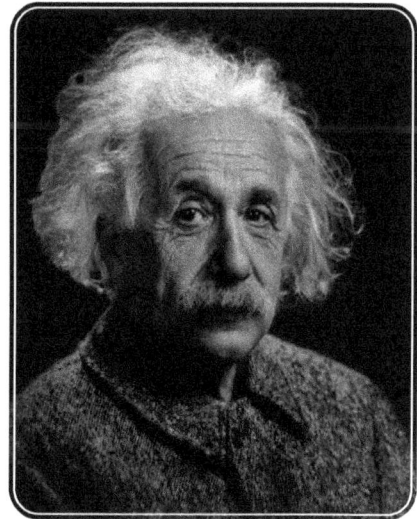

Image 8. *Albert Einstein was one of the early 20th century scientists and researchers who wrote papers and made discoveries about electromagnetic radiation, quantum physics and light.*

What is plasma?

The growth of life on Earth is affected by EMF and also by plasma. So it also is relevant to consider plasma in relation to the *Light Garden* model. The light coming from the Sun, the stars, living creatures, lightning, welding arcs, neon lights and fluorescent tubes is all plasma. All these forms of plasma conduct electricity. Many other phenomena such as the solar wind and the auroras in the ionosphere that envelops planet Earth are also plasmas. Plasma exists when the atoms in a gas become ionised and a roughly equal number of positively and negatively charged particles exist. They are affected by electromagnetic and gravitational fields, as described later in this chapter.

There are many different types of plasma. Lying on the beach sunbathing, one is basking in the plasma of sunlight that has reached the surface of the Earth. Here it interacts with the biosphere, which is that part of planet Earth where life occurs – in the air, land, water, rocks and the like.

Before the plasma of sunlight reaches a beach, it has been through a plasma filter known as the atmosphere. The plasma that streams from the Sun past Earth is referred to as the solar wind. At altitudes more than eighty kilometres above the Earth's surface, charged particles from the solar wind collide with the atmosphere, (or the magnetosphere), as it is referred to at that distance.[62]

> *"As they collide with atoms of gases in the atmosphere, the atoms become energised. Shortly afterwards, the atoms emit their gained energy as light."* [63]

> *"When the solar wind is perturbed, it easily transfers energy and material into the magnetosphere. The electrons and ions in the magnetosphere that are thus energised move along the magnetic field lines to the polar regions of the atmosphere causing the aurora."* [64]

The type of light emitted by the auroras may be referred to as fluorescence. Similarly, the atoms of gas and mercury vapour contained within the glass tube of a fluorescent lamp emit light when the passage of an electric current through the tube energises them. Just switch on a light to witness this!

The leaves of plants are another plasma filter between the sunlight that reaches the Earth's surface and the internal electrical, biochemical and biofield activity within living plants.

Other forms of plasma that have been captured for particular purposes include the ionised gas used to illuminate the screens of plasma televisions. These televisions were developed as large screen devices that produced images with good colour and contrast. However since 2007, plasma displays have been gradually replaced by LCD and OLED flat panel displays, which consume significantly less electricity and dissipate less heat than the plasma ones. Temperatures of the ionised gas in the plasma devices reached at least 1200 C. [65 66 67]

Although many forms of plasma operate at high temperatures, others are known as cold plasmas. Thermal plasma has electrons and heavy particles (neutrals and ions) existing at the same temperature. Cold Atmospheric Plasma (CAP) is said to be non-thermal because it has electrons at a hotter temperature than the surrounding heavy particles at room temperature.[68]

Many of the original cold plasmas existed at temperatures of around 70 to 100 degrees Celsius, which is cold compared to the Sun. Temperatures at the Sun are in the order of 15 million degrees Celsius.[69] During the late 1990s, room temperature cold plasmas were first created in the laboratory.

> *"Cold plasmas are extensively used in industry for critical surface cleaning and have been proposed for multiple applications in Plasma Medicine, including sterilisation or*

decontamination processes. Thermal plasmas are characterised as being macroscopically hot and have widespread industrial use in materials cutting, and more recently broad use in surgical procedures." [70]

For example, a cold plasma jet wand can be used to quickly and effectively disinfect hospital rooms.[71] It utilises the ability of oxygen-based ions in the plasma to destroy bacteria and viruses. The carbon is literally pulled out of the cell walls or protein casings of the bacteria and viruses.

This cold plasma action operates on a similar principle to that used to make homemade anti-bacterial and anti-viral plasma with the technology made available to the world by the Keshe Foundation.[72] All those who partake of this freely available, non-patented technology must first sign a World Peace Treaty. The treaty signatories declare they *"shall never think about getting involved or incite war or develop or use any tools of war."* [73] The supporting rationale for the use of this plasma technology is that

> *"There are better economic alternatives now available for immediate development through new technologies. These technologies provide vast new investment and employment opportunities that far exceed what has existed to date, at a fraction of the cost and complexity. Based on Plasma Science a completely new era of peace and prosperity is opening up to all mankind."* [74]

Another peaceful use of plasma technology is plasma surgery:

> *"It is used for open and laparoscopic surgical procedures and the cutting, coagulation and removal of soft tissue by vaporisation in gynaecology, oncology, general surgery… ovarian cysts and for tumor debulking. The system was selected as the 2008 Innovation of the Year by the Society of Laparoendoscopic Surgeons."* [75]

To a blood donor or a surgeon, the term plasma also may bring to mind blood plasma. Blood plasma makes up about 55% of the content of human blood. It appears as a pale yellow liquid if it is separated from normal red blood. Plasma carries all the different particles found in the blood that circulates throughout the body. These particles include red blood cells, white blood cells, hormones, water, salts, enzymes and waste products.[76]

Some questions and answers about plasma

Why is plasma important? Without the plasma of sunlight, Life on Earth would not exist as we know it. 99% of the visible universe exists in the form of plasma.[77] It's pretty remarkable to exist as living "matter" here on planet Earth, rather than as "plasma" somewhere else in the universe!

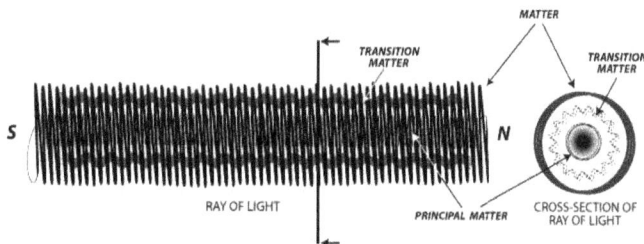

Image 9. *Diagram of the structure of sunlight plasma as it travels through space by Mehran Keshe*

As part of the model for the structure of light that was developed by Mehran Keshe,[78] light has mass and hence its own gravitational field. Light travels from the Sun to Earth as plasma. A simple description of the process is given here. Far more details are included in Mehran Keshe's books.

As illustrated in Image 9, when light plasma travels large distances, it has a helical motion and an internally dynamic, cylindrical shape. When this plasma encounters environmental plasmatic magnetic fields on Earth, it converts to a spherical and rotational form.

When light strikes a leaf on planet Earth, this plasma conversion provides energy for photosynthesis. As it moves, light plasma creates friction between itself and the magnetic and gravitational fields occurring in its environment. Due to this friction at the interface,

> *"the conversion…to matter fields strength leads to creation or release of plasmatic fields in the soft x-ray which is the essence of the creation of life…"*[79]

Matter is created in a leaf when sunlight plasma strikes the surface of a leaf and photosynthesis occurs. Nitrogen is the most abundant element in Earth's atmosphere and it is a vital component of chlorophyll. Plants use chlorophyll and nitrogen in conjunction with sunlight for photosynthesis. Although there are other processes, photosynthesis in plants is the primary way in which light combines with oxygen, carbon, hydrogen and other elements to form the food that underpins plant and animal life on Earth.

Image 10. *The magnetic and gravitational fields of the environment and matter interact with the plasma of sunlight during photosynthesis. Matter forms in a leaf with amino acids and other plant compounds.*

Why is plasma relevant to the Light Garden model?

Life on Earth is greatly influenced by the interaction of the solar wind (plasma), with the Earth's atmosphere and the Earth's gravitational and magnetic fields. The diagram below illustrates how these interact. The solar wind is a stream of ionised particles, (with positive or negative electric charges), that emanate from the Sun in all directions. Some of these particles flow past Earth as the solar wind. The solar wind is labelled as the incoming yellow line on the left-hand side of the image below. This image was prepared by the USA's National Aeronautical and Space Agency (NASA) and included on the Wikipedia website for all to see.

In contrast to planet Earth, Mars lost its planetary magnetic field less than a billion years after it was formed. Before that time, water had been abundant on Mars and there were oceans, rivers and rain. Scientists are examining fossils taken from rocks on Mars. They think it is likely that there was life on Mars that is similar to life as we know it on planet Earth.

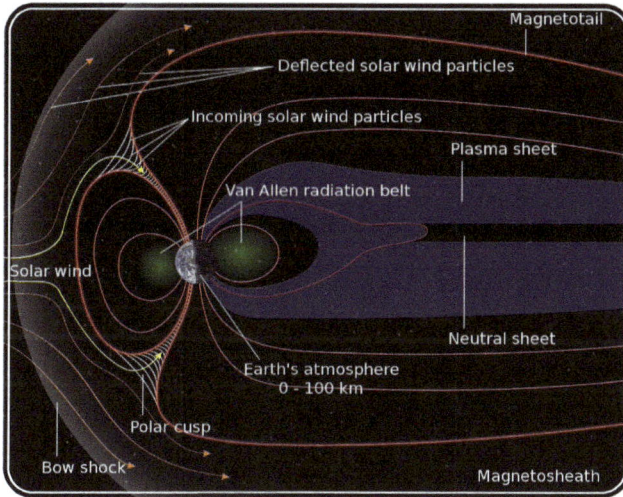

Image 11. *(Above left) solar wind plasma affects life on Earth. (Above right) solar wind bombards planet Mars, which has lost its protective atmosphere and no longer supports life.*

However once Mars lost its internally generated magnetic field, it also lost its principal protection against the impact of the solar wind, (plasma), and its atmosphere was eroded away. Today, only a thin atmosphere remains on Mars. NASA reported these scientific findings in 2016, as part of the Marven mission to Mars.[80] In 2020, NASA planned to launch the Mars 2020 rover mission. That mission aimed to look for carbonised deposits of minerals called carbonates. On Earth, carbonates help form seashells and coral, which are capable of surviving in fossilised form for billions of years.

Carbonates form when carbon atoms combine with oxygen atoms to form CO3 ions. These negatively charged ions combine with positively charged metal ions to create the carbonate minerals found in fossils and other places. It is not only carbonates that draw carbon atoms from the atmosphere. Removing atoms from the atmosphere is an integral part of life on Earth. Trees, soils and oceans are all known for that ability.

Drawing carbon from the atmosphere is one of many ways to tackle climate change. For example, as described earlier, in 2019, Professor Tom Crowther of the Swiss university ETH Zürich, announced his research team's findings. They had been looking at the best ways to tackle climate change. They had found that tree planting was by far the most effective solution. 1.2 trillion native trees would need to be planted on 11% of the Earth's total land area to tackle the problem. *"That area is about 11% of all land and equivalent to the size of the US and China combined",* he said.[81]

In the final chapter of this book, the *Light Garden* model's usefulness for tackling climate change is considered in more detail.

Quantum biophysics

Planting 1.2 trillion native trees is a huge task. Given the high levels of concern about climate change worldwide, engaging people who are happy to be paid to work on this task is probably not a problem. There is currently plenty of available labour, due to the high levels of underemployment of the human population in many countries. In addition, there are vast sums of money available because of government programs to generate money in the first quarter of the 21st century. As a fourth factor, the affinity between biophysics, quantum principles and how we manage light can contribute too. That is explained in further detail as this book progresses.

Quantum biophysics is concerned with discrete, naturally occurring units, such as photons of light. This concept of discrete natural units that behave as both particles and waves also pertains to the atoms that are the subject of biophysics in general. As noted by Encyclopaedia Britannica,

> *"submicroscopic mechanical vibrations in the layers of atoms comprising crystals also give up or take on energy and momentum in quanta called photons."* [82]

Encyclopaedia Britannica has described the meaning of the term 'quantum' in the field of physics as a

> *"discrete natural unit, or packet, of energy, charge, angular momentum, or other physical property. Light, for example, appearing in some respects as a continuous electromagnetic wave, on the submicroscopic level is emitted and absorbed in discrete amounts, or quanta; and for light of a given wavelength, the magnitude of all the quanta emitted or absorbed is the same in both energy and momentum. These particle-like packets of light are called photons, a term also applicable to quanta of other forms of electromagnetic energy such as X rays and gamma rays."* [83]

The connection between light and quantum phenomena is thus apparent. Light is a form of electromagnetic energy, which in the 21st century is commonly referred to as EMF. In 2015 Kaftos et al. elaborated further upon this when commenting upon the evidence of biofields and their connection with light, quantum phenomena, electromagnetic fields, molecular biology and biochemistry:

> *"...any electromagnetic-based definition [of biofields] is limiting, since it does not encompass quantum and holistic effects. EMF theories are also themselves special cases of quantum field theories, the latter being more natural and general, and therefore able to account for the properties of coherence, non-locality, and entanglement... which are strikingly relevant to living organisms."* [84]

Kaftos et al. go on to identify further areas for research around the subject of a living universe and the application of quantum biophysics to human health and other fields. The properties of coherence, non-locality and entanglement referred to above are some of the prevailing attributes of quantum biophysics phenomena. For example, the statistical similarity of an electromagnetic field, or a quantum wave packet at two different points in either space or time, is referred to as the degree of coherence.

Entanglement: an example of the link between quantum biophysics and society

In quantum theory, entanglement refers to the phenomenon that particles cannot be perceived or described independently of each other. Entanglement occurs where multiple objects are linked together because they exist in the same quantum state.

The prospects for *disentanglement* have also been part of the debate by physicists since the early days of quantum physics. A detailed review of that subject is not necessary here. However, it may be found in Antony Crofts' work, from the Department of Biochemistry and Centre for Biophysics and Computational Biology at the University of Illinois.[85]

To set the framework for the *Light Garden* model being applied at all scales from the tiny to the large and in spheres that overlap with social and economic movements, some examples may be helpful. The quantum biophysics concept of entanglement has parallels in the strategies of social and political movements. For example, as described in the first chapter, Dr Vandana Shiva has identified the entangled, simultaneous impact of digital, financial and biotech technologies in the 21st century. Speaking of the situation in East Asia and Japan, Professor Akihiro Ogawa of the Asia Institute at the University of Melbourne also describes how it is the combination, [or entanglement] of events, that often prompts change:

> *"The triple disaster of the Great East Japan Earthquake, its related tsunami and the Fukushima Daiichi nuclear power plant accident on 11 March 2011 was a turning point in the history of social movements in post-Second World War Japan."* [86]

Similarly, a 21st century Japanese student leader has drawn attention to another combination of factors required for the exercise of a citizens' democracy. Authoritarian rulers often challenge the combination of three factors that he described:

> *"The three pillars of this country are kihonteki jinken [basic human rights], kokumin shuken [sovereignty of the people], and heiwa shugi [pacifism]. Those represent the history of our country."* [87]

The centuries-old Japanese Zen aesthetic principles also present a suite of concepts to be used in unison, (just as the *Light Garden* principles are designed to be used in unison). Zen concepts are described in more detail in a later chapter but they include:

- Kanso, meaning "simplicity or elimination of clutter."
- Shizen, meaning "naturalness" and
- Yugen meaning "subtlety."[88]

Entanglement and disentanglement are also terms that social scientists use. For example, in describing the history of social change movements in the 20th and 21st centuries, Giorel Curran of Griffith University noted that:

> *"In disentangling social change strategy from its institutional focus, and in eschewing links to political parties and the route of statist power in general, the new social movements problematised the role of the 'old' labour movement within their ranks…*
>
> *"Others lamented the movements' championing of the 'hyper-individualism' that played into the very hands of their capitalised opponents who were promoting just that."* [89]

The whole concept of quantum biophysics illustrates how the Laws of Nature foster a coordinated approach to our visions for economics, environment, society and governance. *Probability* is another fundamental feature of the quantum perspective. Living processes are described in terms of a likelihood of something being present or occurring, rather than a precisely measured and independent outcome. Considering the interaction between living systems and economic systems, one could say that to continue to plan for an abstract concept of economic growth that is detached from other *Light Garden* considerations has a high probability of failure.

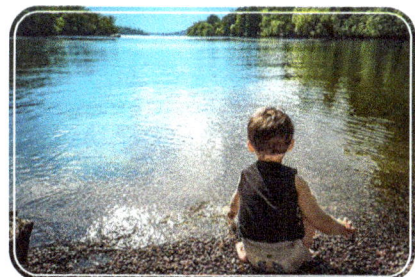

Image 12. *Photo of child.*

Light Garden Principles derived from the principles of quantum biophysics

1. ENERGY. Enhance and work with the energy flows of nature. These direct movement & determine the optimal relative placement of particles and waves. Energy from the sun is one example.

2. SPACE and TIME. Allow space and time for the processes that rejuvenate life to occur. Work with these. For example, allow the space and time through which particles and waves move; through which the seasonal migrations of birds occur and through which the transfer of pollen between flowers occurs.

3. WAVES and PARTICLES. Consider the waves and particles that move in energy fields. Work with the simultaneous wave and particle-like behaviour of many living systems, including human activity.

4. LINES, PATTERNS and PROBABILITIES. There are the lines of motion that we perceive and patterns of motion that form. In addition there are uncertainties and probabilities. Probability theory is widely used in activities such as finance, insurance, gambling, artificial intelligence, machine learning and physics, as well as in understanding of living systems. Work with probability that supports, not degrades, living systems.

5. MULTIPLICATION. Multiplication effects arise due to the cumulative effect of several activities. For example, similar entities may cluster into materials that we can feel and touch. A group of carbon atoms clustering together to form graphite is an example of this. Another group of carbon atoms might cluster differently to form a brilliant pink diamond.

6. ENTANGLEMENT and FOCAL POINTS. There are points where energy paths intersect and where we perceive focal points to arise. In addition there is the related concept of Quantum entanglement, where particles cannot be perceived or described independently of each other. This relates to the following principle of Perception and Measurement.

7. PERCEPTION and MEASUREMENT. Human perception and measurement of phenomena is a significant factor to be aware of. Although perceptions may vary from person to person, there are many human, plant and animal attributes which have genetically evolved over millennia in conjunction with the wider world of nature. Contemporary technology needs to be harnessed to support this connection, rather than creating artificial realities.

8. CONTEXT and ENVIRONMENT. There is the wider environment in which particular activities occur. Light Garden activities contribute positively towards the rejuvenation and maintenance of healthy, biodiverse living systems and are appropriate for their context. The quantum biophysics principle of coherence between the macro and the micro scales of living systems and climate applies here.

9. HUMAN USE. There may be intelligent, restrained human use of resources for particular purposes, such as education, food production; delineation of a parcel of land, water or space, and so on. Consider the interdependence of Life with quantum biophysics principles and quantum field theories, which are able to account for the characteristics of living systems, such as coherence, entanglement and non-locality.

10. STORAGE AND SHARING OF INFORMATION are needed to communicate and pass on the knowledge, skills and organisational capacities to support rejuvenation of living systems.

Image 13. *Light Garden Principles 1-10*

Light Garden Decision Making Criteria

1. ENERGY. Manage energy flows giving priority to supporting living ecosystems and stopping carbon emissions.

2. SPACE and TIME. Allow ecosystems the space and time they need to rejuvenate. Manage human activities within limits to allow this to occur.

3. WAVES and PARTICLES. Foster human activity with a a wave of cooperative laws to support ecosystem rejuvenation at the international level, plus particles of initiatives at the local scale.

4. LINES, PATTERNS and PROBABILITIES. Make decisions based on the probability that ecosystems will endure.

5. MULTIPLICATION. Make decisions about how to manage natural resources and engage human populations in meaningful roles by incorporating the multiplier effects that arise naturally through application of quantum biophysical principles.

For example, in the Indian State of Sikkim where the government has legislated for a fully organic agricultural system, there are meaningful roles for all citizens. They grow and market organic food, rejuvenate soils and forests, cooperatively and equitably manage water, participate in local decision-making forums, education, care-giving, building and so on.

6. ENTANGLEMENT and FOCAL POINTS. Proactively seek benefits for the common good to rejuvenate life systems through anticipating and planning around the principles of entanglement that naturally occur at the small and large scales.

7. PERCEPTION and MEASUREMENT. Acknowledge the bio-physical concepts of non-locality and aesthetics, as principles to be applied when considering human perception and measurement.

8. CONTEXT and ENVIRONMENT. Work for the common good. Make decisions based on opportunities to respect and rejuvenate context and environment.

9. HUMAN USE. Manage human use with intelligent, radical restraint, within the capacity of the planet's life systems. For example, cease over-fishing the oceans so fish populations and ecosystems have the opportunity to rejuvenate.

10. STORAGE AND SHARING OF INFORMATION Store and share information that supports knowledge, skills, human potential and natural resource management for the common good at the local and planetary scales.

A mnemonic to help remember these criteria in the order of 1 – 10 is: **"Every summer we love mother eating perfect, crimson, heavenly strawberries."** *Every* prompts the letter *E*, which is for is for *Energy*. *Summer* prompts the letter *S*, which is for *Space and Time*. *We* prompts the letter *W*, which is for is for *Waves and particles*. *Love* prompts the letter *L*, which is for is for *Lines, patters and probability*. *Mother* prompts the letter *M*, which is for is for *Multiplication effects*. *Eating* prompts the letter *E*, which is for is for *Entanglement and focal points*. *Perfect* prompts the letter *P*, which is for is for *Perception and measurement*. *Crimson* prompts the letter *C*, which is for is for *Context and environment*. *Strawberries* prompts the letter *S*, which is for is for *Storage and sharing.*

Image 14. *Light Garden Decision Making Criteria*

In addition to the concept of probability, (which is a construct of the human mind), it is important to include other ideas associated with the human mind in any set of *Light Garden* principles. Encyclopaedia Britannica also notes the importance of the human mind, when describing how quantum physics underlies theories of biochemistry, neurobiology and electromagnetism. Accordingly, *"Perception and Measurement"* by the human mind is included as a broad *Light Garden* principle.

Image 15. *The role of the human mind is an area of ongoing research.*

The role of the human mind is an area of ongoing research. So too is the quantum property of coherence that acts as a bridge between the macro and micro scales in living organisms. The property of coherence has already been applied in devices used in medicine. For example, these devices prepare visual images of living tissue through the technique of optical coherence tomography. It is used in radio antenna arrays, in astronomical optical interferometers and in radio telescopes. Fields such as quantum wave packets and electromagnetic fields display statistical similarities between two points in space or time. This is referred to as coherence.[90]

Light Garden principle number 3:
Waves and particles

The energy of ocean currents brings particles of sand to beaches in discrete waves. This is a metaphor for the quantum principle that light and energy travel in discrete parcels, like sand.

Light Garden principle number 4:
Lines, patterns and probabilities.

The particles of sand are deposited as the waves retreat...and in their wake, new wave patterns form on the shore. As in quantum physics, the probability that one particular grain of sand will come to rest in a specific place is low. However, when many grains of sand combine, they make the familiar rippled pattern of small sand ridges found on tidal flats the world over.

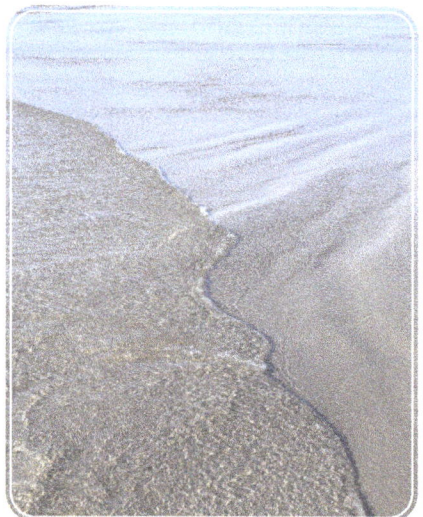

Image 16. *The seashore as a metaphor for the principles of quantum biophysics.*

Light Garden principle number 5: Multiplication effects

Touch one part of a mattress or a body of water and the vibration moves through the whole. Reminding us of the quantum theory that *matter is forever moving as a resonant, responsive, multifaceted whole*, the pattern of sunlight in the waves is forever changing but forever following the principles of quantum biophysics.

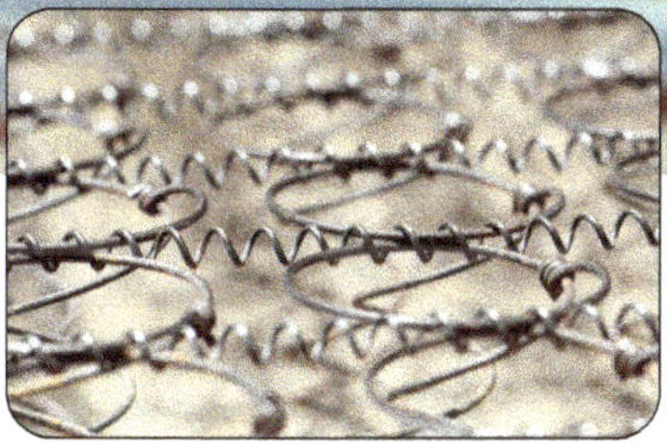

Image 17. (Top) *Light garden principle of Multiplication effects.*
Image 18. (Bottom) *The inner spring mattress analogy: touch one part of the quantum field and the vibration moves through the whole.*

Analogies with sunlight in ocean waves and with an innerspring mattress illustrate how important it is to manage Earth's natural resources so that the integrities of the quantum field, the magnetic field and the gravitational field are retained. That way, when one part of the innerspring mattress is touched and a vibration moves through the whole mattress, it is not broken but it can absorb the impact and allow it to ripple through. In the wider world, a vibration may be experienced in the form of a physical movement, a shock, a change, or a social movement.

In writing about forests, *light gardens* and biophysics, I have chosen the broad sense of the word "gardens." It encompasses traditional agricultural practices, temples, sacred sites, management of biodiversity and urban environments and leads to the concept of whole Earth as a *Light Garden*.

Consciousness is growing that we are all part of the global community. So too, awareness is increasing that natural beauty and natural light are essential natural resources to be shared equitably: they are not peripheral or ancillary facets of modern life. Humans replace the energy and electrons in their body in three ways: from food; from sunlight and from walking barefoot on the ground.

Natural beauty arises when Nature's processes are understood and allowed to flow, rather than being negated by human activities. Landscape design is

Image 19. *Light shines through the translucent petals of a tulip.*

a process where gradually, layer by layer, detail, diversity and resilience are built into the design. Traditional cultures did this with their gardens and Nature still does this.

This book aims to build that capacity for all people, firstly by giving practical examples from each continent and secondly by developing the *Light Garden* model to address the resource management issues of the 21st century at the global scale.

Image 20. *Children at play in a field of tulips, while the broader scale landscape with trees frames this.*

As we have seen in the details of Image 14, *The Light Garden Decision Making Criteria* on page 45 of this chapter, these principles can be applied to address practical day to day decisions and well as the related global issues. Those people who live in close alignment with the natural world instinctively know that all living creatures, (and the quantum world), are interconnected. They know there is no separation between decisions made at the local day to day level and at the global level. Others can learn about this, if they have not lived that way themselves.

No creatures or people are excluded. All creatures observe, co-create and interact. *The Light Garden Decision Making Criteria* embodies this mindset. It translates what may be the less familiar terminology of quantum biophysics into more readily accessible terminology that reflects familiar, day to day lived experiences.

As depicted in Image 20, children delight in brushing the petals of flowers as they run through a field of flowers. At the same time, they have the freedom to do so because they are also safely enclosed within a broader landscape frame of trees, under the watchful eyes of their parents.

Swedish schoolgirl Greta Thunberg caught the world's imagination and attention in 2019 when she spoke at the World Economic Forum in Davos. With her clarion call for immediate effective action on climate change, she articulated the spirit of the quantum principle of entanglement between the smaller and the larger scales:

> *"I want you to act as you would in a crisis. I want you to act as if our house is on fire. Because it is."* [91]

3

North Asia, including Feng Shui influences

Light and Feng Shui: what an ideal match! It is one where there are some interesting concepts to explore, as humanity cooperatively manages the natural resources of our planet in the 21st century. Light is a form of energy and Feng Shui works with balancing the energies of the earth, air, fire, water and wood. Feng Shui practitioners also work with balancing yang and yin, the masculine and feminine energies.

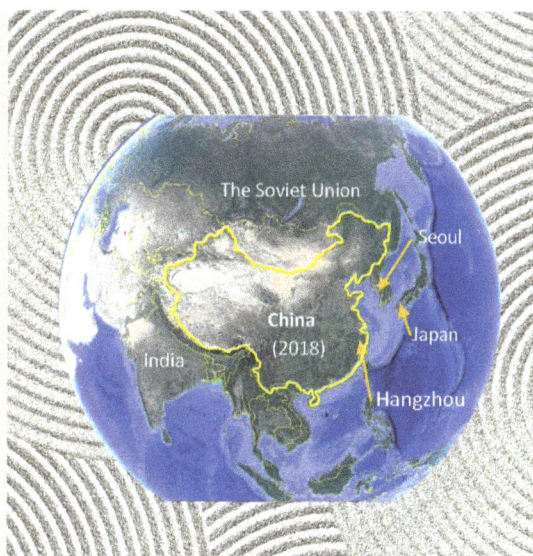

Image 1. *(Above left)* *Feng Shui and Yin Yang symbol.* (Above right) *Location Map of North Asia.*

Feng Shui has been practised in North Asian cultures for centuries. The way it has influenced the management of natural resources, energy, society and light in different countries within this region highlights some potential contributions of the *Light Garden* concept within these cultures. The map included above shows the location of some examples of various sites discussed in this chapter.

Some aspects of Japanese garden design and the Buddhist perspective on enlightenment are also reviewed in the latter part of this chapter, adding depth to the concept that the energy of light is a conscious design factor in these cultures.

China and Feng Shui

Go Puo, Chinese: 郭璞; (AD 276 – 324), was an eminent writer and commentator on ancient texts. He was the author of *The Zangshu,* otherwise known as *The Book of Burial.* He is considered the first and most authoritative writer on the ancient doctrine of Feng Shui.[92] Stephen L. Field, PhD, translated *The Zangshu* to English in 2001.[93] An extract from his work defines the meaning of the term Feng Shui as "Wind Water." [94] The verse reads as:

經 曰	
氣乘風散	*"when qi rides the wind it is dispersed,*
界水則止。	*when it meets a boundary of water it is retained.*
古人	*The Ancients were able to gather it to prevent dispersion,*
聚之使不散,	*to guide it and retain it,*
行之使有止,	*hence it was called Wind Water"*
故謂風水。	

This translation of the concepts behind Feng Shui refers to *"qi"*. Min Li (2009) has described *Qi* or *Chi* as:

"Natural Laws are regarded as the highest guidance of all aspects of human endeavours and Chi is the very essence of the universe…" [95]

This concept of Chi aligns strongly with the flow of plasma and the manner in which electromagnetic and gravitational fields interact throughout the universe. As described in Chapter Two, these fields guide the patterns living organisms follow in their growth, repair and reproduction. Several areas of research into this phenomenon were discussed. They are drawn together and presented as the basis of the *Light Garden* model in this book. This model has been developed for natural resource management that follows Nature's laws or natural laws, as referred to above by Min Li. He continues:

"We all want to reside in a living environment that nourishes us with good health, harmonious relationships, career success, and overall happiness." [96]

Feng Shui provides a system for working towards that goal, with an understanding of what aspects of the "living environment" will support it. Describing the difference between Chinese traditional landscape design and Western landscape design, Junying Pang, a 21st century landscape planning student, said

"Chinese traditional landscape design emphasized the understanding and development of the natural beauty, whereas Western landscape focused on the refining of the natural elements as an abstract sense of order and formal beauty." [97]

Junying Pang's statement is infinity debatable but relevant to the concept of *Light Gardens.* It will be considered it in more detail later in this chapter and subsequent chapters of this book but firstly some particular examples of the application of Feng Shui concepts will be described. These examples are drawn from China, South Korea and Japan.

As an indication of how universally valued is the beauty of Feng Shui gardens, a number of them are included in UNESCO's register of World Heritage sites. Two of these gardens within their landscape settings are considered in this chapter: West Lake in the city of Hangzhou in China, plus Huwon in South Korea.

The symbolism of light in North Asian gardens is quite different from the symbolism in Hindu, Islamic or Christian gardens. In the North Asian cultures, there is a greater emphasis on being in an environment that emulates Nature, with the enlightenment experience arising from meditation and the realization of

the "oneness" of all beings. This concept aligns well with the *Light Garden* concept of this book because ten *Light Garden* principles need to act in unison to create the overall synchronicity of the *Light Garden*. This synchronicity also aligns well with the Buddhist concept of oneness of all beings, where the needs of all are met in diverse, interactive ecosystems and societies.

Highlighting the *Light Garden* affinity with North Asian symbolism is not to imply that other cultures have less affinity with the *Light Garden* model. This will become apparent as one reads through the examples from different cultures that are discussed in this book.

Traditional Feng Shui was developed in the northern hemisphere. Feng Shui has many variations, which have developed over thousands of years. The Eight Life Aspirations style of Feng Shui is referred to in this book. The same Feng Shui principles apply in the southern hemisphere as in the northern hemisphere, except that North and South are reversed, while East and West remain the same. There is some controversy over how to interpret all the details of this concept but there are some basic agreed principles.

For example, in the Northern Hemisphere, the *Fire* Element is located in the South. The diagrams in Image 2 may be used for reference in the southern hemisphere. The chart at shown above right includes the feature of Love and Marriage in the North West, between the *Fire* Element in the North, and the feature of Children and Creativity, which manifests in the West. The Bagua below right was prepared by Anne Whittingham from multiple sources to draw together many related elements and features used in garden and landscape design.[98]

North West Earth Element Love and Marriage	North Fire Element Flame	North East Wood Element Wealth
West Metal Element Creativity/children	Centre Heart Yin/Yang point	East Wood Element Health
South West Metal Element Helpful people/Blessings	South Water Element Careet/Path in Life	South East Earth Element Spiritual Growth/Cultivation

Direction	Element	Function	Feature
South	Water	Career/Life Path	Water feature
North East	Wood	Wealth	Gold bells in water feature
East	Wood	Family & Health	Greenery & wood dragon
South East	Earth	Spiritual Growth	Spiritual symbol
North	Fire	Fame & recognition	Lights, BBQ
South West	Metal	Helpful people	Business seating area
West	Metal	Chikdren & inner child	Playground & yogo area
North West	Earth	Love and Marriage	Flowers, Outdoor furniture

Image 2. *Feng Shui Bagua for the Southern Hemisphere and a lotus flower, popular in Feng Shui gardens.*

Examples of Feng Shui in Landscape Design

Feng Shui principles can be applied to the design of a place, garden or landscape. For example, as illustrated below, I have used them in the landscape design to re-establish native vegetation and make a recreation area around a former quarry site lake in the southern hemisphere.

Feng Shui Around a Lake

Red is in the North with the element of fire and the function of fame and recognition. Place lights or fire pits here.

Purple and gold in the North East is the element of wood, with the function of wealth and prosperity. Add features such as gold and purple flowers.

In the East is green and the wood element, with the function of health and family. A wooden dragon may be placed here.

In the South East, beige, pink and earthly colours are associated with the earth element and the function of spiritual growth and knowledge.

Pink in the North West with the element of earth and the function of marriage and happy personal relationships.

White in the West is the element of metal, with the function of children and play.

Blue in the South with the water element and the function of career and life path.

Grey in the South West is the element of metal, with the function of helpful people and travel. Add outdoor furniture here for meetings.

Lake

Island

Image 3. *Example of location of Feng Shui features around a lake.*

The lake design involved placing relevant Feng Shui features in the different compass directions around the lake. For example, a children's playground was located on the western shore of the lake. This location corresponds with the Function of "Children and the Inner Child," which is assigned to this direction in the Bagua. Similarly, to reflect the Water Element of the South, a low rock waterfall was added on the edge of the lake where a stream flowed into it. This area was also stabilized with revegetation works.

At the northern end of the lake, in the direction of the element Fire, lights and campfire sites were added. Purple flowered native waterlilies and gold flowered aquatic plants were included in the species list to re-establish native vegetation on the lake's adjoining northeastern shores. A walkway for visitors to the site was extended past this area to the lake's eastern shore. Here the revegetation works included plenty of green trees and shrubs. The direction of the East is associated with greenery and the Element of Wood. A carved wooden dragon sculpture was installed here.

On the southeastern shores of the lake, quiet areas for contemplation and meditation were established in lawn areas. Clumps of native vegetation were planted around the lawns. The southeasterly direction is associated with spiritual growth and the Element of Earth in the Feng Shui Bagua. Thus, we see how the design combined a balanced range of Feng Shui activities around the pathway circuit.

Hangzhou and West Lake in China

Image 4. *Map of West Lake near the Qiantang River in Hangzhou, China.*

Feng Shui encourages a mindful abundance of natural light. For example, there are rules for the placement of mirrors that reflect light in interior design. Mirrors are placed to reflect light into areas needing more energy. They also are set to avoid directing light away from areas where it needs to be retained. In landscape design, instead of a mirror reflecting light indoors, a pond of water might reflect light and bring energy into an outdoor area. An example of this is described below at the West Lake site in China. This concept of designing with water can be considered in conjunction with the description of *wind water* given earlier in this chapter:

> *"when qi rides the wind it is dispersed, when it meets a boundary of water it is retained."* [99]

West Lake (Chinese) pinyin Xī Hú; Wu Si-wu) is a freshwater lake in Hangzhou, China. By the 21st century, Hangzhou had grown to be a city with a population of 9.2 million. It may be reached by a one hour train journey to the south-west of Shanghai. After centuries of dredging, three main causeways now divide West Lake into five sections. There are numerous human-made temples, islands, pleasure craft, walkways and gardens around the lake.[100]

The cultural history of West Lake includes many themes from Feng Shui and Buddhism. It also abounds in practical schemes for water storage and water distribution for agricultural, recreational and urban purposes. West Lake was once a lagoon adjoining the nearby Qiantang River. In AD 610, the Qiantang River was linked via the construction of the Jiangnan Canal to the other four major rivers of China, (the Yellow, Hai, Yangtze and Huai).[101] This waterway linkage boosted Hangzhou's regional economy, which in turn supported the development of a class of poets, painters, and travellers who celebrated the West Lake landscape.

The West Lake Cultural Landscape of Hangzhou illustrates the profound metaphysical importance of natural beauty in Chinese culture. Writers and artists have celebrated the beauty of this landscape since the Tang Dynasty (AD 618-907). In the view illustrated below, we see an example of how this aligns with principle number nine in the *Light Garden* model: human use does not dominate the natural beauty. It is restrained within the capacity of the natural resources to accommodate it.

The name "West Lake" is recorded as first appearing in the poems of Baui Juvi. One of these is known as

> *"Bestowed on guests as returning from West Lake in the evening and looking Back to Gushan Temple".* [102]

The appreciation of the beauty of the light of the setting sun is underlined by the naming of the lake as *West Lake*. This name has remained in use ever since the days of Baui Juvi. Millions of visitors continue to come to the site each year. In 2011 it was listed on the United Nations Educational, Scientific and Cultural Organisation's (UNESCO's) World Heritage List.[103]

The West Lake Cultural Landscape in China is one of the inspirational landscapes that underpin the art of Chinese landscape design and planning. The factors contributing to the beauty of West Lake and other inspirational landscapes were analysed long ago and gradually recorded into the system of Feng Shui that we know today.

The idyllic lake scene depicted below appears as though the pavilion has been placed in the natural setting surrounded by forested hills and sky. However, the West Lake landscape has been modified over a period of at least 1,500 years. The lake's main human-made elements, (two causeways and three islands), were created as part of repeated dredgings between the 9th and 12th centuries.[104]

The location of particular structures in and around the lake was determined with Feng Shui in mind. The viewing platform depicted in Image 5 is an example of this

Image 5. *West Lake (Chinese pinyin: Xī Hú; Wu: Si-wu)*

Feng Shui principles are applicable at all scales when designing landscapes. In the three photographs below, looking from left to right, we see the progression from a closeup view of a lakeside pavilion to a more distant view across the lake.

Image 6. *West Lake. Lakeside pavilions - as seen in a series of views from close up to further away.*

Since the Southern Song Dynasty, (thirteenth century), ten poetically named Feng Shui scenic places, have been identified at West Lake. They embody idealised, classical Chinese landscapes that are regarded as examples of the perfect fusion between man and Nature.

The UNESCO World Heritage listing information for the site noted that to make the islands, causeways and the lower slopes of the hills around West Lake "more beautiful", they have been "improved." Numerous temples, pagodas, pavilions, gardens and ornamental trees were added for this purpose. These structures merge with the surrounding farmed landscape.[105] Although you don't see crowds of people in the photographs above, the 3,322 hectare West Lake site caters to over one million visitors per day during peak holiday times.[106] In comparison, the highest recorded average daily attendance at the 341 hectare[107] Central Park site in New York is 220,000 people.[108]

South Korea

The site of Huwon is an example of the unique Korean form of Feng Shui, which is known as Psungsu – jiri – seol. This form was developed by Doseon Guksa, a Korean Buddhist monk, AD (826 – 898). He is honoured in Korea because of his genius in studying, then adapting existing Chinese Feng Shui theories for use in the different conditions of Korean culture.

Doseon Guksa emphasized the effects of Feng Shui theories on communities and the nation as a whole. He gave work for communities and the nation a higher priority than more individual endeavours, such as creating personal fortunes, or the placement of furniture. Korean Feng Shui and the cultural connection to Nature can be traced to the Korean religious spectrum known as Seondo. This includes prehistoric traditions of animism, shamanism and the belief in mountain and forest spirits, as well as Feng Shui.[109]

In comparison to Chinese and Japanese gardens, early Korean gardens emphasised creating a naturalistic setting and the experience of walking through the actual landscape in which the garden was located. Korean landscape architecture and garden design hinge on reverence for Nature. The theory is that structures and garden features are used sparingly – and they are carefully located to complement natural settings.

The garden at Changdeokungi includes *"a small rice field, where the king would farm rice to aid his understanding of the hard work of farmers and show his solidarity with the farmers. The dried rice plants would be used to thatch Cheonguijeong"*.[110]

Huwon garden was designed to embrace the topography by following *pungsu,* (or Feng Shui), principles on the Changdeokgungi Palace site in Seoul. This site dates from the fourteenth century to the present times. There is a hill behind the buildings on the site and a small stream to the front, which is regarded as good *pungsu.* The entry and palace buildings were located on the southern side of the site, that is associated with the Sun element. Huwon, the 32 hectare rear garden, was constructed on the northern side of the site. The northern side of the site is associated with the Water element.[111]

Huwon is also known as Biwon, or the Secret Garden. It was originally constructed for the use of the royal family. However, it is not an extravagant garden. A signboard at the front of the garden was inscribed by King Jeongjo. The inscription translates to English as 'Gather the Universe'. Joseon kings chose to relax, study and write poems in the tranquil setting of Biwon. Pavilions were built on the edge of a square lily pond that was set in a forest glade. Other halls and a library were located nearby.[112]

At Huwon, small pavilions were built along the stream flowing through the site. There were also areas provided for privacy, archery, banquets, military drills and entertaining guests. Kings and Queens used their time in the gardens to perform court rituals, experimental farming and silk cultivation. These ceremonies were designed to show leadership to the people of Korea.[113]

Changdeokungi Palace dates from the 14th century and is located within the modern-day city of Seoul. Another Korean Palace that was built at the end of the 14th century in 1395 was Gyong Palace. It survives to the present day, after being reconstructed.

Image 7. (Top right) *Ongnyucheon stream (Hangeul:* 옥류천 *; Hanja* 玉流川*), in the rear garden of Changdeokgung Palace, Seoul. In the sensitive carving of a rock formation, we see an example of how the Koreans designed around natural features of the landscape.*

Image 8. (Above) *A historical painting of Changdeokgungi, showing the landscape setting. This site is located within the city of Seoul and dates from the 14th century to present times.*

As indicated in the illustration below, the character of the buildings in Seoul is relatively austere. This austerity may reflect the military imperatives that were predominant in its reconstruction after it was destroyed during the Japanese invasion of 1592 – 98. The South Korean capital city of Seoul also was rebuilt after devastation during the 20th century Japanese occupation and the Korean War of the 1950s.[114]

Although the Korean Kings and Queens are no longer in residence at Huwon, the enthusiasm of the people of Korea to develop their connection with Nature and rural enterprises continues to grow.

In contrast to the millions of daily visitors to the gardens of the West Lake Cultural Landscape District of Hangzhou, visitor numbers to Huwon are limited to fifty per tour. Visitors must book one of the two or three popular daily guided tours to enter this garden. Surrounding the site is a city of twelve million people.[115]

Another example of the Korean enthusiasm for connection with Nature is the Bukhansan National Park near Seoul. It is reported to have the highest number of visitors per square meter of any National Park in the world. An average of five million visitors per year come to the Park, exemplifying the national enthusiasm for hiking in the countryside and celebrating the changing seasons.[116]

Image 9. (Left) A gate at Changdeokungi Palace in Seoul. A palace was originally built on this site in 1395.

Image 10. *(Above)* A temple in the mountains of Korea.

Up to the light: a Sky Garden in Seoul

The modern approach to gardens in Seoul reflects the nation's cultural ethos of connecting with Nature. Trees and gardens are planted in all available public spaces along roads and on private balconies and rooftops. Seoul's *Sky Garden* is a 21st century example of this trend. Opened to the public in 2017, it illustrates how a congested inner city area can be literally opened up to the sunlight.

Celebrating the rejuvenating, life-enhancing properties of access to sunlight, *Sky Garden* has caught the imagination of local residents. It demonstrates creative re-use of a 1970's motorway flyover that was no longer deemed safe for its original purpose. *Sky Garden* aims to regenerate and connect pedestrian spaces around the central railway station in Seoul. Roads and railway tracks previously had fragmented these public spaces. Now the *Sky Garden* is open 24 hours per day and is part of a larger plan to transform Seoul into a more pedestrian-friendly city. [117]

Image 11. *Seoul by night*

Restoration of Qi

Feng Shui principles also have been applied at the scale of landscape planning around the city of Seoul. Image 13 illustrates how the planning aims to incorporate the symbolism, character and guidance of the five Feng Shui elements. These include *Earth* (the mountains); *Water* (the river) and *Wood* (the forests). The fourth and fifth Feng Shui Elements of *Metal* and *Fire* are not represented on this broad scale conceptual map. [118]

The Cheonggyecheon (Stream) restoration project in urban Seoul is

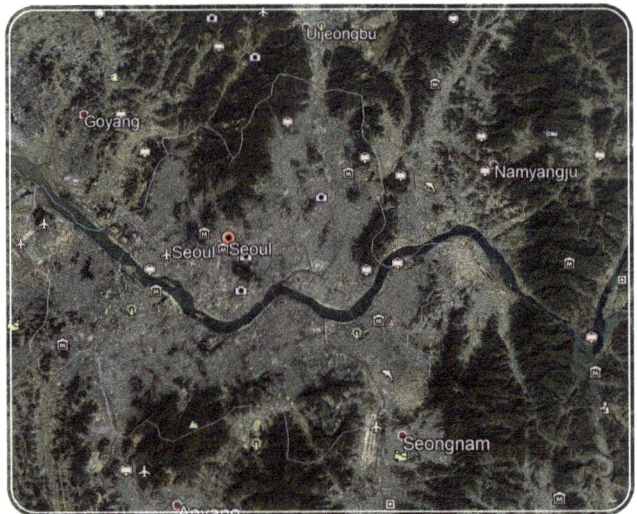

Image 12. *Google Earth image of Seoul in 2020. The steep green, vegetated terrain around the edges of the city contrasts with the grey urban area. By the end of the second decade of the 21st century, Seoul had a population of approximately 12 million people.*

an example of applying Feng Shui principles to city planning and design at a more detailed scale. In particular, this project represents the restoration of *Qi*, which is described as the life force, as living energy, or the energy flux.[119]

A raised motorway had covered Cheonggyecheon before the restoration project was undertaken. The stream was no longer visible beneath bitumen and cars. The landscape design for restoration of Qi through the city involved the restoration of the stream corridor and opening it up to sunlight. Work was planned along a riverbank of eleven kilometres. The design aimed to create a wide river corridor with sloping grass banks that included plenty of space for pedestrian access to sunny lawns, amidst the surrounding dense urban environment.[120]

As illustrated below, the proposed sloping grass banks were not constructed.

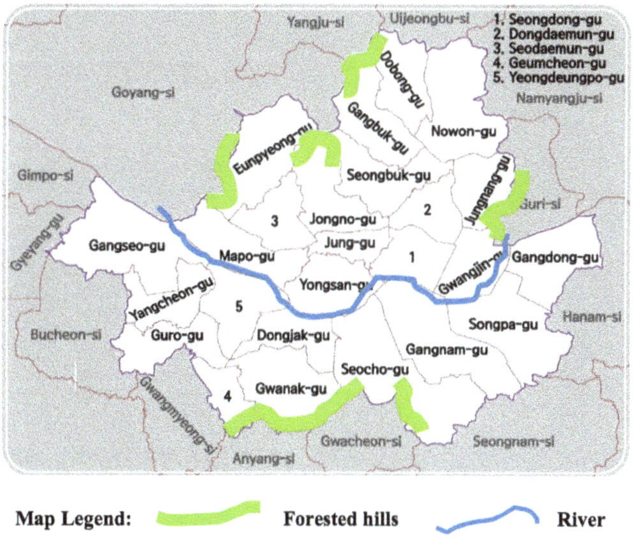

Image 13. *Map derived from the Seoul Green Network Plan for major green-spaces and its potential network in Seoul. (Seoul Metropolitan Government, 1997.)*

Map Legend: ▬▬▬ **Forested hills** 〜〜〜 **River**

Image 14. *Cheonggyecheon Stream restoration project in Seoul, South Korea.*

Feng Shui: supplementing and suppressing

Feng Shui theory also has some parallels with techniques used in the 21st century for ecological restoration. In North Asia, the explanation of such projects to the general public may engage two main streams of Feng Shui concepts. Firstly there is the concept of adding or supplementing elements in the landscape. This is called "Bibo" in the Korean language. An example of Bibo is a forest restoration project that supports ecological restoration through improvements to the local climate, biodiversity, soil and water systems.

Secondly, there is the concept of removing or suppressing elements in the landscape. These elements can include what are regarded as improper or unnecessary open spaces and structures in the landscape. The Korean term for this is "Apseung". The removal of nuclear power plants in geologically unstable areas is an example of Apseung. This type of planning can support long term ecological restoration and management of the planet's natural resources.[121]

Japanese and Chinese gardens provide more examples of the suppression and addition of elements in the landscape. In the series of photographs in Image 15, the top image shows Roan-ji in Kyoto, Japan. Roan-ji is an example of suppression or removal of elements in a garden. The uncluttered open space lined with white gravel is conducive to meditation.

The middle photograph depicts the entry to the Japanese Garden at the Mount Coot-tha Botanic Gardens in Brisbane. This design contains a mixture of garden elements that suppress and supplement.

Image 15. *Suppressing and supplementing elements in a garden.*

For example, the simple white walls suppress clutter around the entrance, while the foreground planting supplements the design. The bottom photograph in Image 15 illustrates a view to West Lake at Hangzhou in China. This is an example of supplementing the features in a garden. The addition of a moon gate in the foreground augments the more distant view to the lake.

Light in Japanese Gardens

The entry to the Japanese Garden at the Mount Coot-tha Botanic Gardens is depicted in one of the photographs on the previous page. There one can see a quite deliberate use of the contrast between light and dark garden design elements. The light coloured walls and paving contrast with the dark timber frame of the entry and the dark trunks of the nearby black bamboo and Syzygium trees. Perhaps it is the combination of the seven principles of Zen aesthetics in this garden that leads to a pleasant sense of natural light, without it being obvious how it is achieved.

There are many principles followed in the design of Japanese gardens, as well as a number of characteristic features, such as stone lanterns. However, English translations of these design principles do not include specific reference to light. Garr Reynolds provides one account of the seven principles of Zen aesthetics in his 2011 book "Presentation Zen":

Simplicity or elimination of clutter – Kanso
Asymmetry or Irregularity – Fukinsei
Naturalness – Shizen
Subtlety – Yugen
Break from routine – Datsuzoku
Stillness, tranquillity – Seijaku
Austerity – Shibui/ Shibumi [122]

The garden at Mount Coot-tha was originally built in 1988 as a gift from the Japanese people to the people of Australia. Constructed on the riverbank site of the World Expo 88 event in Brisbane, this Japanese Garden proved so successful that it was later relocated to at a permanent site at the Mount Coot-tha Botanic Gardens.

After passing through the entry gate of the garden a larger view unfolds, as depicted in Image 16. A grey stone lantern beside the path is located in the centre foreground of the garden. In keeping with the relative subtlety, (Yugen) of the design, this lantern is much smaller than the one depicted in Image 18.

Image 16. *View inside the entry of the Japanese Garden at Mt Coot-tha Botanic Gardens, Brisbane.*

The Mt Coot-tha garden falls within the *stroll garden* category of Japanese garden design. The rounded forms of the clipped, light green shrubbery and lawn in the centre of this garden correspond well with the pool of light that falls upon them. The purpose of neatly clipping so many shrubs in this garden is evident, as the form of each is subsumed within the pattern of the whole.

The right hand half of this view shown in Image 16 is illuminated by a large light well in the surrounding tree cover. The light well occurs over the central garden pond. The water's surface serves as a source of reflected light throughout the garden, as people stroll along the path around the pond. This type of light well in the centre of the garden may be compared to the more mottled pattern of sunlight and shade in the Korean garden depicted below.

The Japanese are less likely to include Buddha's statue in a garden than Buddhists in other parts of the world. In the subtle Japanese way, the analogy of Buddhist enlightenment is provided through lighting, lanterns and the opportunity to stop and reflect upon Nature in the stillness, simplicity and tranquillity of the garden. After all, it was while sitting outdoors under a tree that Buddha gained enlightenment.

Lanterns and pools of light

By day and night, the stone lantern is a key focal point in the oriental garden depicted in image 18. By day and by night, the bright red footbridge handrails are another focal point. Their role as a focal point is enhanced by their bright, contrasting colour and distinctive form amidst the foliage. The pool of light reflected from the surface of the pond in this garden is much smaller than the one in the Mount Coot-tha Botanic Gardens. It illustrates how a combination of symbolic garden elements, (the lantern, bridge and pond), can be used to evoke a broader experience of being in contact with Nature.

Image 17. *The pattern of sunlight and shade in a public park in Seoul, South Korea.*

Space and light in this part of the Image 18 garden are used subtlety in combination with the focal points to create *legibility*. The bridge is not only a means of passing through the garden; it also adds to the legibility of the garden in another way. The bridge allows us to pause and stand upon it, suspended for a moment in space and time. Safely above the water, yet in close proximity to the plants and aquatic organisms, our minds can relax and derive meaning from the experience of being in contact with Nature.

Buddhism: enlightenment beyond the dualism of light and dark

"Beyond dualism, every object – by whomever or in whatever manner it is made – finds salvation." [123]

The concept of dependent origination is one which distinguishes Buddhism from Christianity and other monotheist religions. It is described in the following text, which is attributed to Buddha Shakyamuni (Siddhartha Gautama), who lived during the 6th century BCE:

"He who experiences the unity of life sees his own self in all beings and all beings in his own Self and looks on everything with an impartial eye." [124]

For those Buddhists who seek liberation from impure dual perception, a garden and landscape may be seen as an expression of the unity of life and an opportunity to immerse oneself in it, in order to more fully develop *an impartial eye.* Seotsu Yanagi comments in his 20th century Japanese text:

"…from the Buddhists' point of view, the 'beauty' that simply stands opposed to ugliness is not true beauty…In the Muryoju-kyo ('Sutra of Eternal Life'), the following statement is attributed to the Buddha:

Image 18. *The lantern and bridge add to the legibility of this oriental garden.*

"…If in the land of the Buddha there remains the distinction between the beautiful and the ugly, I do not desire to be a Buddha of such a land…" [125]

As an example of the Buddhist way of life, the former Korean royal families chose to immerse themselves in gardens within natural settings. Their chosen activities, dedicated to the benefit of the nation, were ritual, study and contemplation around the natural streams that flowed through the palace grounds.

Thus the symbolism of light in Buddhist gardens is quite different from that in Hindu, Islamic or Christian gardens. Not surprisingly, there is a greater emphasis on Naturalness (*Shizen*) in Buddhist gardens, wherein the enlightenment experience arises from meditation. It is a different concept of light from the symbolic role of light found in other religious cultures. For example, as described in various scriptures, light may be a symbol of divine inspiration; a symbol lighting the way to an understanding of God, or a symbol of the triumph of good over evil.

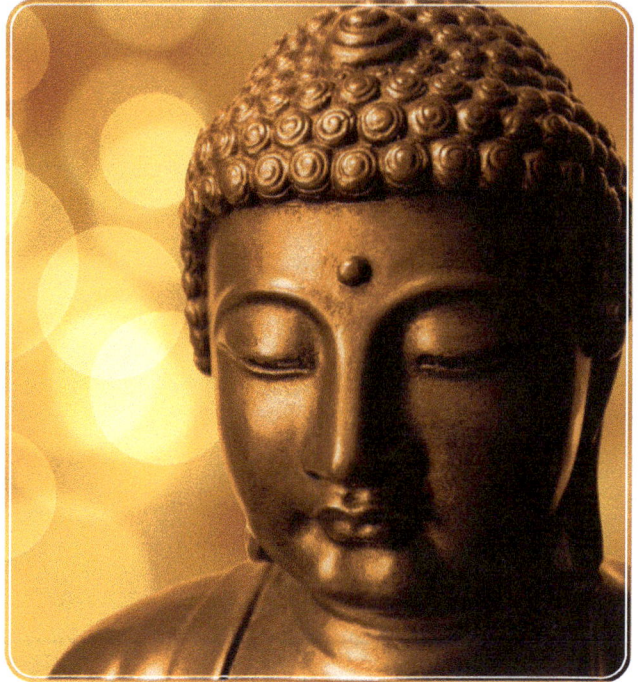

Image 19. *A Buddha statue: an aid to meditation.*

4

Islamic countries

Islamic paradise gardens appeal to the human soul.

Islamic gardens are often described as paradise gardens and are based on the principle that there are four rivers in paradise. The rivers are represented in a garden by four channels of water. These channels or rivers divide the land into four quadrants, each of which is filled with flowers, plants and birds.[126]

> *"God is the Light of the heavens and earth. His Light is like this: there is a niche, and in it a lamp, the lamp inside a glass, a glass like a glittering star, fuelled from a blessed olive tree from neither east nor west, whose oil almost gives light even when no fire touches it - light upon light - God guides whoever He will to his Light; God draws such comparisons for people; God has full knowledge of everything - shining out in houses of worship. God has ordained that they be raised high and that His name be remembered in them, with men in them celebrating His glory morning and evening."* [127]

In Islam, as in Judaism, God is not depicted. However an understanding of God may be developed through reference to light. This practice is described by the Qur'an, which Muslims believe to be the actual word of God given to the Prophet Muhammad. [128]

> *"God guides whoever He will to his light."* [129]

From this mindstream, the Islamic garden emerges. As I will try to describe in this chapter with reference to examples, it is almost as though the role of light, like that of God, cannot be described through reference to the physical world, or to the four quadrant principle of paradise gardens. However, through the experience of being in such a garden, one can approach an experiential understanding of these concepts. This may occur in a similar way to the description from the Qu'ran that is quoted above, where the Light of God shines "out in houses of worship."

Although Islamic gardens were not designed for use by non-believers, several of these sites, such as The Alhambra and the Taj Mahal, are often included in lists of the world's most famous pilgrimage and tourist destinations.[130] These sites are also listed as being of World Heritage significance by the United Nations Educational, Scientific and Cultural Organisation (UNESCO).[131]

As described later in this chapter, although these gardens were built with high ambitions, their patrons probably never imaged the worldwide influence they would have upon people's consciousness in so many nations during the 21st century. The internet has facilitated the spread of beautiful images of these sites worldwide and more people than ever before have travelled to visit these sites.

This widespread appeal illustrates the underlying ability of these Islamic gardens to appeal to the human soul, regardless of culture. Many visitors to Islamic sites cannot read the inscriptions they contain but visitors are none the less inspired by the experience of being in the gardens. This is testimony to the validity of the goal for peaceful, spiritual coexistence between human souls that is upheld and promoted by many Islamic religious leaders and other religious leaders of the 21st century. One of the goals of this book is to support evolution in that direction, through greater conscious use and sharing of the resource of light on Earth.

The map at right focuses on that part of the globe where Muslim majority countries are located, as of the year 2019. Places referred to in this chapter are labelled on the map.

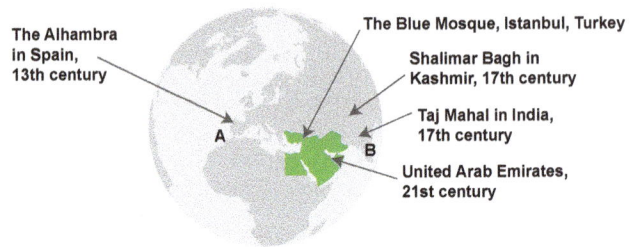

Image 1. *Location map of cultures referred to.*

There are significant Islamic populations in all the countries in the band between point A in North-West Africa and point B in Indonesia. For example, the county of India falls within this band. Although India is not regarded as an Islamic culture in the same way as say Saudi Arabia, there is a significant Islamic population in India.

In Islamic countries, the call to prayer that rings out from the mosques five times per day sets the rhythm for the whole community. Illustrating the importance of sunlight in this ritual, it is the passage of the sun through the sky that defines these five times: [132]

"*Salat al-fajr:* **dawn, before sunrise.**

Salat al-zuhr: **midday, after the sun passes its highest.**

Salat al-'asr: **the late part of the afternoon.**

Salat al-maghrib: **just after sunset and**

Salat al-'isha: **between sunset and midnight.**"

Image 2. *The five times of prayer each day*

The Light of Paradise

Many of the famous Islamic Gardens are built to take full advantage of light from sunsets over water. Shalimar Bagh is no exception. High in the Himalayas, its central watercourse steps down through a series of four terraces across a length of 539 metres to the swamp meadows that line the shores of Lake Dal. Built during the period 1569 – 1627 as a retreat from the scorching summer heat of the Indian plains,[133] such visions of paradise have ongoing appeal to earthly, as well as heavenly sensibilities.

In Islam, rather than providing an analogy for God, light is recognised as a quality that can be perceived and understood by humans, whilst also being a quality that most closely resembles God.[134] For a more detailed discussion of this subject in relation to Islamic thought, refer to the references for this chapter.

As depicted in Image 3, the setting sun shines over Lake Dal and the terraced gardens of Shalimar Bagh. It is not difficult to see how successful Emperor Jahangir was in celebrating the inspirational light of the Islamic

Image 3. *Shalimar Bagh and the setting sun over Lake Dal in Kashmir*

scriptures. It is also recorded that he built this garden to celebrate his Queen Nur Jahan. The Queen's name translates to English as "light of the world."

The Vale of Kashmir has been immortalised through ancient myths and plays that are set in this area. One of the earliest preserved historical records tells us that amidst the natural springs that flow from the foothills into Dal Lake, the Hindu ruler Pravarassena II built a garden there in the 1st century CE.[135]

> *"Agar Firdaus bar rōy-e zamin ast, hamin ast-o hamin ast-o hamin ast".*

> *"If there is a paradise on earth, it is here, it is here, it is here."* [136]

Foreshadowing these words of the Persian poet Amir Khusrau which are inscribed at Shalimar Bagh, the Sanskrit word *Shalimar* translates to English as "abode of love."[137] *Shalimar* was an ancient sacred site long before *Shalimar Bagh* was created there by the Moghul Emperor Jahangir in 1619. For

centuries since then, the dazzling play of light in the fountains has entranced all those who behold them.

Inviting us to walk and pray in the colonnades of paradise, the design of the formal gardens of Shalimar Bagh illustrates an understanding of the interplay of light and dark in the Islamic scriptures. Creating such experiences was regarded as an activity fit for rulers such as Emperor Jahangir.

Image 4. *Fountains at Shalimar Bagh*

Around the shallow edge of Lake Dal, below the formal gardens of Shalimar Bagh, is a band of swamp meadow about 1.6 kilometres wide. Groves of willow trees, rice paddies and vegetable gardens were established there centuries ago.[138] As is still the case today, plenty of food was needed for all the visitors in this paradise garden!

By the 21st century, approximately fifty thousand residents and visitors lived around the edges of the lake. Despite the early good intentions, the lake now has weed-choked waterways and floating islands. Residents and visitors live in the town of Srinagar and on the many tourist houseboats anchored around the edges of the lake.

Government programmes with the aim of rejuvenating *paradise* have been commenced. Problems include lack of law enforcement to stop pollutants such as untreated raw sewerage, excess sediments, rubbish and other materials that flow into the lake.[139] Applying the *Light Garden* decision making criteria as described in Chapter 12 could be a valuable tool to decision making for how to rejuvenate the natural beauty and natural resources of this treasured Himalayan region.

For example, applying the first decision-making criteria for managing energy flows to support living systems and stop carbon emissions would also address many of the lake's pollution problems. Waste would be captured and composted to stop carbon emissions. The composted material would then be utilised to rebuild the soil structure in nearby areas with degraded soils. Another example of applying the *Light Garden* decision making criteria in this community is to make decisions based on the probability that ecosystems will endure. Here at Lake Dal, the whole waterway ecosystem is stressed. The probability that it will continue to degrade is quite high, unless decisions are made to implement positive changes.

Comparison of Moghul Gardens and Versailles

The landscape design for the paradise garden at Shalimar Bagh included channelling a natural stream through terraced ponds. Approximately one century later, a grand water channel with fountains was also constructed at Versailles. Recognising the universally appealing qualities of the Islamic paradise gardens, some observers have noted that they may have influenced the design of Versailles in France.

Versailles was commissioned by the French king Louis XIV in the 1660s. As illustrated on the following page, the plan of Versailles includes a prominent, central intersection of water channels. Some observers have interpreted this plan view as reminiscent of the plans of Islamic gardens.

However, contrary to the analogies of God's light in Islamic gardens, Louis XIV considered himself king by divine right. He chose the sun as his personal symbol, naming himself the Sun King (*Roi Soleil*). The 800 hectare site of Versailles was built to impress others with his power, not as a place to help others invoke an understanding of God.[140] As noted in the following text, the Islamic concept of God transcends many of the individual *Light Garden* parameters, such as energy, space and time. Possibly the synchronistic action of all ten *Light Garden* parameters flowing in unison comes closer to the *transcendent and unknowable* totality of God.

> *"According to Isma'ilism, God is absolutely transcendent and unknowable; beyond matter, energy, space, time, change, imaginings, intellect, positive as well as negative qualities."* [141]

The aesthetic impact of views at Versailles is entirely different from that at Shalimar Bagh. Applying the *Light Garden* parameters to identify why this is so, it can be observed that human use of the landscape is more restrained at Shalimar Bagh, (Principle Number 9). Views to a natural landscape of mountains and water are more integrated into the garden experience at Shalimar than at Versailles. This integration of human experience with the broader natural landscape illustrates the application of Principle Number 8: "*Context and Environment.*" In contrast, at Versailles, the whole of the visible landscape is sculpted to a particular human-centred goal.

The garden of the *Roi Soleil* is depicted below. To facilitate an appreciation of this site's scale, points A and B have been marked on this aerial photograph. The long geometric axis of Versailles terminates at point A, which is at a distance of approximately 3.5 kilometres from point B. Point B is located at the entrance to the palace.

Image 5. *Versailles, Google Earth image. The visual axis of the site is 3.5 kilometres long from A to B.*

Image 6. (Above left) *Versailles and* (above right) *Shalimar Bagh. Point A in the photograph of Versailles corresponds to point A in Image 5. Versailles was constructed approximately one hundred years after Shalimar Bagh.*

Image 7. *Symbols of Le Roi Soleil (the Sun King) at Versailles.*

Another interesting comparison between Islamic gardens and Versailles is found in the type of detailing and inscriptions. For example, as illustrated in Image 9, at the Taj Mahal, we see inscriptions from the Qu'ran. At Versailles, we see Louis XIV's self-appointed symbol: the Roi Soleil, (the Sun King).[142]

Arches and Inscriptions

Less than ten percent of the inscriptions on the walls at another famous Islamic garden, (The Alhambra), are quotes or verses from the Qu'ran.[143] These inscriptions were documented in a comprehensive 21st century study conducted by the Spanish Government. Although the name of Allah was frequently inscribed by the masons, this study identified that many of the other inscriptions extol the virtues of the architecture itself, or of the rulers who commissioned the work.[144]

Other textural inscriptions at The Alhambra, such as those in the Hall of the Two Sisters, give us an insight into the imagery of light that pervades the poetic stream of Moorish thought and infuses its garden with light:

> *"The portico is so beautiful that the palace competes in beauty with the sky...How many arches are high on its summit, on the columns that are adorned by the light, like spheres that turn above the glowing pillar of the dawn!"* [145]

Archways *"adorned by the light"* and covered with inscriptions are often an important part of Islamic paradise gardens. They gain significance as symbols of the passage between light and dark, life and death, paradise and hell.[146] Further illustrations of this concept are provided in Chapter 6 at the Taj Mahal site in India.

If anyone doubts the importance of light in the Islamic Mogul Gardens of India, let them remember that were it not for Shah Jahan's vision that the Taj Mahal should be fully reflected in the waters of a wide river, it is likely that it would have been built some 800 kilometres to the south of its current site.[147]

Shah Jahan initially chose a site for the Taj Mahal in Burhanpur, by the banks of the Tapti River in central India. Burhanpur was the headquarters from which Shah Jahan spearheaded his military campaigns into central India. It was there that Mumtaz Mahal died in childbirth with her fourteenth child, whilst accompanying her husband on his military campaigns.

To honour Mumtaz Mahal, the Shah wanted the Taj to be built of white marble, which could only be sourced from Makrana in Rajasthan. That site was a long way from Burhanpur. He also found that the River Tapti was not wide enough at Burhanpur to fully reflect his intended vision for the Taj Mahal. In addition, the rock foundations may not have been strong enough for the enormous weight of the intended structures.[148]

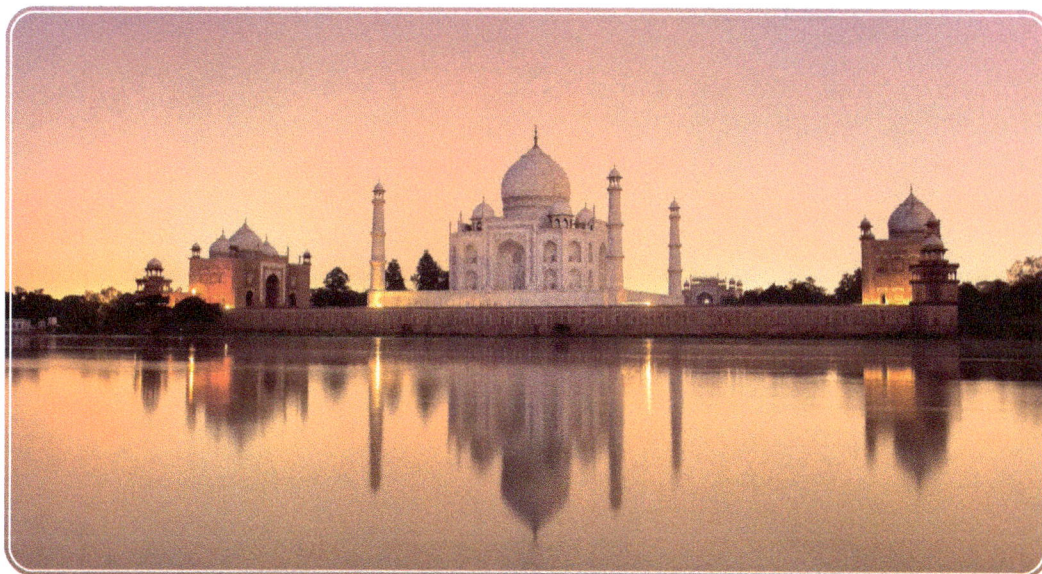

Image 8. *The Taj Mahal*

So upon finding a site with firm foundations, with reasonable access to the white marble supplies of Rajasthan and on the banks of the wide Yamuna River at Agra, the decision was made to build there. Such tombs were disapproved of by some Islamic leaders because of the Muslim tradition forbidding elaborate decorations on graves. There is also debate about whether the Taj was primarily a symbol of human love or power. Others point to the inscriptions from the Qur'an on the walls of the building and say the Taj Mahal is far more than a grave.

Regardless of these concepts, the bodies of Mumtaz and Shah Jahan were placed in a relatively plain crypt beneath the inner chamber of the Taj Mahal tomb, with their faces turned to the right and towards Mecca.[149]

Image 9. *Arches, Inscriptions, Symbols and Light at the Taj Mahal.*

After construction of the Taj Mahal, Shah Jahan was overthrown and locked up by his son, Aurangzeb. Legend has it that the only thing Shah Jahan could see across the waters from his prison cell was the Taj Mahal. From that distance, he could not have read the marble inscriptions of the Qur'an on the walls and arches. However, gazing upon the reflections in the river, it is likely that they ran through his mind.[150]

The Alhambra

Built during the 13th to 15th centuries CE, the hilltop fortress of The Alhambra in Spain is quite different from the Taj Mahal and Shalimar Bagh in India. However, these three places were all built to reflect the same principles of Islamic paradise. These principles, including an appreciation of light, influenced all these designs. The difference between these places is determined by more than the different geographic locations and climatic zones where they are located.

Challenging the notions that appreciation of beauty is constrained by culture and that *beauty is in the eye of the beholder*, there is a high degree of consensus about the beauty of The Alhambra.

The site has World Heritage status under the United Nations Educational and Scientific Organisation, (UNESCO) accreditation programme.[151] It also is the second most visited site in Europe, according to information published by tripadvisor.com.[152] Its popularity demonstrates the cross-cultural nature of the principles considered in this book - and which underlie all beautiful gardens and the natural world.

The Alhambra was initially established in the mid-thirteenth century as a Moorish palace on the site of earlier Roman fortifications that date back at least as far as the 8th Century CE. The Alhambra now exhibits a blend of Medieval Islamic, Renaissance Christian and Modern styles.[153] As illustrated below, there are some similarities between The Alhambra and sites built in Italy during the Italian Renaissance period. However, the impact and character of the places is quite different.

Image 10. *Unlike Islamic gardens, the rectangular form of this Italian Renaissance style garden at Pisa in Italy does not include water courses that divide the lawn into four quadrants.*

Set high in the southern mountains of Spain, The Alhambra takes advantage of its hilltop location and glorious views to distant mountains. It masterfully juxtaposes these views with the more intimate surrounds of walled Islamic paradise gardens on the site itself. As described earlier in this chapter with reference to Shalimar Bagh, "paradise" is not just here, ("Agar Firdaus bar rōy-e zamin ast, hamin ast-o hamin ast-o hamin ast").[154] Paradise also lies in the juxtaposition between what is here, with what is far away in the sky and hills.

The Garden of the Partal, (Jardines del Partal), depicted in Image 11, is an example of the type of image featured in travel brochures for The Alhambra. Such views tend to attract endless streams of people to admire and photograph them.

Phi in the Sky

This Islamic garden demonstrates an awareness by the designers of how to apply principles that people of all cultures will respond to favourably. Application of these principles also enhances the perception of connection with the cosmos. One of these principles is the presence of the phi ratio (1:1618).

In this case, we also see the presence of *Light Garden* principle number five, "*focal points*" and principle number six, "*multiplication factors*." As illustrated overleaf in Image 12, multiplies of the phi ratio frame the focal point in the central arch. Two golden mean rectangles with sides in the ratio of 1:1.618 were superimposed over the photograph. Both the pink and the red rectangles frame the distant central arch.

Fountain in The Alhambra

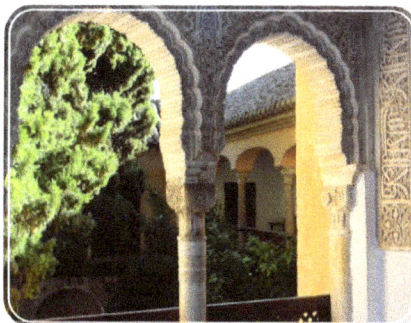

Arches in The Alhambra

Image 11. *The Moorish gardens have water courses that divide them into quadrants. This is in accordance with descriptions of paradise contained in Islamic texts.*

In this view, the pink golden mean rectangle is formed when the **building's arched facade is framed by the roof and the foreground hedge.** I think this would have been consciously designed because, for example, the dark green hedge is trimmed so that it is just the right height to form the base of the pink rectangle. The upright date palm and conifer trees add foreground presence and balance as they frame the view.

Image 12. *The golden mean and focal points, illustrating an application of Light Garden Principle Number Six, Entanglement and Focal Points.*

This view's sense of perspective is heightened by the second red golden mean rectangle that frames the whole scene. It runs from the edge of the foreground pool and out to the countryside beyond.

In the case of The Alhambra, the Phi ratio is used to frame our perception of movement from discrete units in the garden foreground, out to the apparently limitless expanse of the distance. How does this relate to the *Light Garden* theme of this book?

Consider the concept of moving our perception from a discrete unit in the garden foreground out to the apparently limitless expanse of the distance. This concept can be seen as analogous to a discrete unit taken from a larger field, which is part of 20th century Quantum Theory. That theory was developed by scientists such as Albert Einstein. It includes, for example, the concept that light travels in discrete parcels called photons.

Building upon that, *Light Garden* principle Number Five, *Multiplication Effects and Scale,* includes the concept that at places such as The Alhambra, the design consciously works with expanding and linking our foreground frame of perception out into the apparently limitless expanse of the distance. In this case, perception includes more than sensory perception. It consists of the associated progressive utilisation of cognitive awareness, metaphorical capacities and human understanding of religion and the cosmos.

Analogies can be drawn here with the Islamic concept of creating paradise gardens in order to help people develop their understanding of God through the experience of being in the garden. The words of the Koran provide inspiration. The presence of design features such as the phi ratio on the site build direct links between the phi ratio in the human body, the human perception of the site and the phi ratio itself, with its capacity for limitless expansion.

Image 13. *above left: inscriptions at The Alhambra. Above right: the Tetracys.*

When we draw, we need light to see what we are doing. We tend to start drawing at a particular point. This is the case whether we are drawing in the sand to make a symbol of something we want to build on the ground, (such as a garden, a farm, or a village), or whether we are drawing with a pen or a computer.

We then move from a starting point to create lines, areas and spaces to represent something that is in our minds. As a way of describing this process, the Greek Pythagoreans are attributed with developing the Tetractys symbol depicted above. It is thought to have been developed during the 6th to 5th Centuries BC.[155] The Tetractys was used to represent the musical, arithmetic and geometric ratios which underlie the way we develop a plan concept.

However, this is a simplified model of the human mind and Quantum biophysics includes many more concepts to address other factors that come into play. These are presented in the *Light Garden* model through principles such as multiplier effects, quantum entanglement and wave motion.

As can be seen overleaf in Image 14, the multiplier effects of a colonnade of arches are quite different from the effects of a single archway in terms of how they define a space. This provides an example of how each of these ten parameters is relevant to the nature of that place - and helps to explain why it has such universal appeal.

Living with the Earth as a Light Garden

Every culture has its own ways of working with light, albeit often unconsciously. The ten Light Garden *principles set out in Chapter One are linked to particular design features of The Alhambra, as illustrated in Image 14.*

Light Garden Principles in a Courtyard at The Alhambra

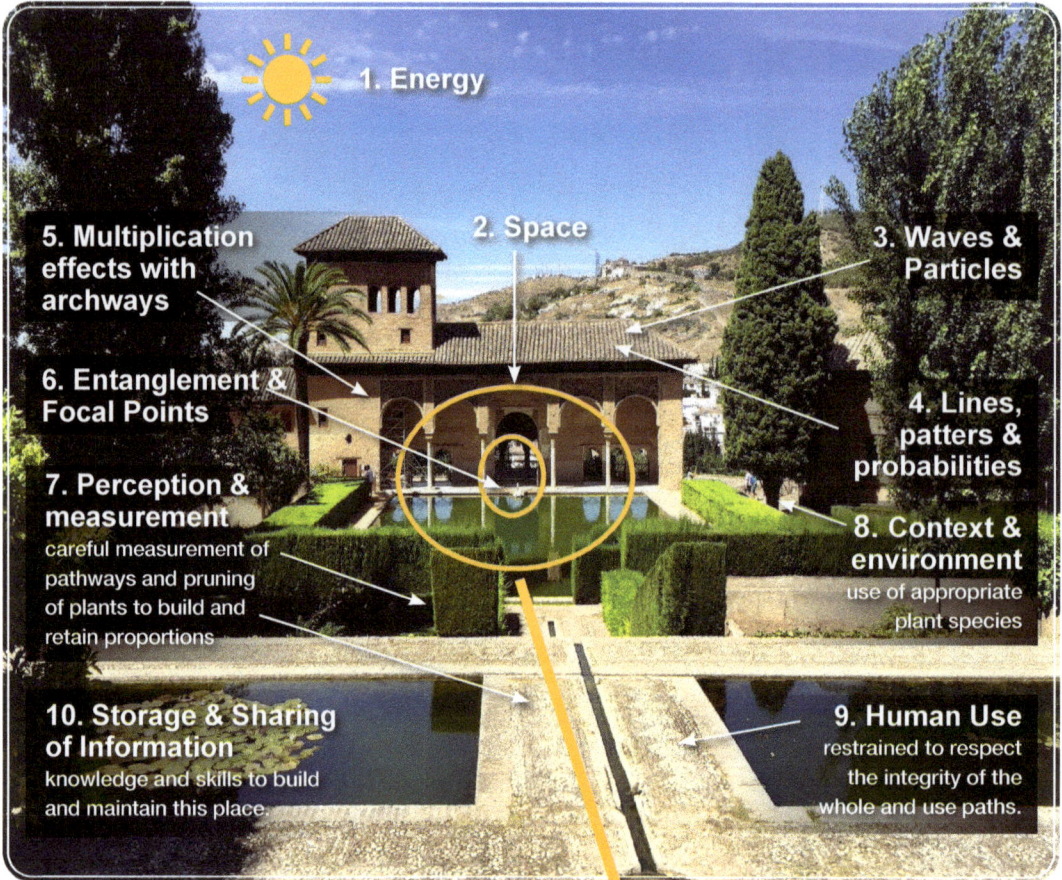

1. Energy

5. Multiplication effects with archways

2. Space

3. Waves & Particles

6. Entanglement & Focal Points

4. Lines, patters & probabilities

7. Perception & measurement
careful measurement of pathways and pruning of plants to build and retain proportions

8. Context & environment
use of appropriate plant species

10. Storage & Sharing of Information
knowledge and skills to build and maintain this place.

9. Human Use
restrained to respect the integrity of the whole and use paths.

Image 14. *One courtyard at The Alhambra: looking for Light Garden principles.*

Further description of the *Light Garden* principles illustrated above is provided in the table that follows:

Descriptions of Light Garden Principles at Alhambra

Component and Description
1 ENERGY: This garden is fully open to the sky and the energy of the sun by day and by night. By night, the light of the stars and moon is reflected in the water.
2 SPACE and TIME: The garden design consciously frames a transition through space from what can be seen in the foreground, through to what can be seen in the distance. For example, in the foreground the space around the pools is framed by paving and hedges. In the middle ground, the space is framed by the walls and arches of the building, plus the tall trees.
3. WAVES and PARTICLES: The motion of light in the form of particles or waves moving through this garden at the visible scale is not an important feature of the design. This is a more static garden, where the light is quite static, even though it changes with the motion of the sun and stars through the sky overhead. This is consistent with Islamic gardens being designed for rest, reflection and contemplation.
4. LINES, PATTERNS and PROBABILITIES: The primary line of perceived motion through this garden is along the central visual axis. The axis moves from the foreground, through the arches of the building and on to the distant hills. The probability of any garden elements falling outside this formal geometric pattern is low. The places where people walk in this garden also fall within the formal geometric pattern.
5. MULTIPLICATION: Atoms multiply and cluster together to form the different basic materials of this garden: water, space, plants, paving and buildings. The archways of the building and the reflections in the pool are examples of shapes that are multiplied. The reflections from the pool are part of way in which paradise is symbolised, or alluded to in this garden.
6. FOCAL POINTS: The beauty of this garden is an example of the concept of quantum entanglement, where the beauty of individual parts cannot be perceived or described independently of each other. It is the sum of all the parts that leads to the beauty of the proportions and the relationship to the landscape beyond.
7. MEASUREMENT and PERCEPTION: The striking beauty of The Alhambra is universally admired. The site has been studied and measured in detail by many scholars and is listed on UNESCO's World Heritage Register.
8. CONTEXT: Islamic principles were applied to help people reach an understanding of God not only in this immediate garden settings but also in the wider landscape setting.
9. HUMAN USE: The paradise garden is specifically designed for human use, including providing a contemplative setting in which people may approach an understanding of God.
10. STORAGE The design of this garden is based on information about the paradise garden concept that has been stored and shared for centuries in the Quran.

Image 15. *Description of Light Garden principles in a courtyard at The Alhambra.*

In addition to the *Light Garden* principles, the Phi ratio and a proliferation of geometric shapes and patterns are found at The Alhambra and Islamic sites in general. This follows earlier developments in the fields of mathematics, design, art and science during the 8th and 9th centuries AD:

> *"the expansion and development of geometry through Islamic art and architecture [was related to] significant growth of science and technology in the Middle East, Iran, and Central Asia…such progress was prompted by translations of ancient texts from languages such as Greek and Sanskrit (Turner, 1997). By the 10th century, original Muslim contributions to science became significant".* [156]

In the case of the Tetractys, the space is a tetrahedron.[157] The influence of the Greek Pythagoreans extended to Islamic scholars, to Plato and many others. As Leonora Leet said of Plato's work, it

> *"implies that every number presupposes a definite and discrete unit taken from a limitless, homogeneous field.*
>
> *Contemplation of it thus provides access to the contemplation not only of a limit but also of the limitless. These extremes are the fundamental tension in Pythagorean thought."* [158]

This concept of discrete units taken from a larger field is analogous to contemporary Quantum Theory. As described earlier with reference to a photograph, the courtyard design depicted at The Alhambra fosters contemplation of what is near and what is far away: of "*a limit but also the limitless.*"

As Petruccioli has described in detail,[159] there are three pre-Islamic roots from which the diverse range of Islamic landscapes emerged: Arab, Turkish and Persian. Although each of these roots had strong agricultural underpinnings and different concepts of nature, space and light, there is some sense of unity within that diversity. It is to that sense of unity that I have tried to refer to in this book, whilst leaving readers to ponder more detailed texts such as Petruccioli's[160] if they need further clarification about the diversity of these cultures.

Image 16. *Geometric shapes and inscriptions at The Alhambra*

The 21ˢᵗ Century

Looking at the nighttime skyline of Dubai, one could call it a City of Lights. However, the people of Dubai in the 21st Century have reinterpreted traditional Islamic values and are developing alternatives to this type of high energy consumption urban development. They are looking to create a future which has a greater emphasis on sustainable, ecologically sound principles.

In 2006 the United Arab Emirates was declared by the World Wildlife Fund as the country with the greatest ecological footprint per capita in the world.[161] Announcing a new vision for the city in 2018, His Highness Sheikh Mohammed bin Rashid Al Maktoum, said that the Sustainability City project is:

"…a key component of our development journey, which is part of the national agenda. We are committed to sustainability, which is a top priority that we strive to implement taking into consideration environment conservation, and balance between economic and social development, to provide people the best quality of life and ensure happiness of community." [162]

Upon completion, the *Sustainability City* project will support Dubai's aims to produce 75% of its energy from clean sources by 2050.[163] The developers of the *Sustainability City* project cite their mission as:

"Striving to safeguard the natural world by helping people to live more sustainably". [164]

As Robert Kunzig noted in his 2017 article for National Geographic:

"A decade ago Dubai had one of the largest ecological footprints of any city in the world. By 2050 it wants to have the smallest." [165]

Sustainability City does not look like a typical town, urban development, educational institution or farming enterprise. Instead, the 46 hectare site has a tree lined, a six-kilometre long exercise trail and eleven food producing "bio-domes" located in a parkland spine that runs through the centre of the site. There are multiple solar panels and solar powered charging stations for electric cars used by residents who live on the site.

There is also a mixed-use zone, which includes a school, an eco-hotel and a hospital and health rehabilitation centre which is open to the public. Although much of the development in this zone looks similar to contemporary international style, some of the features of traditional settlements in the Arabian Peninsula area have been included. These include wind funnels to help cool small outdoor squares where people can gather in

Image 17. *The night skyline in Dubai.*

A Story of Evolution in the Form of Domes

Islamic gardens have strong agricultural roots. They are usually part of a landscape of settlements, shelters and food cultivation oases which are situated in a more harsh environment, or desert. Although the sequence of moving from the old to the new may have occurred slowly over the centuries in some parts of the Islamic world, big changes have occurred in Dubai within a short historical time frame. As illustrated in the images below, the symbolism of mosques has been retained.

The white Taj Mahal at sunset in India.

"The Sustainable City", is the first "Net Zero Energy" development in Dubai. The concept of "Net Zero Energy" has emerged during the 21st Century to refer to developments that have zero energy requirements from the energy grid because they generate as much of their own electricity as they consume.

Solar energy as well as energy from on-site composting is being used. This project, costing an estimated 1.25 billion Emirati Dirhams, has received personal support from His Highness Sheikh Mohammed bin Rashid Al Maktoum, the Vice President, Prime Minister and Ruler of Dubai.

The Blue Mosque. A recently constructed mosque in Dubai uses traditional dome shapes in its construction and modern blue electric floodlighting at night.

A 21st century biodome constructed at Sustainability City in Dubai.

A related concept of "Net Positive Development" was proposed by Dr Janis Birkeland in her 2008 book "Positive Development: From Vicious Circles to Virtuous Cycles through Built Environment Design". Net positive development means a project contributes more to, or rejuvenates more for environmental, social and economic well being than it consumes or takes away.

For example, an urban development project is net positive for energy if it contributes more electricity to the grid than is consumed, after allowing for relevant set up costs, use of resources and so on.

Image 18. *A story of evolution as illustrated above by the three different types of domes.*

the evenings and palm trees to foster an oasis-like atmosphere.[166]

Sustainability City has some notable statistics that illustrate how the *Light Garden* concept can be applied in 21st Century settlements. For example, with over ten thousand trees on the site, there is a ratio of five trees for every residence. With careful planning, it also has been possible to locate a 10,000 Kilowatt/h/p solar installation over buildings and car parks.

The on-site light-harvesting solar installation produces 20 Kilowatts of electricity per residence. This illustrates the efficiencies that can be gained with this type of 21st century *Light Garden* technology when applied at the community scale. Composting of waste material is also carried out. The system provides sufficient electricity to operate the free charging stations provided on the site for long-range, subsidised electric vehicles and free buggy transport in residential areas.

Being located in the desert fringe of Dubai, Sustainability City also demonstrates that *Light Garden* living is achievable in other harsh desert environments and remote locations such as refugee camps and military settlements. As the 21st century proceeds, this type of landscape and community is likely to proliferate. We need to conceive of these camps and settlements as opportunities to create viable, liveable places for the millions of people who will call them their long term *Light Garden* home on planet Earth.

With an investment of appropriate security, training and technology for waste recycling, food production and the like, living conditions and vocations in these new settlements could be better than what has been left behind in war torn areas.

The innovative MyHive project established at Sustainability City in 2018 aligns with another vital aspect of the *Light Garden* concept. Bees are essential for pollination of food species and for biodiversity, (not to mention when trying to establish plants in harsh environments where bees may be scarce or absent). The popular MyHive project engages local residents to learn how to look after bees and produce honey. It maintains an interesting website; sponsors beehives and offers ongoing training and support.

In the 21st century, Dubai is also known for its innovative high rise buildings. For example, as depicted on the following page, the *Buri Al Arab* is shaped like the three cornered sail found on traditional fishing dhows in the Persian Gulf.

Rising from the sea on an island, Buri Al Arab is now a city icon for Dubai. At night, floodlighting of the structure makes its unique Arabian character all the more apparent.

Dubai has been a fishing village and trading port for many centuries. In the 20th Century, an oil boom and a real estate boom transformed it into a city with one of the world's most dense collections of skyscrapers; the world's tallest building and as of 2018, the third busiest port in the world.

Image 19. *The International Centre for Biosaline Agriculture, another project in Dubai which has a broad sustainability agenda and which is transforming formerly arid lands. The desert fringe may be seen in the background of the illustration.*

Modern critics such Salmar Samar Damljui have said of the Buri Al Arab,

> *"…both the hotel and the city, after all, are monuments to the triumph of money over practicality. Both elevate style over substance."* [167]

Bearing in mind that these structures perform many functions, the same could well be said for World Heritage Listed sites such as the Sydney Opera House, the Taj Mahal and many other structures that have been deliberately designed as cultural icons, memorials or landmarks.

Another cultural icon for which Dubai has become world-renowned in the 21st century is the cluster of artificial islands constructed along the waterfront. Construction commenced in 2001 and has continued since then. Two islands in the shape of palm trees and another in the shape of a world map have been built. Other nations such as China and Korea, also have been busy in the 21st century building artificial islands. Often these are purposed as military bases. Tiny island nations facing inundation from rising sea levels and climate change around the globe must look by with incredulity at the priorities for global natural resource management that are implied by these activities.

On the other side of the coin, Damluji has also noted that:

> *"Viewed in the context of the specific environment and cultural fabric of this desert region in Arabia, the coming of modern architecture has been coupled with extensive cultivation projects implemented in an originally barren landscape. Simultaneously, the cities have also remained true to their heritage and recognised the importance of their vernacular architecture and, in a fascinating contrast to the rapid modernisation, today there are also many reconstruction and heritage projects underway."* [168]

Damluji, like many others, has acknowledged the massive changes occurring in Dubai and how the cultural heritage is being celebrated and expanded with modern technology.

The Buri Al Arab Hotel   A fishing dhow

Image 20. *The new and the old in Dubai*

5

Africa

Biodiversity is a strength of smallholder farms, which preserve
climate resilient varieties of plants and animals.

Africa is a wonderfully vibrant and culturally diverse place.

However, It is a sad truth that Africa has been the battleground of colonial powers for centuries.

In considering the following two questions, it is perhaps not surprising that a disturbing theme of exploitation emerges:

- What is unique about African landscapes, gardens and places?

- What is unique about the way in which the energy of sunlight is used to sustain them?

In a report published in February 2018, the Rights and Resources initiative estimated that 500 million people had been a target for foreign governments and investors looking to produce food for populations outside of Africa. These 500 million people depend for their livelihoods on 3.46 billion acres of farmland in sub-Saharan Africa. Examples abound throughout the continent of foreign interests coming in to plant crops like sugarcane, palm oil, and jatropha. They have gained control of vast tracts of land that local people already inhabited, or that could be used for growing food to feed these people, or to grow forests to rejuvenate the planet's biodiversity and climate.[169]

What is the *Light Garden* model's relevance to the management of African natural resources and cultures? In formulating a response to that question, several traditional and contemporary examples of African cultures are considered. The location of each country referred to in this chapter is illustrated on the map in Image 1 overleaf.

Despite the exploitation, the economic champions of these colonial cultures that have exploited African resources are under no illusion about the competency and benefits arising from their leaders supplanting traditional African gardening, farming and land management practices. Milton Friedman, as one of those 20th century economic champions, said:

> *"If you put the federal government in charge of the Sahara Desert, in five years there'd be a shortage of sand."* [170]

Maps & Images of African Locations & Climatic Zones

Map of African Locations

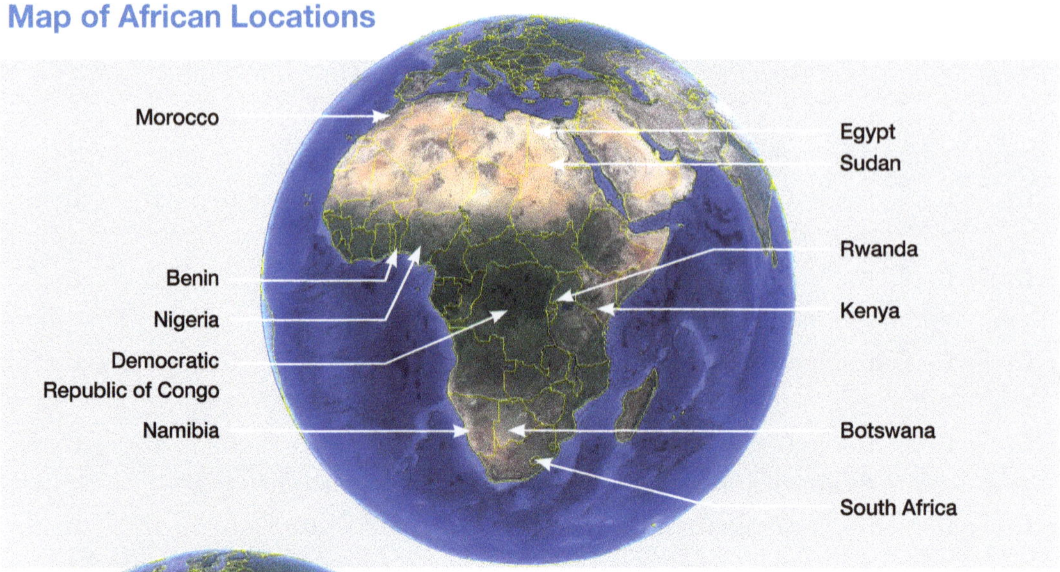

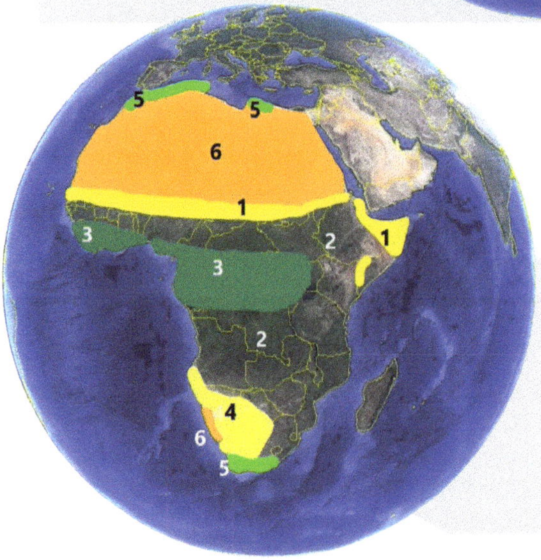

Borders of countries in Africa. There are 54 countries in Africa (2018). In summary, some of those referred to in this chapter are labeled on the map.

Climatic Zones in Africa

1. Sub-Saharan Africa – (bright yellow)
2. Tropical Savannah (lighter green)
3. Tropical rainforest (dark green)
4. The Kalahari Basin (yellow)
5. The Mediterranean coasts (olive green)
6. The Sahara and a patch of the West Coast (orange)

Women farmers walking through a garden in Sudan.

Fynbos Heathland with white flowers near Capetown.

Children in Botswana

Desert in Nambia

A quiver tree

Image 1. *Maps and images of African country locations and climatic zones.*

His political philosophy advocated a free market economic system with minimal government intervention. However, his statement about the Sahara indicates that he realized the limited value of America seeking to act as a colonial power that managed African resources and lives.

"A free market system with minimal government intervention" could not be said to describe the ancient Egyptian culture of the Nile under the Pharaohs. However, that concept does apply at least in part to aspects of the traditional tribal systems of governance that prevailed in Africa prior to the colonial period. Although Friedman's ideas continue to influence conservative governments' policies in the 21st century, he also had more liberal views. For example, he announced publicly that his proudest achievement was his work towards eliminating military conscription in the United States.

Giving us hope for people and systems to change towards a more equitable and less exploitative future, a similar progressive development of views during the course of his lifetime occurred for another well-known 20th century leader and thinker: Albert Einstein. After contributing significantly towards the development of the atomic bombs that America dropped on Japan at the end of the Second World War, Albert Einstein awakened to the destructive power that his ideas had unleashed. For the rest of this life, he was a public advocate *against* nuclear proliferation and *for* peace.

Perhaps in a similar way, Milton Friedan realized the destructive power of the economic policies he had advocated when they were unleashed by colonial powers upon Africa and other places. He then chose to turn his mind towards the more humane concept of eliminating military conscription, which so often goes hand in hand with objectives for economic and political power. Against this background, we begin to see the relevance of the *Light Garden* concept to manage natural resources and maintain traditional cultures in Africa. It is relevant because it provides an integrated approach to economic, social, governance and natural resource management issues, within the capacity of the planet's natural systems to support human use.

The rapidly expanding Sahara desert in Africa could be considered an example of unsustainable natural resources management and one that is not consistent with the *Light Garden* model. Attempts to curb this expansion are underway in the 21st century through projects such as tree planting in Chad. The global extent of arid lands and deserts is apparent in Image 2. Vast areas of the Earth are deserts, as indicated by the beige colouring on the maps. Areas of snow and ice are white. Forests are green. The huge Sahara Desert - the largest on Earth - has steadily expanded in recent centuries. Research published in 2018 shows that during one century alone, (the period 1920 – 2013), the Sahara grew by ten percent.[171] The yellow line on the Image 2 map shows the northern extent of sub-Saharan Africa.

When seeking to curb the expansion of deserts, the *Light Garden* model can be applied. As illustrated in Chapter Two, a quantum field is like an innerspring mattress. Touch one part and the vibration moves through the whole. In quantum theory, "matter" is forever moving as a resonant, responsive, multifaceted whole. Considering economic resources and natural resources in this way is consistent with how the ecosystems of nature operate. They are diverse, interconnected networks, (like the innerspring mattress), where one impact will reverberate through the whole.

In sub-Saharan Africa, we find some examples of cultures that *do* engage in the sustainable management of natural resources, limit the growth of their economies and co-exist with Nature. These are consistent with the *Light Garden* model. Some comparative examples of life in rural and urban areas of Kenya illustrate this concept's relevance in more detail.

Image 2. *A composite satellite image of Africa (centre) with the other continents.*

A traditional shamba in Kenya

South of the Sahara in equatorial Kenya, live the nomadic Maasai tribes of the African Great Lakes region and the non-nomadic, agriculturally based cultures that live in shambas. A shamba means an area of cultivated land. Traditional cropping, garden and pastoral activities in the shamba of Jorama Onjimba are illustrated on the following page, as an example of relatively sustainable management of natural resources. This plan view of Jorama's nine hectare property shows the extent of pastures for grazing and fields for cropping. The associated photographs were taken in northern Kenya during the 1980s. At that time, Jorama lived with his two wives and eight children. Six other children who had been born into the family had died earlier in infancy.[172]

Approximately one third of Jorama's shamba was devoted to pasture. Jorama had two cows in milk, two calves, one heifer, four oxen, three sheep, and half a dozen chickens. The animals were a vital part of the diverse range of agricultural activities conducted by this self-sufficient family. One third of the property was used to grow maize for consumption by the family, with some surplus for local sale. In addition to pastures and crops, one third of the property was used for a diverse range of activities, including dwellings, cassava, taro, beans, vegetables, trees and waterways. The family lived in a cluster of thatched huts that is shown on the plan of the shamba.[173]

Image 3. *Thatched huts in Jorama Onjimbo's shamba.*

SHAMBA OF JORAMA ONYIMBO
(North of Kakamega)

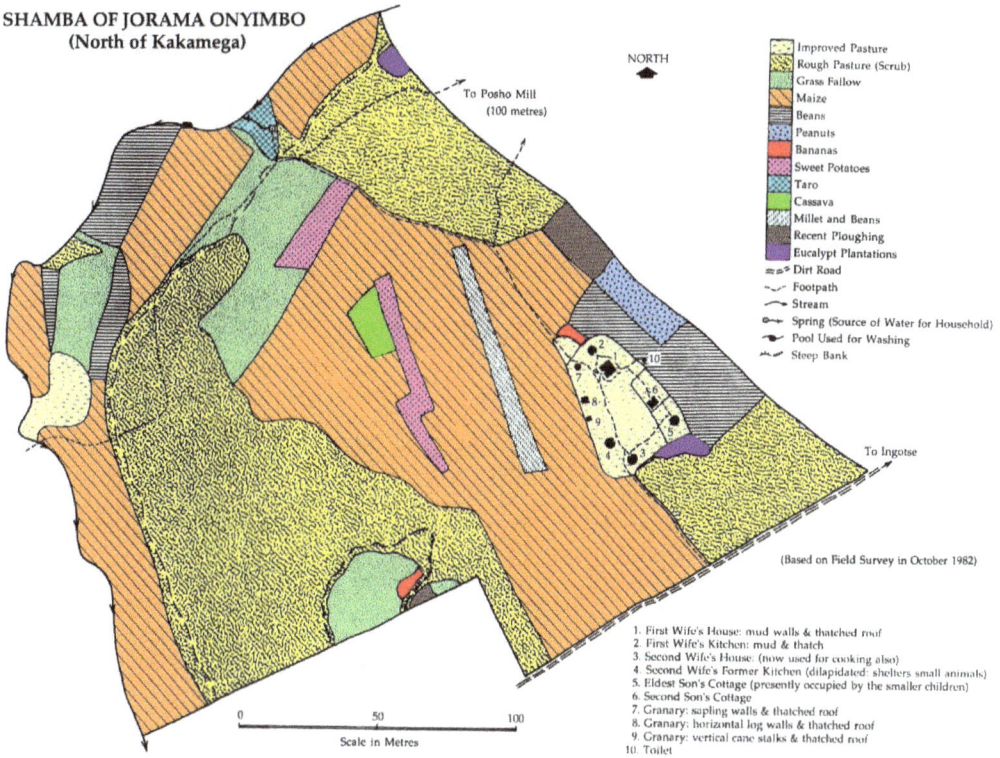

NORTH

To Posho Mill
(100 metres)

Improved Pasture
Rough Pasture (Scrub)
Grass Fallow
Maize
Beans
Peanuts
Bananas
Sweet Potatoes
Taro
Cassava
Millet and Beans
Recent Ploughing
Eucalypt Plantations
Dirt Road
Footpath
Stream
Spring (Source of Water for Household)
Pool Used for Washing
Steep Bank

To Ingotse

(Based on Field Survey in October 1982)

0   50   100
Scale in Metres

1. First Wife's House: mud walls & thatched roof
2. First Wife's Kitchen: mud & thatch
3. Second Wife's House: (now used for cooking also)
4. Second Wife's Former Kitchen (dilapidated: shelters small animals)
5. Eldest Son's Cottage (presently occupied by the smaller children)
6. Second Son's Cottage
7. Granary: sapling walls & thatched roof
8. Granary: horizontal log walls & thatched roof
9. Granary: vertical cane stalks & thatched roof
10. Toilet

Image 4. *A scale drawing of a traditional family shamba garden and pasture in Kenya, Africa. Below the plan are illustrations of Jorama with some of his livestock and a thatched hut, similar to the ones in the family shamba.*

In many ways, this family lived in accordance with *Light Garden* principles. By using local materials to build their own dwellings, Jorama's community was more self-sufficient than the Amish communities of North America. Although quite self-sufficient, the Amish allow the use of building materials that are purchased off-farm. The Amish communities are described in more detail in Chapter 9.

Jorama's farm property was considered quite large compared to farms in the more southerly regions of Kenya, where the population was higher and the roads more highly developed. Traditional pastures had survived in Jorama's region. Commercial pressures there were fewer than in the southern regions. An illustration of another shamba in Kenya – that of Jimmy Adanje – is shown below.

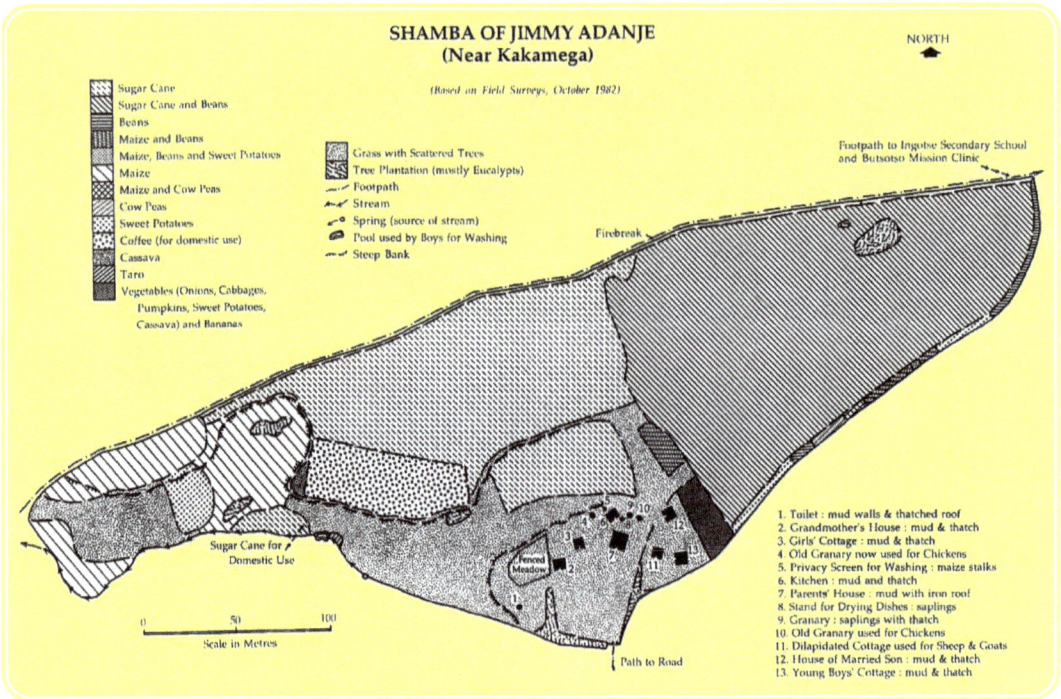

SHAMBA OF JIMMY ADANJE
(Near Kakamega)

(Based on Field Surveys, October 1982)

NORTH

Sugar Cane
Sugar Cane and Beans
Beans
Maize and Beans
Maize, Beans and Sweet Potatoes
Maize
Maize and Cow Peas
Cow Peas
Sweet Potatoes
Coffee (for domestic use)
Cassava
Taro
Vegetables (Onions, Cabbages, Pumpkins, Sweet Potatoes, Cassava) and Bananas

Grass with Scattered Trees
Tree Plantation (mostly Eucalypts)
Footpath
Stream
Spring (source of stream)
Pool used by Boys for Washing
Steep Bank

Footpath to Ingotse Secondary School and Butsotso Mission Clinic

Firebreak

Sugar Cane for Domestic Use

0   50   100
Scale in Metres

Path to Road

1. Toilet : mud walls & thatched roof
2. Grandmother's House : mud & thatch
3. Girls' Cottage : mud & thatch
4. Old Granary now used for Chickens
5. Privacy Screen for Washing : maize stalks
6. Kitchen : mud and thatch
7. Parents' House : mud with iron roof
8. Stand for Drying Dishes : saplings
9. Granary : saplings with thatch
10. Old Granary used for Chickens
11. Dilapidated Cottage used for Sheep & Goats
12. House of Married Son : mud & thatch
13. Young Boys' Cottage : mud & thatch

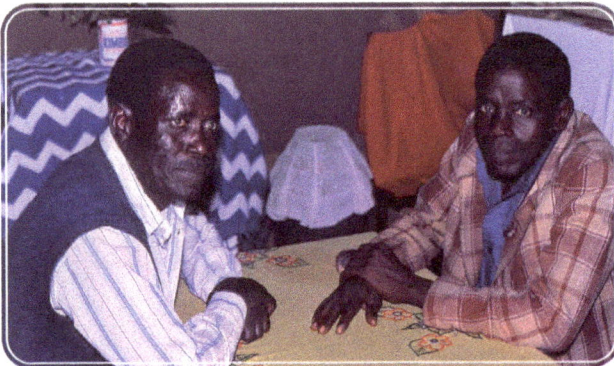

Image 5. (Above) *A plan of Jimmy's property shows that although he has sugar cane, he has virtually no land upon which to graze his animals. In addition, the proportion of his land devoted to vegetable and taro growing is much smaller than in Jorama's garden, despite Jimmy having two wives and fifteen children to feed.*

(Left) *Jimmy Adanje seated at a table on the far left.*

(Right) *Jimmy's wife of thirty years, as she tends the vegetables.*

Although both Jimmy Adanje and Jorama Onjimba began their lives in traditional Kenyan shambas, Jimmy has not worked in his village all his life. His shamba was different from Jimmy's too. The photographs of Jimmy's shamba included below were taken during the same historical period as those of Jorama's property.

When Jimmy was growing up as a child on his family shamba, vegetables were grown for household use. The family owned ducks, several chickens, three goats, three cows, one calf and four sheep. In contrast to this focus on healthy food for local consumption, by the 1980s, the amount of land devoted to pasture, maize and vegetable growing had been significantly reduced from the traditional allocations of earlier years. This change was to accommodate the export crop of sugar cane.[174]

Sugar production requires centralised planning in order to organise the harvest. The mill owners determine the dates of planting and harvesting sugar cane. The dates are staggered between districts to provide a continuous supply of sugar for the mill. The small-holder does the planting and the weeding, (seven times), but the company provides the fertilizer and the cane.[175]

Jimmy Adanje served in the British Royal Air Force during the Second World War and was later employed for many years on construction work in Tanzania and other parts of East Africa. The money he earned helped him develop his shamba, finance his marriages, and pay for his children's education.

Jimmy lived near Ingotse, 10km north-west of Kakamega, and his *shamba* was small for that area -- only half the average size. As can be seen on the plan in Image 5, over half of the good arable land was devoted to sugar cane production. Sugar provided him with a cash income. However, he was compelled to buy much of the corn needed to feed his family. His family was no longer self-reliant in food production. The strip of unharvested land around the cane field's edge reflects the sugar company's policy: growers are required to maintain a firebreak of evergreen crops around the cane.[176]

Jimmy owned some sheep and it is possible that his family may have participated in a program run by groups such as One.org/us. That group is devoted to working with African women to encourage the artisan economy as an additional income source for households. For example, as an outcome of one project in Rwanda, 72 percent of women participants reported in 2016 that they now never run out of food. Before participating in that project, only five percent of women in the area were able to report that they never ran out of food. [177]

Image 6.
A panoramic view of Jimmy Adanje's shamba taken in the 1980's. By then the former layout of this property had been changed to incorporate sugar cane production. A field of sugar cane may be seen in the foreground.

Violence makes refugees

Although Jimmy Adanji's lifestyle has changed several times during his lifetime, he is more secure than millions of other Africans. During the past century, millions of African people have been forced to move from life in villages and rural areas to live in cities and refugee camps. The need for greater security from violence and warfare was one of the prime causes for making these moves.

An estimated 18 million people in sub-Saharan Africa were of concern to the United National Humanitarian Commission for Refugees (UNHCR) in 2018. This sub-Saharan population represented about 27 percent of the total global population of refugees and displaced persons.[178]

Image 7.

(Above left) *Homes destroyed gives a clear message to local people. Abandon your property and livelihood. Flee for your life. You are now a refugee.*

(Above middle) *With water tanks destroyed by gangs, what chance is there for gardens here?*

(Above right) *With no police assistance, men sit under the stars all night, defending their families as best they can.*

(Right) *Forced to flee to a refugee camp to escape a killing spree in her home area, this woman was separated from her children, her husband, her home and her livelihood.*

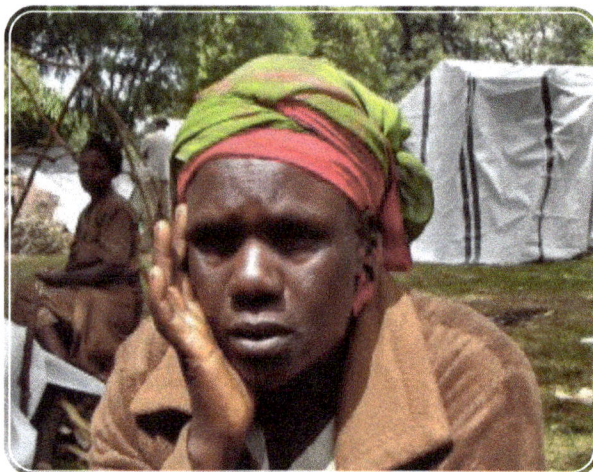

In addition to escaping violence and warfare, there are other reasons why people chose to move from the relative self-sufficiency of rural village life, to live in the urban areas of Africa. Let us consider what these motivating reasons are, in the context of cultures that have traditionally used sunlight as the energy source to grow crops, raise livestock and manage natural resources in Kenya.

Reasons commonly cited for making a move to cities include over-population in the villages, droughts and a shortage of productive land for gardens and farms. Dr John Tyman has described the story of Kibera, one of the largest peoples' settlements in Nairobi. Nairobi is the capital city of Kenya. People have moved there to an urban lifestyle and subsequently demonstrated great determination and resourcefulness in order to survive:

> *"… Thousands of families and single men and women struggle to survive in a community with almost no services and few opportunities for remunerative employment. Kibera is situated 7 kilometres from the centre of the city, on the Motoine Ngong, a tributary of the Nairobi River, and overlooks the Nairobi Dam, which is highly polluted with waste from the settlement." [179]*

Life and Trees in Kiberia

Kiberia is located on marshy ground but clean water is in short supply. As one mother said,

"Water is Life but here it can mean Death." [180]

This woman was speaking of death due to contaminated water and disease. Muddy, open, waste disposal drains run among the homes in Kiberia. This waste management system is so different from the composting toilets, clumps of vegetation and recycling of materials found in the traditional thatched hut Kenyan villages. These features are shown on the plan of Jorama Onyimbo's shamba provided earlier.

There are no trees and gardens on one side of the railway track that runs past Kiberia, as illustrated below. Once there was a forest of trees and a peaceful settlement at Kiberia. But now, with over 250,000 people relocated from their rural farms and villages to live in the crowded, insecure conditions of Kiberia, no trees remain there. In contrast to this, the more affluent Nairobi citizens who live on the other side of the railway track have trees nearby.

Many of the young men in Kiberia grow up surviving from day to day. They have few prospects for land ownership, traditional male roles in their community, paid work, business opportunities, or training. In most cases, they have no legal right to occupy the land, no security of tenure and virtually no police protection.

Image 8. (Top left and right) *Images of life in Kiberia.*
(Middle left) *No trees on the Kiberian side of the tracks.*
(Bottom left) *Thousands throng to the bus depot in Nairobi.*

During the early 1980s in Nairobi, rival election candidates represented different tribal groups. These groups enlisted gangs of youths who roamed the streets. Amidst the terror, looting and burning that occurred when the gangs set forth to do the bidding of those who enlisted them, over a thousand people (1,133) lost their lives in nationwide violence; 3,561 were wounded, and 117,216 properties were either damaged or destroyed. Roads were barricaded. Drivers were dragged from trucks then beaten or killed. The trucks were torched.[181]

Image 9. *Street violence in Nairobi during the 1980's, following by a gesture of tree planting.*

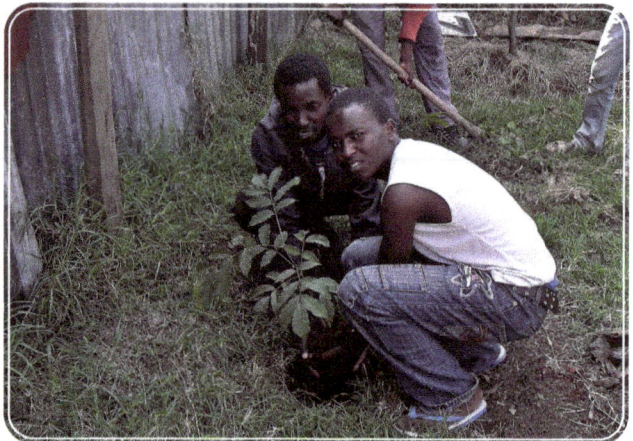

What could be done to change things for these young men after all this? In a gesture of peace, a tree planting program was commenced. After the violence subsided, young men planted trees in symbolic gestures as illustrated above. But more than this is needed. Kibera has been described as the biggest slum in Africa and one of the biggest in the world. Of the 3.5 million people living in the city of Nairobi, 2.5 million live in such areas, which are located on 6% of the land. The land is often on the fringes of the city.[182]

Light and Human Rights

... that there is light despite all the darkness

Hope is being able to see that there is light despite all of the darkness.

Archbishop Desmond Tutu

Archbishop Desmond Tutu and Nelson Mandala are but two of the brave and tireless African leaders who have sought to redress injustice and bring the light of international human rights principles to the structure of societies in contemporary Africa.

Foreign governments have targeted Africa for a long time. For example, refer to the quote by Tewodros II, Emperor of Ethiopia in the mid 19th century.

I know their game. First, the traders and the missionaries; then the ambassadors; then the cannon. It's better to go straight to the cannon.

Tewodros II

Article 23 of the Universal Declaration of Human Rights

1. Everyone has the right to work, to free choice of employment, to just and favourable conditions of work and to protection against unemployment.

2. Everyone, without any discrimination, has the right to equal pay for equal work.

3. Everyone who works has the right to just and favourable remuneration ensuring for himself and his family an existence worthy of human dignity, and supplemented, if necessary, by other means of social protection.

African women at work, growing food for their families.

Image 10. *Light and Human Rights*

How did a word from the ancient and revered kingdom of Nubia come to be the namesake of the large settlement at Kiberia? *Kibera* is a Nubian word for *forest*. The following historical account is worth telling because it reveals how access to land, resources and light has been at the core of the creation of this settlement and others like it. It is also a tale of just how vital it is for human welfare to have access to adequate sunlight, space, land, and clean water. Thirdly, it reveals a process that has been replicated in similar ways around the globe to disenfranchise traditional communities and gain control of the sunlight, space, land and clean water that

Image 11. *Kiberia. Residents have limited access to sunlight between the dwellings.*

they once were able to rely upon for their livelihoods. When we speak of sunlight and *Light Gardens*, we are speaking of the energy that supports human survival, as well as forests, climate and natural systems.

The Nubians came from their homelands of Egypt and Sudan to live at Kibera following a mutiny in 1897 amongst warriors who had been recruited to fight for the British. At that time, the British military rescinded its earlier decision to repatriate the Nubian warriors and instead dispersed them to Kenya.

When they first came to live in Kenya, the Nubians called the forested military base where they were stationed *Kibera*. They continued to be excellent soldiers. However, by denying them title deeds to land, the British ensured that Nubians could only build temporary structures. Many warriors from Nubian villages in Kenya fought for the British in World War I (1914 – 1918). However, after the war, they were demobilised without compensation, unlike the Indian soldiers who had fought for the British.

Nubians were not accorded the privilege of British citizenship, despite their long and loyal service to the British Crown. When constructing Kenya's social structure, the British colonial authority consolidated ethnic groups and designated them to native reserves. They deliberately excluded the Nubians from the process because they considered them a detribalised community, rather than a Kenyan tribe. This Nubian position was ameliorated to some degree by the passage of a new Kenyan Constitution in 2010. The constitution recognised the Nubians as the 43rd tribe of Kenya. However, earlier in 1963, the Kenyan government had already taken control of the land at Kiberia and made it available for informal occupation by other people moving into the area.

African gardens and farms, old and new

As the story of African culture is vast, let us now return to comparing the old ways and the new ways, when it comes to managing light and gardens. Ancient Egypt and Morocco are renowned for paradisiacal garden pools and clear, flowing water but rarely are these seen in the daily lives of Africans today. Food, gardens, land, people and light are not superficial or whimsical subjects for approximately 500 million African people. They are hotly contested subjects. In Kiberia and the following examples, perhaps the relative stability of the ancient Egyptian dynasties has some appeal.

The annotated map located overleaf illustrates some examples of African people being displaced from their homes, land and access to natural resources. As we have seen on the preceding pages, this includes being displaced from free access to the energy source of sunlight.

For example, at least 8.8 million acres of Ethiopia's most arable land has been leased to China. China has established export cropping enterprises on this land. As documented by the organisation Human Rights Watch, at least 70,000 people have been displaced from the leased land.[183] In addition, as reported by Friends of the Earth International, numerous elephants have been displaced too. An Ethiopian elephant sanctuary has been cleared, so that more land can be devoted to agrofuel export cropping. However, China is not the only nation engaging in such activities. Companies from the United States, Norway, Germany, Israel and other places are involved too, as illustrated overleaf.

As also noted in the Friends of the Earth report which documented the above situation about elephant displacement in Ethiopia, "agrofuel" or "biofuel" crops are often seen by overseas-based governments and companies engaged in biotech and agricultural industries as a way to enter the African market. For example, these organisations are researching genetically modified crop varieties to use in Africa. Modified crop varieties exclude local farmers from participating in the market with traditional, locally used crop varieties. Export industry proponents also claim that their activities will help the global community tackle climate change.

Based on the Rights and Resources Initiative report (2018), the Image 13 map below shows several projects in Africa where local farmers have been displaced by land deals with international corporations. The corporations then use the land, water and light to grow export crops such as sugarcane, jatropha and oil palm. Such activities would not pass the *Light Garden* model test from the perspective of African citizens' human rights. That is because *Light Garden* decision making entails reference to criteria such as '*Storage and Sharing of Information.*' More comprehensive detail about *Light Garden* decision making processes is provided in Chapter 12.

A particular example from the Congo region of Africa, where information and resources have not been shared with local people, is summarised as follows:

"In Congo-Brazzaville, President Sassou- Nguesso has ceded 10 million hectares of fertile land to South-African farmers to grow staple food crops for export without any percentage to remain in Congo, alongside 70,000 hectares granted to the Italian oil company ENI to plant oil palm monoculture plantations for agrofuel production, threatening Africa's last precious tropical primary forest." [184]

The shambas in Kenya that were illustrated earlier in this chapter are examples of what are referred to as smallholder enterprises. That term is used by global agencies such as the United Nations when compiling data about food production, arable land and use of other natural resources such as fisheries and forests.

Smallholder enterprises generate more food per acre than industrial scale, export-oriented agriculture. In addition, they are often more biodiverse than large scale, export-oriented agricultural enterprises. However, there are large scale enterprises that rejuvenate the biodiversity of the region where they are located. For example, as described in a later chapter, in South America, Kris and Doug Tompkins purchased thousands of acres in Chile's wild Patagonian region. Over a period of twenty years, they managed the land to support the rejuvenation of biodiversity. One million acres of land was then gifted back to the government to be managed as National Park. In that case, and with the *Light Garden* model in general, it is the aims and decision making priorities, rather than the scale of the enterprise, that are the key issues.

African Gardens, Old and New

An irrigation system supplies water to a farm

Drip irrigation reduces water consumption because the water is delivered directly to the soil root zone.

Comparison of food produced in the 21st century food garden shown at left with the diet of of the ancient Egyptians highlights how in ancient Egypt the diet consisted of much more than plants and livestock that could be raised in specific gardens or farms. The diet included a variety of fish and wildfowl caught in the reeds along the waterways, plus beef, goat and mutton. The ancient Egyptians also grew onions, leeks, garlic, beans, lettuce, lentils, cabbages, radishes, turnips, dates, figs and melons.

The transfer of drip irrigation technology to African village gardens during the past century illustrates principle number ten of the global *'Light Garden'* concepts described in Chapter One: Storage and Sharing of Information.

Hieroglyphics at Karnak

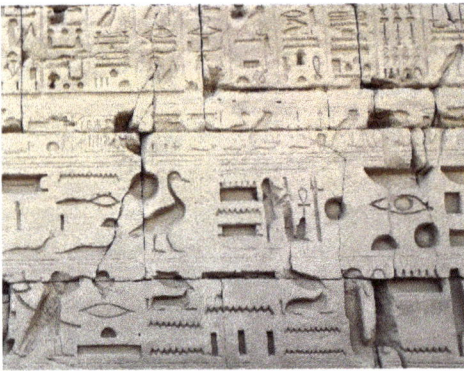

Sacred Flowers

The two sacred flowers of ancient Egypt were the lotus and the papyrus. They both grow along the Nile River. The lotus, Nymphea caerulea, was regarded as a symbol of the sun.

"At Heliopolis, the origin of the world was taught to have been when the sun god Ra emerged from a lotus flower growing in "primordial waters." At night, he was believed to retreat into the flower again." [185]

Image 12. *African gardens, old and new.*

Export Projects in Africa

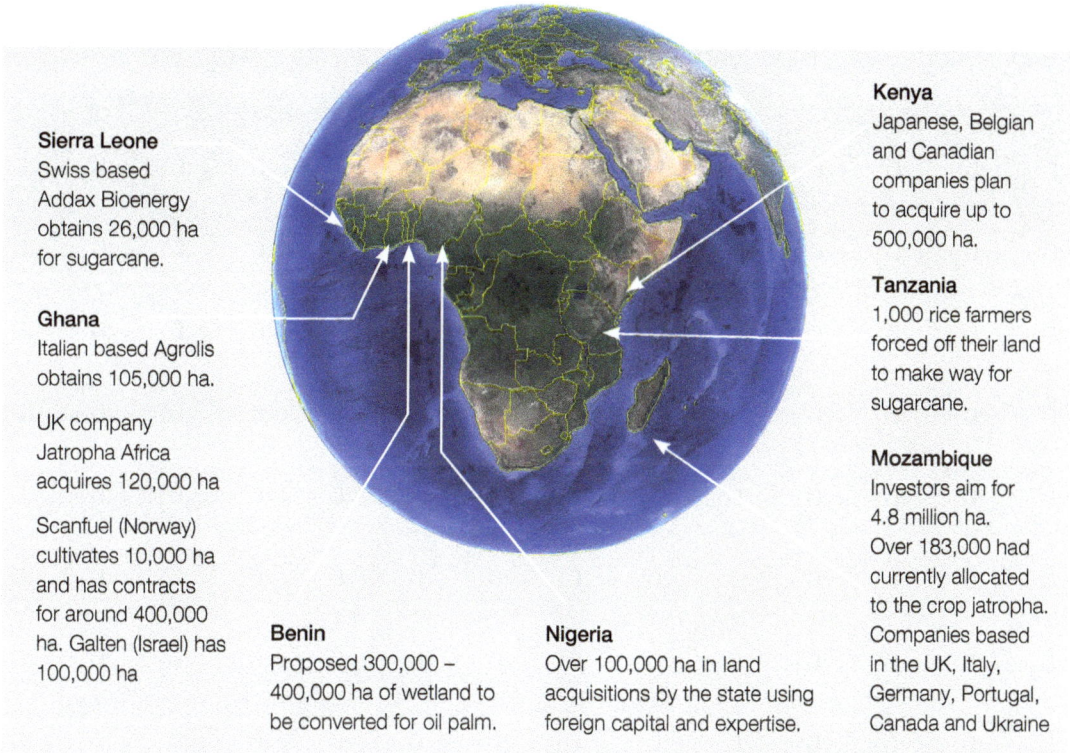

Sierra Leone
Swiss based
Addax Bioenergy
obtains 26,000 ha
for sugarcane.

Ghana
Italian based Agrolis
obtains 105,000 ha.

UK company
Jatropha Africa
acquires 120,000 ha

Scanfuel (Norway)
cultivates 10,000 ha
and has contracts
for around 400,000
ha. Galten (Israel) has
100,000 ha

Benin
Proposed 300,000 –
400,000 ha of wetland to
be converted for oil palm.

Nigeria
Over 100,000 ha in land
acquisitions by the state using
foreign capital and expertise.

Kenya
Japanese, Belgian
and Canadian
companies plan
to acquire up to
500,000 ha.

Tanzania
1,000 rice farmers
forced off their land
to make way for
sugarcane.

Mozambique
Investors aim for
4.8 million ha.
Over 183,000 had
currently allocated
to the crop jatropha.
Companies based
in the UK, Italy,
Germany, Portugal,
Canada and Ukraine

Uganda's food production and economy (2018)

The Ugandan National Flag

Population 36.3 million.

Main Exports: Tea, cotton, tobacco and sugar.

Main diet of the local population in terms of food
and agricultural commodities: plantains, cassava,
potatoes, sorghum, corn and groundnuts.

A young farmer in Africa.

Image 13. *Map of some export projects in Africa.*

Small Holder Gardens and Farms

Approximately 50% of form work is done by women in sub-Saharan Africa. Some more data, as provided below, helps to flesh out the picture of the agricultural base of *'Light Gardens'* in Africa.

75% of the world's food is generated from only twelve plant species and five animal species. This makes the global food system highly vulnerable to shocks.

Biodiversity is a key strength of many smallholder systems that keep thousands of rustic and climate-resilient plant varieties and animal breeds alive.

Bees are part of this living network. They are needed for pollination of many food plants.

80% of food Smallholders supply 80% of the overall food produced in Asia, sub-Saharan Africa and Latin America. This includes farmers, artisan fisher folk, pastoralists, landless and indigenous peoples.

570 million The majority of the 570 million farms in the world are small. In addition, 70% of the 1.4 billion extremely poor people live in rural areas and 75% of these rural poor are also smallholders.

<10 hectare Smallholders are small-scale farmers, pastoralists, forest keepers and fishers who manage areas varying in size from less than one hectare, up to ten hectares.

Image 14. *Smallholders, biodiversity and food*

Africa: unique and ubiquitous

Image 15. *Proteas are part of the unique African ecosystems.*

As part of the *Light Garden* model, application of Principle Number 4, *Lines, Patterns and Probabilities,* leads to decision making based on the probability that ecosystems will endure. This implies a reordering of priorities away from the exploitation of resources and towards the rejuvenation of living systems. A change of this nature inherently presents a challenge to export-oriented, monoculture agricultural ventures in Africa but not to more diverse enterprises, regardless of the scale. Planning for rejuvenation of biodiversity benefits from a broadly based, well-coordinated approach that considers the ecosystem scale of natural systems. The contributions of larger scale enterprises and government are most welcome in this context.

The world renowned Kirstenbosch National Botanic Garden on the outskirts of Capetown in South Africa is a good example of government's potential role in the rejuvenation of biodiversity. Here a vast range of plant species is presented. Although the gardens feature the somewhat ubiquitous style of gardens and lawns found in Botanic Gardens the world over, amidst and around it all, the unique, wild, African landscape shines through.

Image 16. *Images of the South African landscape and the Kirstenbosch National Botanic Garden at Cape Town.*

Carefully designed so that planting appears to blend seamlessly with the wild landscape beyond, the gardens give visitors the opportunity of safely experiencing something of the grandeur that exists when the natural systems of the wild African landscape are allowed the space and time they need to function in a healthy manner. This is *Light Garden* Principle Number 2 in action: allow ecosystems the space and time they need to rejuvenate.

The significant educational value of Kirstenbosch is without doubt, as over one million visitors, including many special interest groups and school children, come to the site each year. This is an example of *Light Garden* Principle Number 10 in action: *Storage and Sharing of Information*. The site is managed by the South African National Biodiversity Institute, (SANBI), as part of a network of sites devoted to biodiversity conservation and management. As noted in their 2016/17 Annual Report, their work extends well beyond the boundaries of each site to the management of natural resources in general:

> *"In addition, SANBI assists in the development of a National Biodiversity Framework, including bioregional plans and strategies; as well as coordinated programmes related to the conservation and sustainable use of indigenous biological resources and the rehabilitation of ecosystems."* [186]

Image 17. *Kirstenbosch National Botanic Garden. The style of the lawns may be ubiquitous but the wild landscape is unique.*

6

India and Bangladesh

In India, light is very much aligned with radiance. It is a radiance with a depth of patina that has been refined and consciously maintained over millennia.

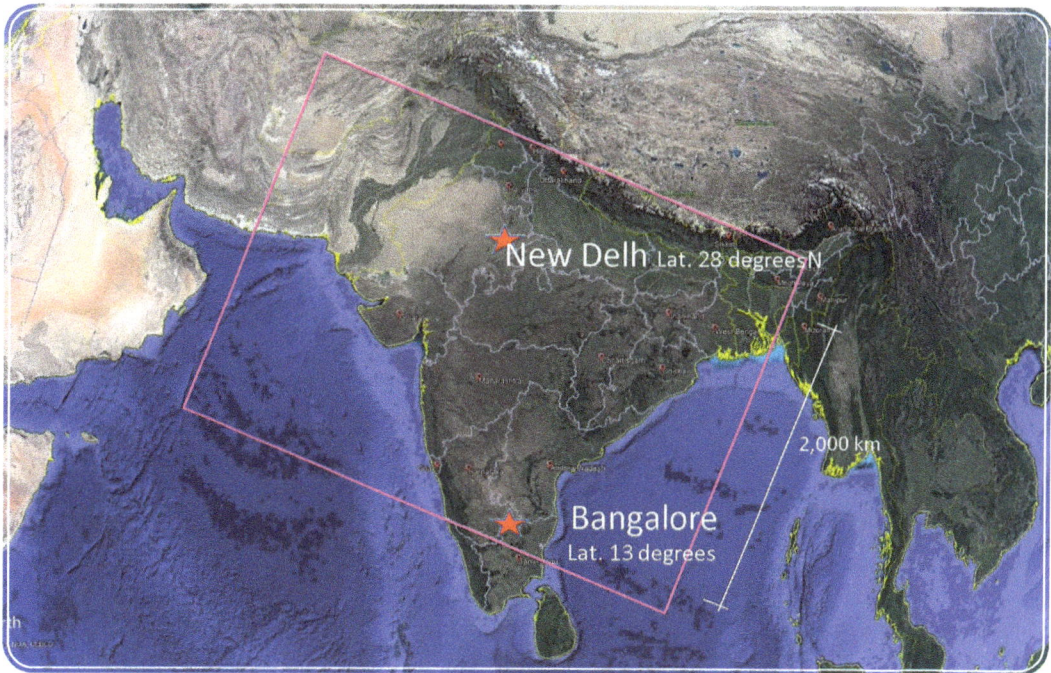

Image 1. *The scale of the Mauryan Dynasty of 265 BCE extended well over 4 million square kilometres.*

The current borders of India, Pakistan and Bangladesh were established after the partition of India in 1947. Over two thousand years earlier, the land in these countries was part of the Mauryan dynasty of 265 BCE. The pink rectangle on the map above shows the extent of the Mauryan Dynasty - one of many that have existed within the current territories of India, Pakistan, Afghanistan and Bangladesh. The Mauryan Dynasty was the first to control large parts of northern India and extend into more southerly regions.

The *Light Garden* model is considered in relation to six themes within the great diversity and complexity of Indian culture. The first theme is the ancient groves of India. The second considers biodiveristy, the *Light Garden* theme and Gandhi's philosophy. For example, Gandhi's philosophy included the concept of *Swaraj*. Swaraj entails adopting a lifestyle of self-restraint, whilst also engaging in community work. In that context, people acting independently with self restraint *and* as part of a group for the good of the community, are analogous with *Light Garden* Principle Number Two: act as both a wave, (contributing to community groups), and as a particle, (as a self-restrained individual).

The *Light Garden* Waves and Particles principle entails people acting as a wave when engaged in group activity and as a particle when focused on individual action. Light itself behaves as both a wave and a particle.

Gandhi's philosophy is much more complex than the simple analogy described above and it will be discussed in more detail later in this chapter. That discussion reveals much about the Indian psyche that people from other cultures may not well understand. It also reveals some of the limitations of the *Light Garden* model, which is intended to be much simpler in its scope than Indian philosophy. The *Light Garden* model is not intended to be a comprehensive philosophical basis for society but it is a tool that can be used in conjunction with various cultures.

This chapter is divided into six parts, which consider ancient and modern culture in India. These six parts are listed in the Map Legend table in Image 2. The examples listed in the table are shown on the map on the following page. Although India's most famous places and gardens tend to be iconic sites such as the Taj Mahal, there are a great many other sites throughout the land.

In addition to considering the six types of places listed above, reference is made to the enduring

Part	Map Code	Type of Garden & Landscape	Examples in this chapter
1		Ancient groves	• Mallur Gutta in Telegana • Shankaracharya in Kashmir • Alupuzza in Kerala
2		Biodiversity gardens & farms	• Navdanya in Uttar Pradesh • Kaplavruska in Gujarat
3		Traditional village gardens & farms	• Ziro Valley, Aranchal Pradesh
4		Temple gardens	• Varanasi and the Ganges • Meenakshi Amman, Tamil Nadu • Bodh Gaya
5		Famous gardens & festivals	• Taj Mahal • Diwali Festival
6		21st century sites & Vastu Shastra	• Kutupalong microgardens • Roof terraces in Jaipur • Floating gardens in Bangladesh • Ahmedabad - Vastu Shastra

Image 2. *Legend for Map and six parts of this chapter*

influence of Mahatma Gandhi. He is one of India's and the world's most well respected historical figures. His work drew upon the ancient Indian traditions and developed a way forward for the nation through complex legal, political and philosophical matters during the 20th century. He also insisted on initiating practical assistance with the day to day lives of the people. Details of the principles for living that Gandhi developed are discussed later in this chapter. They are also discussed in relation to the *Light Garden* model and how humanity is moving forward in the 21st century. For example, the Indian biodiversity movement is one of many groups that still quote and cite Gandhi's principles.

The Ancient Groves of India

As reported by the Indian Ministry of Environment, Forest and Climate change, there are over 18,000 species of flowering plants in India. This category includes conifers, flowering trees and other forms of flowering plants, such as shrubs and groundcovers.[187] Statistics recording the number of tree species

Image 3. *Location Plan for sites considered in India and Bangladesh.*

in India are not available. However, the Indian government is currently engaged in documenting the nation's forest cover and an estimate of the number of tree species may be made available in the future. According to information available in 2018 from the United Nations Food and Agricultural Organisation, in Bangladesh, there were 750 – 800 known tree species.[188]

In Europe, there are 250 - 500 tree species, compared to 40,000 – 53,000 species of trees that grow in the world's tropical forests.[189] There are an estimated 60,000 tree species globally.[190] The biodiversity of Europe in the 21st century is less than one percent of that found in the tropical forests of the world.[191] Thus we see how vital it is that any *Light Garden* proposals put forward in this book support the cultural base upon which the protection and veneration of sacred groves have rested for thousands of years. Speaking of sacred groves in India

> *"Experts believe that the total number of sacred groves could be as high as 100,000…*
> *It is estimated that around 1000km² of unexploited land is inside sacred groves."* [192]

In contrast to the protection of sacred groves by Hindus, Buddhists and ethnic cultures in India and Bangladesh, in past centuries the religions of Christianity and Islam have regarded the worship of trees as idolatry. Following from this, although there are many other contributing factors, we now find vast areas of Europe and the Middle East devoid of ancient groves of trees. Throughout the world, cultures have incorporated various ways of worshipping nature. The protection and veneration of sacred groves and forests are some of these. In India, these practices have existed for millennia.

Shankaracharya sacred grove in Kashmir

Kashmir is located in the mountains of northwestern India. The oldest of the Hindu scriptures, which some claim are dated back to 7,000 – 4,000 BCE, were probably composed in the northwest region of the Indian subcontinent. The Rig Veda, a collection of Vedic Sanskrit hymns to the gods, is likely to have been written around 1700 – 1100 BCE.[193] The sacred groves of the Himalayas are not unlike a form of *Light Garden* because of the striking natural beauty which has acted as a magnet and inspiration for scholars, singers, musicians and many other visitors over the centuries.

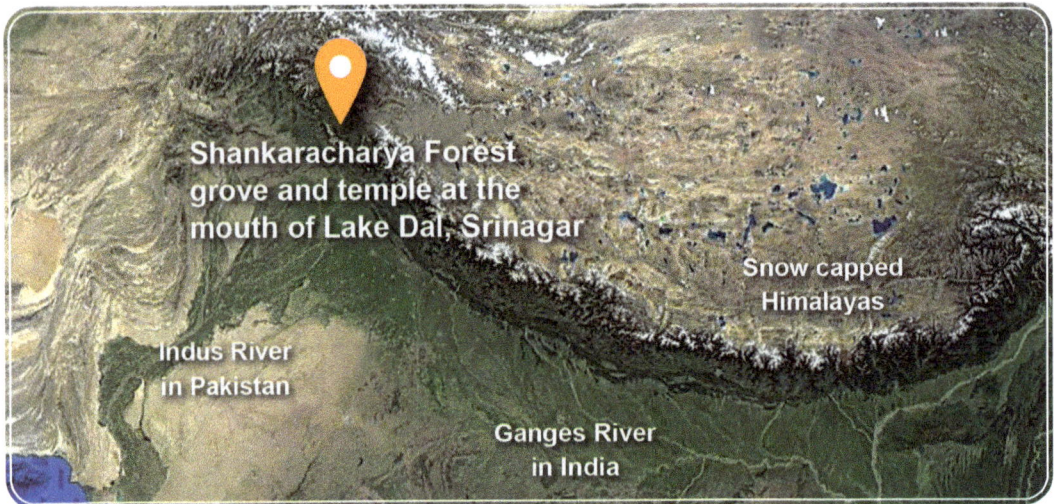

Image 4. *Location Map for Shankaracharya Ancient Grove on Lake Dal in Srinagar*

The Shankaracharya hilltop forest grove is strategically located at the southern end of Lake Dal in the town of Srinagar in Kashmir. Ancient Islamic texts describe 'Paradise' as a garden where four rivers intersect at a central pool, surrounded by lush green trees and beautiful flowers. The natural landscape and beauty of Lake Dal in Kashmir may once have mirrored this.

A 2011 survey by Kewal Kumar identified a total of 256 plant species at Shankaracharya forest grove. They had a thought-provoking range of uses:

> *"The forest had 112 medicinal species, 68 weed species, 36 poisonous plants, 23 exotic species, 14 fodder species, 12 species used in regional art and crafts, 12 edible species, 9 religious species with sacred value for both Hindus and Muslims, 5 species utilised in the making of houses …and the Shikara (the floating house boat) and 3 parasite species."* [194]

Image 5. *The town of Srinagar runs along the five kilometre length of Lake Dal. It extends southwards towards the Shankaracharya sacred grove at the southern end of the lake, in this Google Earth view.*

Image 6. *Shankaracharya Sacred Grove on the hill behind Lake Dal at Srinagar in Kashmir*

Mallu Gutta sacred grove

The Mahua (Madhuca longifolia) tree is worshipped by local people in the Mallur Gutta sacred grove. Its seeds may be seen in the photograph below.

Mallu Gutta is a sacred grove in the forested hill country near the city of Hyderabad. Although this grove is more extensive than many, the reasons local people value this grove are typical of the reasons why sacred groves have been valued all over India for millennia. In most places, local people still care for and protect the groves. Despite this, in the 21st century accumulated plastic litter left by tourists, lack of legal protection and intrusion by large development corporations have become problems in many areas.

In 2016 a team from Hyderabad University published their studies about Mallur Gatta.[195] During the previous six years, they had worked in consultation with local people to document 470 species of plants found in this 1500 hectare grove. This diversity of plants highlights why local communities value such vegetation communities as sources of medicinal plants.

Also found within the grove are Hindu temples for Lord Sri Laxminarasimha Swamy and Lord Hanuman, as well as prehistoric burial sites, the sacred "Chintamani" perennial stream and sites for ethnic worship of the Mahua tree.[196] This tree species is keenly conserved by those dwelling near the grove, as fat from its numerous seeds is used in skincare, vegetable butter, and fuel. Its flowers are used to produce a ceremonial alcoholic drink and several parts of the tree, including the bark, are useful for medicinal purposes. No wonder it is regarded as sacred.[197]

Although we do not have all the details, this description of the use and protection of the Mahua tree starts to build a picture of the management of the sacred Mallur Gutta grove in accordance with *Light Garden* principles. One of these principles, Number Three, is based around the concept of 'Act as both a Wave and a Particle, (as light does).' One could say there is a wave of diversity with many individual particles, where the people who act as protectors of cultural and biological diversity are the particles.

As reported by the Indian Ministry of Environment and Forests in 2001, they manage a network of 85 National Parks and 448 Wildlife Sanctuaries. These cover 4.2% of India's land area and contain 20% of the world's recorded plant species. Of the eighteen documented biological diversity hotspots in the world, two are found in India: the Eastern Himalayas and the Western Ghats.[198]

Image 7. *The Mahua (Madhuca longifolia) tree is worshipped in the Mallur Gutta sacred grove.*

Paralleling this diversity of ancient groves is the multiplicity of languages and human cultures in India. Census data from 1961

> *"identified no fewer than 1,652 mother languages... Twenty-nine of these, according to a census taken 40 years later in 2001, are spoken by over a million citizens each."* [199]

Alapphuza sacred grove in the Western Ghats

Ancient groves are part of the Hindu, ethnic and Buddhist cultures of India but numerous pressures are dampening the flame of faith that keeps these groves alive and well. The Western Ghats are a chain of mountains that runs down the entire west coast of India from north of Mumbai to the nation's southern tip. Although there are no comprehensive studies of the area under sacred groves across the Western Ghats, it is known that

Image 8. *Visitors at Alapphuza sacred grove. The remnant trees are behind the foreground fence.*

> *"There are hundreds of groves which have not been documented at all...*"Many tribal communities consider areas within forests to be sacred, but these are not even acknowledged as sacred groves."* [200]

In 2014, researchers who set out to update the current status of documented groves in Kodagu, a rural district in the Western Ghats, found that many groves were smaller than previously reported. More than two-thirds of the smaller groves were not forested, or could not even be found .

> *"...many family owned groves have been destroyed by the lack of faith in old cultural beliefs, lores and myths among the youth, and the migration of outsiders to the neighbourhood who do not understand the cultural significance of groves..."* [201]

In Maharashtra and Kodagu, roads have been made inside groves and elaborate temples constructed. A research associate at the Nature Conservation Foundation has studied attitudes towards groves.

He asked local residents if the change that has occurred in groves was culturally significant to them. He referred to forests changing from dense, biodiverse forests into quite disturbed patches of forest remnants. He found that only 14% of respondents said the change was culturally significant to them.

Parking lots at temples in forest groves are now common. People can be driven right up to the temples, without walking through the forest. In Kerala, the Mannarshala temple parking area accommodates at least 200 four-wheel drive vehicles.

> *"The forests seem to be becoming less important than the temple within it,"* says Anand M. Osuri, research associate with the Nature Conservation Foundation... *"It is important to understand what this means for conservation"* he says. [202]

Biodiversity Culture

The sacred groves at Alapphuza, Mallu Gutta and Shankaracharya are three of innumerable, valuable remnants of vegetation that contribute to the Indian subcontinent's biodiversity. Consciously conserving and supporting this biodiversity has been part of a movement towards rejuvenating a culture of biodiversity. Ancient 'Vasudhaiva Kutumbakam' philosophy was applied in the early years of the 21st century as part of developing the concept of a 'biodiversity civilisation.'

'Vasudhaiva Kutumbakam' is a Sanskrit phrase found in some Hindu texts such as the *Maha Upanishad*. It translates to mean *'the world is one family'*.[203] It is the Indian philosophy of living in harmony with every living being on the planet. It is an appeal to transform from a more narrowly focused industrial mindset to one of with a much greater emphasis on living as part of the planet's biodiversity.

This theme has inspired hundreds of thousands, if not millions of people to join the movement *towards* organic biodiverse gardens and farms in India and *away* from industrial agriculture, monocultures, farmer suicides and debt during the first two decades of the 21st century.

Such transitions might seem huge but they are already underway, through local and broader scale activities. For example in the Dal Swaraj Yatra of 2016, Navdanya representatives travelled over 1200 kilometres from East Uttar Pradesh to Madhya Pradesh in Northern India to spread organic dal seeds. They met and walked with over two thousand farmers during the twelve day yatra (journey).[204] Following on from this, the central theme for the 2018 International Biodiversity Congress in India was *"Biodiversity for Ecological Civilization: Vasudhaiva Kutumbakam."*[205] The title theme illustrates how the forward-looking concept of biodiversity civilisation is paired with India's ancient knowledge preserved in the Hindu teachings.

Mohandas Gandhi was accomplished at combining his forward-looking vision for India's future as an independent nation, with his knowledge of how the ancient traditions of India influence the everyday life of the people. For example, Gandhi publicly supported the continuation of the caste system in India, in order to avoid the chaos that dismantling it would entail. He none the less spent huge amounts of energy promoting the welfare of the weakest citizens amongst the power hierarchy of Indian society. His approach was both philosophical and practical. This conjunction between visionary inspiration and practical implementation is characterised today by the guiding light that gardening and farming have become as a way of implementing the principles that Gandhi advocated for the nation as a whole. It also aligns with the *Light Garden* principles of this book.

As he is commonly referred to, Mohandas, or Mahatma Gandhi, is best known for this work towards gaining Indian Independence. *Mahatma* translates to English as 'great soul.' Mahatma Gandhi was assassinated in 1948, the year after the British Parliament passed the Indian Independence Act. However, his words live on, for he was concerned with a revolution in Indian society that went far beyond gaining independence from British rule.

Dr Vandana Shiva has been an advocate of Gandhian principles for several decades. They are included in the guests' guidebook at the organic farm *Navdanya*, where Dr Shiva may be found engaging with farm work. Dr Shiva and other likeminded people have built upon Gandhi's concepts for society in the 21st century. They have significantly strengthened them by linking them to sound ecological and biodiversity principles. As an internationally renowned advocate for social and environmental justice, scientific research, the rights of women, biodiversity conservation and organic farming, Dr Shiva also speaks of her heart connection with this work:

"When you are doing the right things for the earth, she gives you great company." [206]

Biodiversity culture, Swaraj and Light Gardens

Biodiverse, small farms are very much in accordance with Gandhi's philosophy of Swaraj, which he worked throughout his life to develop and implement. To Gandhi, *Swaraj* entailed the fruits of tireless work and devotion to the good of the community. For example, he bridged the gap between being a negotiator at international forums and being an advocate for individual citizens by making statements such as:

> *"Recall the face of the poorest and weakest man you have seen, and ask yourself if this step you contemplate is going to be any use to him".* [207]

The manner in which the nation of Bangladesh has accepted nearly a million desperate refugees from the neighbouring country of Myanmar during the 21st century provides an exemplary contemporary example of this principle. Further description of this refugee community is provided later in this chapter.

Inherent in Swaraj is a philosophy of universal participation and empowerment of citizens. This philosophy incorporates implementation techniques such as restraining and eliminating discrimination, oppression, domination and segregation. In addition, proactive government policies for the rejuvenation of society are required.

The relevance of this concept to the 21st century society is only too apparent. Throughout the world there are significant levels of underemployment of the population. The omnipresent threat looms that more and more people will find that their services are unwanted by employers, as digital technology is used to replace the human workforce. Amid this, most governments seem strangely paralysed and unresponsive to calls to use their power to restructure our economies, unless those calls are for returning to *business as usual* scenarios. For example, calls to create meaningful employment for all the population through labour intensive, decentralised programs targeted to the rejuvenation of natural resources and society seem to fall outside their agendas.

But these calls do align with the principles of Swaraj as described by Gandhi. Swaraj is achieved firstly through each person voluntarily adopting a lifestyle of self-restraint and regular self-cleansing. In addition to this, each person engages in constructive work.[208] The role of government includes implementing policies that support a network of village scale, largely self-reliant local economies, where there are meaningful roles and work for all.

The concept of Swaraj overlaps with the *Light Garden* model. It may be compared to particular to *Light Garden* principles, such as number nine, which involves *restrained human use* of natural resources. However, Swaraj incorporates a more sophisticated concept: the Seven Social Sins.

Gandhi is widely credited with this concept, although it had been published in an earlier sermon at Westminster Abbey by Fredrick Lewis Donaldson in 1925.[209] Gandhi read this and published it later that year in his weekly newspaper *Young India*. His paper had a huge readership and it spread the message far and wide. The list of the *Seven Social Sins* is:

> *"Politics without Principles. Wealth without Work. Pleasure without Conscience. Knowledge without Character. Commerce without Morality. Science without Humanity. Worship without Sacrifice."* [210]

We can assume that this set of principles was firmly embedded in Gandhi's mind in subsequent years, as twenty two years later, he wrote it on a slip of paper. He gave the paper to his grandson Arun Gandhi, as they parted company for the last time. Shortly afterwards, Gandhi was assassinated.

Another example of how Swaraj is being implemented in the 21st century is through partnerships between governments and citizens in the north Indian State of Sikkim. In 2017, this Himalayan area was recognised as India's first, (and the world's first), entirely organic farming state. The government has legislated, so the use of commercial pesticides and fertilisers is now illegal in Sikkim and there is meaningful work for local people. The people typically work in growing and marketing organic produce; rejuvenating soils and forests; managing the water supply; participating in local decision-making forums; building homes; care-giving, hospitality and educational roles.

As part of an integrated approach to environmental management, tourism, employment and food production, the Government of Sikkim has recognised the need for financial planning and support for the State's farmers.

The success that has been achieved in Sikkim was celebrated at the 2018 International Biodiversity Congress held at Dehradun in India. Participants announced a goal that all the eight Himalayan states in India would become devoted to organic, biodiverse farming and environmental management.[211]

This type of farming is healthy for people, society and the environment. And as Dr Vandana Shiva has said:

> *"For fifteen years we have been analysing the small farms of India - in the wet areas of Kerala, in the high Himalayas, in the deserts of Rajasthan - and our research has shown, again and again and again, that biodiverse small farms using ecological inputs, produce three to five times more food than industrial monocultures."* [212]

The film "Economics of Happiness", was released in 2011 by Helena Norberg-Hodge, Stephen Gorlick and John Page. It gives an international perspective to work being done in India and other nations around the globe. It includes numerous interviews with people such as the Indian farmer who said:

> *"All I need is a complete integrated farm of one acre and I can feed twenty people. We don't need agricultural scientists; we don't need hybrid seeds; we don't need GM."* [213]

Image 9. (Above left) *Dr Vandana Shiva. An internationally recognised advocate for biological and agricultural diversity, women's rights, seed sovereignty and related causes. She has successfully advocated for these advancements, building upon Gandhi's moral compass for human civilisation.*

Image 10. (Above right) *Cattle often live on biodiverse farms in India.*

Although people who are not literate in Sanskrit may not understand the full significance of each stage in the historical tableau included on the following page, the iconographic illustrations convey the general ideas. For example, the thin, shirtless, seated body of Mahatma Gandhi may be seen in the icon at the lower right, final timeline position for the year 1947. It conveys the message: Gandhi's campaigns for national independence were based on satyagraha techniques to awaken the inner voice of the oppressors to the truth and rightness of their own heart.

Mahatma Gandhi progressively developed these satyagraha techniques, drawing upon the inspiration and embedded knowledge of a culture that had developed over millennia. In many ways, the concept of an Indian biodiversity civilisation in the 21st century is a natural extension of India's cultural heritage.

Accounts of the worship of Surya, the Hindu Sun God, are found in the *Rigveda*. This text was composed between 1500 and 1000 BCE. The *Rigveda* is the oldest of the Hindu sacred texts, which are known as the Vedas.[214] Surya is the dawn rider who brings in the sun and rides his chariot across the sky throughout the year.

As indicated in the top row of the Image 11 timeline diagram, the Indus Valley Hindu civilisation is dated from 3,500 BCE. Light and sunlight feature in Hindu civilisation from the earliest times. Celebration of Diwali, the Festival of Light, dates back at least 2500 years. Diwali is still widely celebrated today. The religious significance of the event varies in different parts of the Indian subcontinent but the symbolism of Diwali often celebrates the triumph of

Image 11. *Timeline of Hindu civilisation in India.*

good over evil. As an indication of the importance of light in the Hindu culture, it is the light and Diwali lamps that symbolise the triumph of goodness. Bringing beauty and the opportunity to celebrate with family and friends, this is a message that transcends language, literacy and different cultures.

Light as a cultural metaphor in Indian civilisation

In India, as everywhere else, light comes from the sun. However in India, the meaning of light is very much aligned with radiance. In India, it is a radiance with a depth of patina that has been refined and consciously maintained over millennia. This radiance has been bestowed by virtue of a conviction to seek and manifest the truth. The radiance can be in a person, a garden, or a place. It may manifest from the morning mist as a vision - as the Taj Mahal does for those who rise early enough to see it. It also has a vigour that is undeniable and not necessarily pretty.

In India, light is not an *abstraction* in which the senses delight. It is a daily part of the struggle for survival. A discourse about light in terms of abstract design concepts inevitably crumbles when discussed in the context of India. It must step aside in favour of India's more robust and compelling debate about justice, empowerment of the people, democracy, self-rule, and the unfolding manifestations of the words of the sages.

For example, Vincent Van Gogh may have exclaimed *Jeune Magnifique,* as his heart and senses delighted in the magnificence of the light upon the yellow cornfields and sunflowers that he painted in the south of France. Gandhi - amid his lifelong struggles for freedom, justice and personal responsibility - referred to light in a more visceral sense:

The influence of Gandhian philosophy is still playing out, despite being resisted during his lifetime by his colleague, the Indian Prime Minister Nehru. Nehru regarded it as impractical to implement in a national political context.[215] None the less, the global reach of

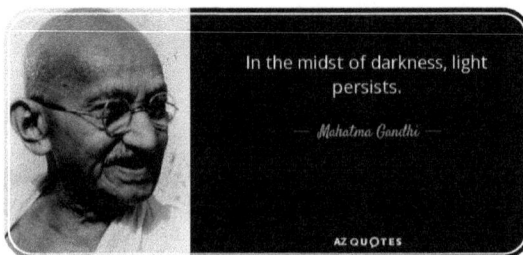

Image 12. *Gandhi referred to light as part of his philosophy: in the midst of darkness, light persists.*

Gandhi's philosophy and its all-embracing principles continue to influence people around the globe as the message spreads.

Underlying this philosophical background is the celebration of light and life. It is so tightly embedded in the Indian culture that it is liable to burst forth with vibrancy at any time of year. The festival of Diwali, (The Festival of Light), is a good example. It draws upon centuries of time-honoured meaning, bestowed through the symbolism of light and darkness. Animating the ancient Vedic scriptures, it celebrates the triumph of good over evil.[216] It is one of the most popular and widespread annual festivals in India and is described in more detail in Part 5 of this chapter.

Although Gandhi's focus was not on themes of this book that relate to biophysics and use of natural resources, the principles that he established for participatory democracies are relevant. They continue to be taken up by many groups who are strong forces behind the movement calling for more effective, responsible, just and equitable management of natural resources. The concept of a biodiversity civilisation in India falls within that movement's scope, so it is worth considering how Gandhi's principles have affected it.[217]

For example, when people come to live and work at the Indian property *Navdanya*, they are given a *Visitor's Guide* that refers to Gandhi's principles.[218] These include additional concepts to Swaraj and the Seven Social Sins that we have considered so far. A deep culture shock can ensue for some visitors from Western cultures who start to live and work side by side with Indian scholars. These scholars may have gained post-doctoral qualifications at the world's most prestigious universities and be renowned as international guest speakers. They may also choose to spend their lives working in communities such as *Navdanya* and helping others. They chose to live simply and happily, adhering to the principles of the community and serving their people, rather than pursuing individualistic Western lifestyles. These Navdanya community principles include Satyam, Ahimsa, Brahmacharya and Swadesh, as briefly described below:

Ahimsa (non-violence...Gandhi...held that total non-violence would rid a person of anger, obsession and destructive impulses.

Brahmacharya (self-perfection through self-control and contentment)...means control of the senses in thought, word and deed. It also means the pursuit of virtue and to strive for excellence in all domains of activity and relationships.

Swadeshi (self-reliance) began as a Gandhian concept during the time of the British Empire in India. Gandhi galvanised masses of the Indian population to abstain from purchasing cloth that was not made in India. In later years, the term came to have a broader meaning associated with the self-reliance of local economies, communities, and government systems.[219]

Satyam (Truth)

> *"The pivotal and defining element of Gandhism is Satyam, a Sanskrit word usually translated into English as 'truth'. The literal meaning is 'what actually is'. Gandhi believed that the principle of Satya should pervade all considerations of politics, ego, society and convention."* [220]

Gandhi believed that each person had to seek their own version of Satyam, whilst adhering to the spirit of the concept and all the other principles as well. Therein lies one great difference between Indian civilisation and many simpler, more individualist Western lifestyles of the 21st century.

Baskar Save, the Gandhi of natural farming

Inspired by the writings of Gandhi and Vinoba Bhave, in 1956 Baskar Save decided to begin an experiment. He would revert to an organic farming system on his family's farm in the State of Gujarat, India. It is interesting to examine how Baskar worked with the natural resources available to him to do this from first principles. As well as tending the soil and water, Baskar consciously developed ways to optimise the use of the available sunlight on his farm. In the early years, he planted short-lived crops such as vegetables, legumes and rice between longer-lived tree species of coconut and chikoo. Later he introduced medium life- span crops such as bananas and papayas.

The Gandhi of Organic Farming: Baskar Save's principles

Baskar's first principle is very similar to Gandhi's Ahimsa principle:
"all living creatures have an equal right to live."

His second principle recognises that
"everything in Nature is useful and serves a purpose in the web of life."

Baskar's third principle is:
"farming is a dharma, a sacred path of serving Nature and fellow creatures; it must not degenerate into a pure dhandha or money-oriented business. Short-sighted greed to earn more – ignoring Nature's laws – is the root of the ever-mounting problems we face."

Baskar's fourth principle is for on-going regeneration of soil fertility. It recognises that the energy of sunlight can, like other natural resources, be cycled back through soil and water to maintain ecologically sound and balanced systems. After harvesting tree products, trees should be retained. The balance of the biomass, (85% to 95%), should be returned to the soil to replenish the fertility. This can be done through direct composting of vegetative matter, or feeding plants to animals, which produce manure for composting back into the soil. [221]

Sixty years after he began this family farm in 1956, Baskar was still alive to see it continuing as a stable and profitable enterprise. By that stage, ninety percent of the income earned was from the long-lived chikoo and coconut trees.The principles that Baskar developed for use on his farm are widely applicable. Many visitors have taken tours of the property, hoping to learn more about how to create prosperous, living, biodiverse enterprises and ecosystems.

Baskar's farming system is consistent with the *Light Garden* model. For example, it aligns with principle number nine, (restrained Human Use) and with principle number eight, (Context and Environment). In accordance with *Light Garden* principle number one, (Energy), Baskar was conscious of working with his available energy source, which was sunlight. He consciously planned his farm activities to utilise the available space and time that different types of crops took to grow. This type of planning aligns with *Light Garden* principle number two, (Space and Time). He initially planted quick growing ground covers and shrubs. Longer lived trees became more important in later years, once they had become established amongst the other crops.

Baskar's organic farming principle number one *"all living creatures have an equal right to live"* echoes the feeling of *Light Garden* principle number six, (Entanglement and Focal Points). All living creatures are enmeshed in the same web of life and the same biophysical fields that underlie life. Baskar's second principle states that everything in Nature is useful and serves a purpose in the web of life. That idea resonates with *Light Garden* principle number seven, (Perception and Measurement). It reminds us of the need to consciously use our powers of perception to seek and find the usefulness of everything in Nature.

Image 13. *Long lived coconut trees provide income on Baskar Save' organic farm*

Traditional Villages

Although they may have many things in common, there is no typical village garden found in the great diversity of places that occur in India and Bangladesh. In addition, due to outside influences since 1950, many villages have experienced changes to traditional practices that had previously endured for centuries.

However, I have chosen to describe one group of traditional villages in the Ziro Valley of the Himalayas that has been preserved, despite outside pressures. Considerable documentation of this culture's authenticity was compiled in the process of nominating the village-based way of life for inclusion in UNESCO's World Heritage list. The people who live in Ziro Valley are also examples of a culture where light is consciously revered as part of spiritual, social, garden and landscape management. Hence it serves to illustrate the theme of this book in more depth. The World Heritage listing documentation provides much of the material I refer to when describing the role of light in this culture.

As shown by eight ⭐ symbols on the map that follows, there are eight Indian States in the Himalayan region: Jammu and Kashmir, Himachal Pradesh, Uttarakhand, Uttar Pradesh, Sikkim, Arunachal Pradesh and parts of Assam and West Bengal. The Ziro Valley lies in the State of Arunachal Pradesh, in the northeast of India.

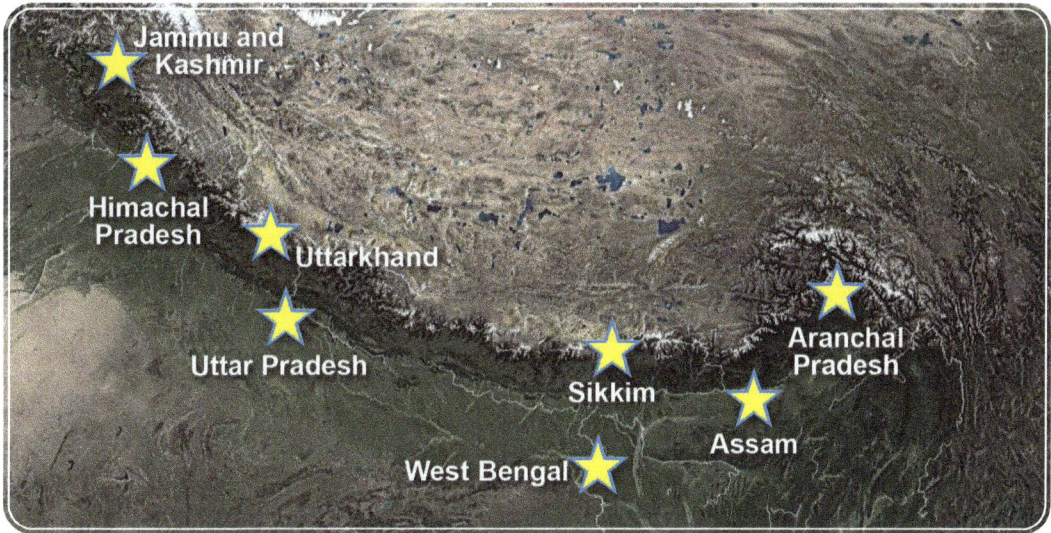

Image 14. (Top) *Map of the Himalayan states in India.*
(Above) *The peaks of Laurabina Yak in the Himalayas*

Image 15. *Ziro Valley Location Plan*

> *"Indians love these peaks because they are a part of every Indian's life. Indians revere the mountains, as they would, the father. Even today, when urban India is racing against time, in the caves of the snow-clad peaks, live hermits – seeking the divine. Not a surprise when you consider that even this century has seen some great philosophers like Raman Maharishi, Swami Vivekananda, Ramakrishna Paramahansa and Krishnamurti."* [222]

For centuries, the Siang River, (otherwise known by the Tibetan name of Yarlung Tsangpo), has also been known as the Brahmaputra River, once it flows south across the Himalayans into India. To the north of the Himalayas, it flows for 1600 kilometres before reaching the border with India.[223] The River Yarlung Tsangpo originates in the Angsi Glacier near Mount Kailash. Flowing to the east, it reaches the "Great Bend" between Namche Barwa and the Gyala Peri mountains. Among the gorges in this northeastern extremity of the Himalayas, is the spot where I have chosen to begin this description of the role of light in the traditional gardens in India.

Ziro Valley is located on a tributary of the Brahmaputra, less than 200 kilometres south of the Himalayan border with China. It is some 2,000 kilometres to the east of New Delhi, the capital city of India. The indigenous religions of the Tibeto-Burmese peoples of Arunachal Pradesh are known as Donyi- Polo.[224] As an example of how integral the concept of *light* is to these religions, the term *Donyi-Polo* means *sun-moon* when translated to English.

The practical expression of the faith in Donyi-Polo can be found in people's daily lives and actions: they call themselves "*Donyi O, Polo Ome*", meaning "children of the sun and the moon".[225] In more depth, *Donyi–Polo* is an analogy for describing God:

"representing the way in which the divine principle manifests itself, that is: eternally veiling, unveiling and then revealing himself in nature; providing harmony and balance to the universe, for example in the alternation of light and darkness..." [226]

As described in more detail on the following page, this belief system around the concept of light underpins the practical organisation of tasks in the traditional village life of the Donyi Polo people. It also is recognised as a significant contributing factor to the nomination of the cultural landscape of the Ziro Valley on the United Nations Education, Scientific and Cultural Organisation's (UNESCO's), World Heritage List.[227]

It has been their ability to maintain their traditional agricultural and belief systems, despite pressures from outside influences, which makes the Donyi-Polo unique. (These people are also known as the Apatinai people).[228] To better understand how they have achieved this, it is worth considering some of the history and detail of their gardening and agricultural systems. [229] [230] [231] Note: these references apply in general to the discussion of Ziro Valley.

The Apatani tribes of Ziro Valley inhabit an area of 1058 square kilometres. In the 21st century, the population is estimated as being between 20,000 and 40,000 people. They consciously worship sacred groves, forests and light in the form of the sun, moon and nature. The religion is called Donyi-Polo and religious rituals and agricultural practices are synchronised with lunar phases.

The Apartani belief system that reveres all forms of Life has underpinned their ability to maintain the forested watershed of Ziro Valley, thus ensuring some biodiversity and a clean flow of water into their fields, gardens and villages. Unlike many parts of Asia where pesticides are now used, the Apartani developed a unique system of organic, wet rice and fish cultivation (Aji-ngyii). Based on estimates by village elders, one hectare of land produces about 200 kg of fish, each in the size range of 140 – 200 grams.

Image 16. *Wet rice cultivation*

The Apartani system of governance through village councils called *bulyañ* has helped maintain their traditional communal agriculture and belief systems, despite pressures from outside influences. That is what is recognised as unique, in the UNESCO World Heritage listing citation for the cultural landscape of Ziro Valley.

Tibetan and Indian sources indicate that the Apatani and other tribes of the Arunachal mountains have probably inhabited the area since around the 8th century CE and certainly since the 15th century CE. Until very recently, traders travelled between Tibet and Assam, through the mountain passes of Arunachal. The Apartani, along with other Himalayan hill tribes, were accustomed to negotiating treaties for co-existence with the Indian Ahom kings of the Brahmaputra valley. The tribes resisted undermining of their local tribal authority and way of life when the British colonial government of the 19th century ousted the Ahom kings. The Apatanis were brought into this colonial conflict situation relatively late, (in 1897), due to the relative isolation provided to Ziro Valley by its elevation of 5,000 metres. [232] [233]

The British tried to force the hill tribes to be porters and work as plantation farm labourers. When forced to work for the British, the Apartani had to leave their own farms and community responsibilities for extended periods.

Ziro Valley: new ways of seeing the light

The landscape of the Ziro valley homeland of the Apatanis has some similarities with other Himalayan valleys. These include the Imphal Valley of Manipur, the Kathmandu Valley of Nepal, and Bhutan's Paro Valley.

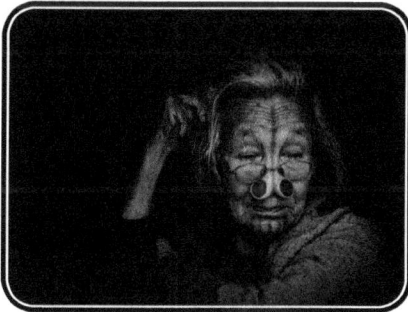

Urbanisation has completely changed the landscapes of the Imphal and Kathmandu valleys. Though Paro valley still retains its charm, agriculture is minimal and mainly due to individual efforts rather than the type of community activity that still occurs in Ziro valley.[234]

Looking downcast, perhaps the Apartani woman depicted at left is thinking of the loss of traditional values amongst the younger generations of visitors who come and go through the Ziro Valley in the 21st century.

Image 17. *In a concession to the modern age, an Apartani woman wears some factory made garments and spectacles, plus and the traditional nose plugs and facial tattoos.*

For millennia, the Brahmaputra has been known as the crystal clear, lifeblood water for gardens and villages in the northeastern part of India. However, as reported by *The Hindu* newspaper in December 2017, the Indian Government at that time was investigating why the river had turned black. The water was unfit for consumption. Natural causes such as earthquakes were suspected.[235]

In November 2017 *The Times of India* had carried similar reports with photographs of the river sludge. It quoted local people saying they seen the river turn dark before after mudslides, but never before had it been like this. This situation prompted speculation that the cause was Chinese activities upstream, leading to release of large quantities of cement into the river, probably in conjunction with underground tunnelling and redirection of the natural flow of waterways away from India and into the dry parts of China.[236]

Despite this, the Himalayas continue to draw many gardeners, pilgrims and visitors, many of whom are seeking to create in their own lives a reverence for nature and for light, such as has been kept alive by the Apartani people.

Famous gardens

Light in a garden in India is not an abstract concept. It is a radiance, a presence - something of awe. Perhaps that is why the Sanskrit and Arabic languages are so rich in terms for such phenomenon, which are not easily or simply translatable.

Popular culture holds that the Taj Mahal celebrates Shah Jahan's love for his wife, Mumtaz Mahal. The Taj Mahal is India's most well-known international icon. What could be more appropriate in one of the world's most successful and enduring matriarchal societies, where the divine light of women and Goddesses is still venerated in daily life? Although eight million visitors come to the Taj Mahal each year and in 2018 the Indian Government introduced a limit of 40,000 domestic visitors per day to the site, its triumphal mystique remains.

There are a number of internationally famous gardens in India, many of which were constructed in the Moghul style of Islamic Paradise Gardens. The Taj Mahal is one of those gardens. When considering the design of that site, many of the concepts discussed in this book may be more widely applicable to other famous Indian gardens.

The Taj Mahal

The plan for this 17 hectare site has five main parts as illustrated and described on the following page.[237][238] The Taj Mahal is not only a masterpiece in its own right; it offers an insight into the beautiful visions and lights of paradise that bejewel the world of Muslim art, philosophy and religion.

According to Islamic beliefs, Paradise consists of a garden and four rivers with lush green trees, beautiful flowers and plants. The plan of the Taj Mahal was designed to reflect this vision and required a great deal of practical site planning to bring it into reality near Agra between 1631 and 1648.[239] Shah Jahan went to great lengths to choose the Taj Mahal site on the banks of the Yamuna River, it being some eight hundred kilometres from where his wife Mumtaz died.

The site initially planned for Mumtaz's mausoleum was found not to have foundations solid enough to bear the weight of the great marble structure that Shah Jahan envisaged. Nor did the original site have a river wide enough to reflect the glory of the structure within its waters. In addition, a site that was accessible for the transport of marble from the quarry in Rajasthan to the riverbank was needed. Shah Jahan foresaw a vision of the incomparable reflection of white light from domes constructed of India's finest marble. The UNESCO World Heritage Listing of the site describes it as

> *"the jewel of Muslim art in India and one of the universally admired masterpieces of the world's heritage."* [240]

Image 18. *White light reflecting from the marble of the Tah Mahal. No matter how large the rivers of pilgrims grow, the mausoleum is visible from all parts of the garden.*

"Charbagh or Chahar Bagh is a Persian and Islamic quadrilateral garden layout based on the four gardens of Paradise mentioned in the Qur'an. In Persian, "Chār" means 'four' and "bāgh" means 'garden'." [241]

Image 19. *The Taj Mahal*

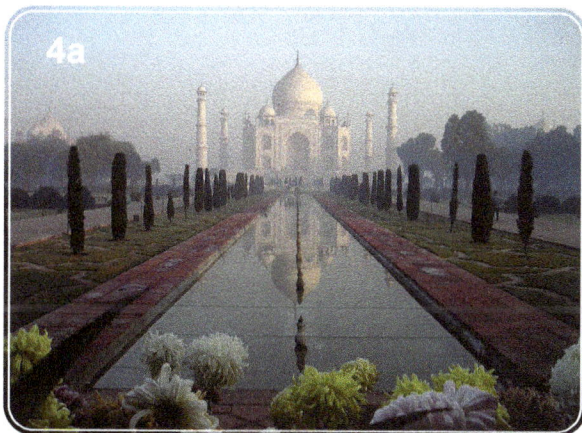

(Above) The Taj Mahal. The plan for this 17 hectare site has five main parts as listed below:

1. The *Taj Ganji*, or paved bazaar forecourt, which has a boundary wall adjoining the dense urban area to the south. This urban area may be seen on the far left of aerial photograph view of the site above left.

2. The large, brown coloured *Jilaukhana*, or front of house area. This was built as an arrival hall for guests with sizeable entourages, including elephants.

3. The *Charbagh*. This is the flat, enclosed garden with trees, flowers, lawns and intersecting water channels.

4. The riverfront terrace, upon which the domed, white marble Mausoleum (4a) and Kau Ban Mosque (4b) stand. An image looking north across the garden towards the mausoleum (4a) is shown above left.

4a. *View across the Charbagh (garden)* towards the mausoleum at the Taj Mahal.

4b. *Women at the Kau Ban* Mosque of the Taj Mahal.

5. The Yamuna River, plus the moonlight garden on the far bank of the river. The far bank of the river is out of view, to the right hand side of the photograph.

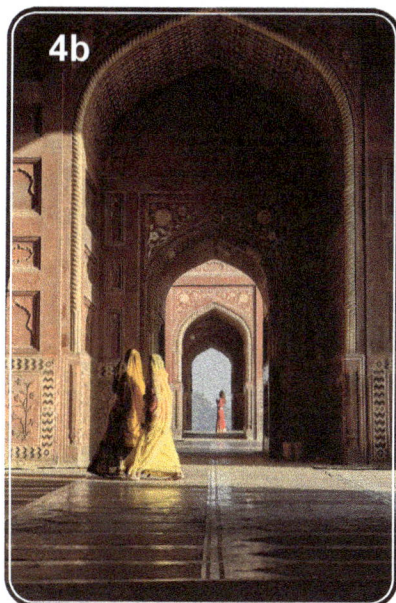

The Char Bagh, or central garden area of the Taj Mahal, covers an area of three hundred by three hundred metres. Four symbolic rivers of paradise separate the garden into quadrants. The rivers are of water, milk, honey and wine. Multiples of the number four are considered the most holy of numbers in the Islamic religion, so the four garden quadrants were further divided into sixteen flowerbeds. The tree species used in this garden are Cyprus, (which symbolise death) and fruit trees, (which represent life).[242]

The design of the Taj Mahal site has been analysed in terms of Vastu Shastra, which is the traditional Indian science of construction and architecture. Vastu Shastra has ancient origins in India and predates Islamic influences. It lends a particular presence to the gardens and sites of India and is concerned with creating a central space surrounded by zones where specific activities occur. The flow of energy and sunlight is carefully considered and is relevant to consider here.[243]

Creating a central space with openness to sunlight is one of the basic principles of Vastu Shastra. Such a space is found at the Taj Mahal. Other features of the Taj Mahal that align with Vastu Shastra principles include open space in the East and North of the site; the presence of the Yamuna River in the East and North of the site and the flow of the river from West to East.[244]

Vastu Shastra

Underlining the significance of light in Hindu design, is none other than the Lord Brahma, Creator of the Universe. He is responsible for bringing light upon the Earth's surface, in an alternating sequence of day and night. It follows that an uncluttered space for Lord Brahma and light must always be reserved in the centre of a design, whether it be indoors or outdoors.[245] The peaceful existence of humans is guarded by nine Hindu Gods of Nature, the *Ashtadhik Balakars'* or *Guards of Directions*. The Vedas contain much scripture dedicated to these Gods. One of the earliest poems in the vast Hindu collection of the Rigveda describes the desire for alignment with the dawning of light.

"An unshaped consciousness desired light And a blank prescience yearned towards distant change" [246]

In turn, such concepts underpin Hindu design principles and remain as powerful influences in the contemporary practice of Vastu Shastra. The surface of the Earth is represented by a square in Hindu cosmology. Firstly, the four sides of this square are defined by the two positions where the light rises at Sunrise (East) and sets at Sunset (West). The directions of North and South represent the other two sides of the square. This geometry provides a tangible indication of how important the concept of light is in the design of Hindu sites.[247]

Image 20. *Lord Shiva. Shiva temples are designed according to Vastu Shastra principles.*

Hindu sites are designed on a mathematical basis, which is encoded in the Vastu Shatra and includes the Purusha Mandala. A Mandala is a plan or chart that symbolically represents the universe. The term Purusha refers to humankind's cosmic nature – to our energy, soul and power. An analogy may be made with the game of chess, which originated at least 1,500 years ago in India. The chessboard symbolises our existence as a field of action on which the Gods engage in combat. Each God has their role within the eternal battle between power-seeking asuras and benevolent devas.[248]

The design of Hindu sites such as cities, temples, gardens, offices and homes, is guided by specific activities which should be conducted in each direction. For example, in a home, the pooja or prayer room should be located in the east because that is the direction from which daylight first touches a site. A pooja room is separate from a bedroom, office or lounge room, as commonly understood in Western culture.

Kandariya Mahadeva Temple in the city of Ahmedabad is an example of an 11th century Shiva temple designed according to Vastu Shastra principles.[249] A larger scale application of these principles is described later in this chapter with reference to the city of Madurai in the south of India.

Temple, festival and pilgrimage gardens

Almost all of the Mughal gardens of India that relied upon open channels and displays of water are dry and derelict today. Some, such as the Taj Mahal, are maintained by a paid workforce. In contrast, the innumerable smaller Hindu gardens throughout the land are still used and maintained by the local people.

Temples as places of pilgrimage

To understand the nature of how light is incorporated in Indian and Bangladeshi Gardens and landscapes, an appreciation of the prevailing and historical Hindu and Islamic religions that underpin these societies is necessary. A brief introduction to this subject is included on the following pages.

" The gods always play where groves are near rivers, mountains and springs, and in towns with pleasure gardens. Temples are therefore sited in relation to rivers and groves. They are places of pilgrimage, not places of congregational worship."

Image 21.
(Above) *Women at Varanasi.*
(Above right) *Hindu women at a Diwali ceremony in the Ganges.*
(Right) *Men bathing at sunrise in the Ganges at Varanasi.*

Diwali

Of the many festivals celebrated in India, the festival of light is perhaps the most widely followed. Known as Diwali, it occurs over a period of five days. What better symbol to signify how important the concept of light is within Indian culture than this event?

Diwali is celebrated at the time of the Hindu New Year, during the lunar month of Kartika (October and November). Millions of Hindus, Sikhs and Jains across the world join in the festivities. Diwali is a time of gift-giving and visiting friends and relatives. Fireworks and lamps are lit; prayers are conducted and special community events are organised. Diwali is equivalent in significance to the celebration of Christmas in Western culture.[250]

While each faith has its reason to celebrate Diwali, the central theme is the triumph of light over darkness and goodness over evil. The legend of Lord Rama and his wife Sita returning victorious to their kingdom in northern India after defeating the demon king Ravana is one to which people of all ages can relate. It is the 15th century historical story behind the present day Diwali celebrations.[251]

The Sanskrit word Diwali means "rows of lamps" and these can be seen in all the homes and shops. Preparation of rangolis surrounded by lamps is a traditional activity carried out during Diwali. Preparing a rangoli involves quiet, contemplative activity to draw the intricate, intersecting lines and patterns on the ground. Reminiscent of the fourth *Light Garden* principle of *Lines, Patterns and Probabilities*, the probability is high that these lines and patterns will include some traditional symbols but also that each rangoli will be a joyful, unique creation, once the finishing touches are added.

Rangoli's are traditionally made from colourful fresh flower petals, coloured grains of rice and similar granular materials. They add to the festive spirit of Diwali.

Unlike the Christian celebration of Christmas with a strong church and home focus, Diwali is traditionally a home based festival. Indian temples are not designed as places for

Image 22. A completed Rangoli surrounded by lamps.

congregational worship but rather as places of pilgrimage. Both Christmas and Diwali are times when people visit and entertain their friends and relatives, deriving joy from the beauty of decorations, good food, celebrations and the glow of lamps and candles.

The preparation of intricate sand mandalas with similarities to rangolis is another symbolic activity carried out by Buddhist monks at various times of the year. Buddhism arose in northeastern India in the 6th century BCE.

Trees and gardens in the life of Gautama Buddha

In contrast to the bright lights, crowds and family events of Diwali, the life the Buddha, (Gautama Buddha) was characterised by quietly taking refuge outdoors, under the shelter of trees. He taught his disciplines in such places as well. Pilgrimage trees have become associated with Gautama Buddha's significant life events. The life of Gautama Buddha was spent not in the deserts of Rajasthan, the beaches of Kerala or the snow clad peaks of northern India but in the fertile plains of the Ganges and the foothills of the Himalayas. Trees, gardens, flowers and forests

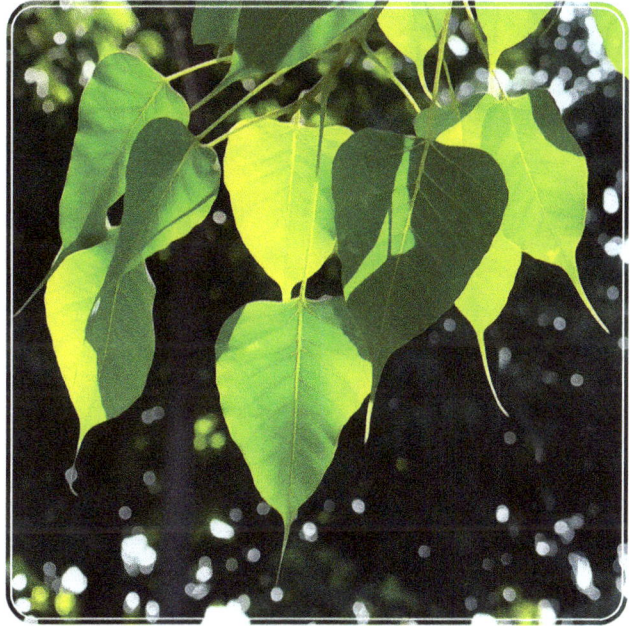

Image 23. *Bodhi Tree leaves*

abounded in those parts of India. No wonder they are interwoven not only through the imagery of Buddhist texts, sculptures and tankhas but also through the course of Gautama's actual life.

Historical accounts indicate that he was born in a garden under a sal tree, about 550 BCE at Lumbini. At the time, his mother was journeying back to her father's kingdom to give birth. Making such a journey was the custom at the time. Buddha's birth en route at Lumbini is somewhat comparable to the birth of Jesus when his parents were travelling to Bethlehem.

Buddha gained enlightenment under another tree: the Bodhi Tree. This tree is also known as the Peepal Tree. Realising that he was close to attaining enlightenment, Buddha chose to trek to this tree and sit in meditation until achieving full enlightenment.

Today the Bodhi Tree is a large and sacred fig in the Mahabodhi Temple at Bodhgaya. It has been maintained by the propagation of successive fig trees from the time of Buddha's enlightenment in about 585 BCE up to the present day. It has large and appealingly heart-shaped leaves, symbolic of the heartfelt sentiments necessary for successful and sustained Buddhist practice.

Multitudes of pilgrims now visit these sites in Lumbini and Bodhgaya each day. As a sign of how important the living trees are to the experience of Buddhism, walls have been erected around them to protect them from physical damage by the crowds. Buddha also chose to pass away under a tree in the forest outside the town of Kushinagar. Buddhism itself became almost extinct as a movement in India by about the 12 Century CE. However, in the meantime, it had spread to many other Asian countries, where it still prevails today.[252][253]

Trees are not as prevalent in some of these Asian regions, (such as the snowfields and glaciers of the Tibetan plateau), but the imagery of trees and flowers remains in the rituals, thankas and sadhanas. All of the *Light Garden* principles are readily compatible with the Buddhist teachings, through common concepts such as *Storage and Sharing of Information,* Restrained *Human Use* of resources and consider *Context and Environment.*

Meenakshi Amman Temple

This temple is located in the southern Indian State of Tamil Nadu. It attracts over a million pilgrims and visitors during the annual ten day Meenakshi Tirukalyanam festival, which is held during the Tamil month of Chittirai. Chittirai usually coincides with the month of April in the calendars of 21st century Western cultures.[254]

The ancient temple site was built without walls. It is said to have been first constructed in the 6th century BCE in the city of Madurai. The city itself is dated as 2,500 years old.[255]

The temple has always been at the heart of the city. Hindus rebuilt the city in the 16th and 17th centuries after Muslim invaders sacked and looted the temple in the 14th century. The Muslims subsequently demanded tribute from the Hindus for centuries but the Hindus remained in control of the city administration.

Image 24. (Above) *Meenakshi Amman Temple - Google Earth aerial photograph*

Image 25. (Right) *Meenakshi Amman temple with crowds of visitors, walls and towers visible.*

The city was built to incorporate Hindu and Vastu Shastra principles. These included having the city face East to greet Surya, the Sun God who rises in the East.[256] The old city's street layout is illustrated below, with yellow coloured linework overlaid to the Google Earth 2019 aerial photograph. The original concentric squares and streets opening towards the East of the city centre can be seen. This street layout contrasts with the modern city's surrounding streets, which now encompass the ancient city. For example, a large transport corridor can be seen running just to the west of the old city street pattern in the aerial photograph below.

Image 26. *Meenakshi Amman temple in the centre of the city of Madurai. The yellow lines show the pattern of streets that were built around the temple.*

Streets in the original city were named after the months of the Tamil Hindu calendar, such as Masi, Adhi, Avani-moola and others.[257] The tradition of festively parading bronze statues from the temple through the city's streets developed centuries ago.[258] It continues today at religiously auspicious times.

The rebuilding of the temple included the addition of courtyard walls to protect the inner shrines. The shrines are dedicated to the Hindu Goddess Parvati, (also known as Meenakshi), and to her consort, Shiva. The shrines are housed in buildings constructed according to Vastu Shastra principles. Millions of pilgrims come each year to experience being in the temple and to join the celebrations.[259]

Madurai is one of the many temple towns in the Indian State of Tamil Nadi. The name Tamil Nadi is derived from the groves, clusters and forests which are each dominated by a particular variety of a tree or shrub. Each variety of tree or shrub is believed to shelter a presiding deity.[260] Despite the huge crowds that visit the site, it is interesting to see in the aerial photographs on the preceding page that there is a ring of large shade trees around the perimeter of the site. These trees help to retain something of the character of the groves after which Tamil Nadu was named.

The significance of light in the rebuilding of the temple and the whole city has been described by Susan Lesandowski:

> *"The Nayaka rulers followed the Hindu texts on architecture called the Silpa Shastras in redesigning the temple city plan and the Meenakshi temple. The city was laid out… in the shape of concentric squares and ring-roads around them, with radiating streets culminating in the Meenakshi-Sundaresvara temple."* [261]

As illustrated on the previous page, in the 21st century the Meenakshi Amman temple is surrounded by vast walls and a series of towers. Like the Taj Mahal in the north of India, the Meenakshi Amman temple attracts tens of thousands of visitors per day. Why is it so popular? The timeless appeal of the non-duality of human and divine romance may provide an answer:

> *"The wedding of the divine couple [Meenakshi and Shiva] is regarded as a classic instance of south Indian marriage with matrilineal emphasis, an arrangement referred as "Madurai marriage."* [262]

In further analysis of the temple, it has been noted that:

> *"This may reflect the matrilineal traditions in South India and the regional belief that 'penultimate [spiritual] powers rest with the women', gods listen to their spouse, and that the fate of kingdoms rest with the women."* [263]

Gardens of the 21st century
Planning for refugee resettlements as *Light Gardens*

What role do *light gardens* and landscape planning have in the daily lives of the millions of refugees in India, Pakistan and Bangladesh, where survival on a day to day basis is the chief concern? Due to years of unrelenting violence, Muslim refugees, driven from their homes in the neighbouring country of Myanmar, have flooded into Bangladesh in recent years. Some enter Bangladesh by wading through the Naf River delta at night, trying to avoid Myanmar soldiers before landfall.

There is a strong case for refugee camps to be internationally funded with no interest, long term loans and the goal of creating *Light Garden*, self-contained, zero-carbon local economies. These would grow their own food; create their own employment; plant trees; collect and store their own water requirements; organise cultural activity and generate their own fuel through a suite of sources such as solar power, gas from waste composting and wind power.

In one of the ironies of the 21st century, we now have the technology to plan for this type of refugee camp, low carbon economy in accordance with the *Light Garden* concepts. Rather than costing the international community money, these communities would save money by not generating greenhouse gases and thus not further exacerbating the costs of international climate change management.

Image 27. (Above) *Four out of five refugees stay in countries next door to their own. We have the technology to plan for low carbon economies in refugee settlements.*

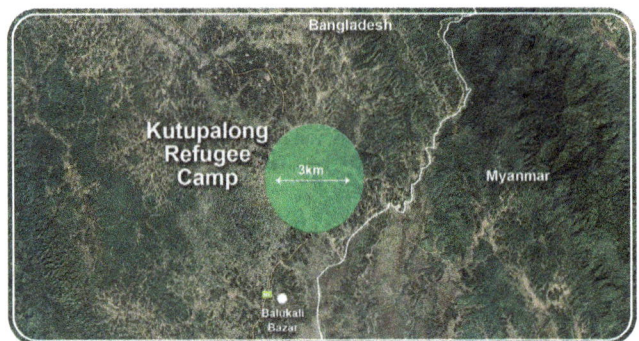

The sheer scale and population density of the Kutupalong camp that houses 900,000 refugees in Bangladesh necessitate and actually facilitate such planning. The camp area is at least 3 kilometres by 3 kilometres, or 9 square kilometres if one calculates this using the bar scale provided on the Google Earth image shown on the following page.[264]

The population density of this camp may thus be calculated as about 100,000 people per square kilometre. (900,000 divided by 9 = 100,000). This density is at least twice that of the most densely populated city on Earth, which is reported to be Manila. The urban density in Manilla is 43,079 inhabitants per square kilometre.[265] In comparison, the density of Beijing in 2016 was 1,146 people. In Shanghai, it was 3,816 inhabitants per square kilometre.[266]

The United Nations Humanitarian Commission for Refugees (UNHCR) Global Trends report of 2017, presents data which shows that 85 per cent of refugees live in developing countries.[267] Many of these countries are desperately poor and receive little support to care for refugee populations.

In addition, there are often flow-on effects such as serious environmental and social problems in the host countries. For example, over 4,000 hectares of forest near the refugee camps in Bangladesh has been stripped bare by refugees seeking firewood. Even the tree roots have been dug out.[268]

Image 28. *Aerial photograph of Kutupalong refugee camp by Google Earth.*

Image 29. *Kutupalong refugee camp.*

Tolerance of other faiths is a consciously cultivated virtue of the inclusive belief system of the Hindu people. This is exemplified by India's willingness to host the Buddhist refugees who fled Tibet in the years following 1959. Similarly, in the second decade of the 21st century, Bangladesh has hosted at least 900,000 Muslim refugees, who have fled for their lives from violence, persecution and death in their neighbouring homeland of Myanmar.[269]

Buddhist-majority Myanmar does not recognise the Rohingya Muslim minority members as citizens, referring to them pejoratively as "illegal Bengali immigrants." Government officials on the Bangladeshi side of the border refuse to classify the Rohingya Muslims as refugees. Bangladeshi authorities consider them as *"forcibly displaced Myanmar citizens"*.[270] The refugees are not allowed by law to work in Bangladesh but many escape the camps and find jobs, forcing down wages for the long term, local Bangladeshi population. This creates local angst.[271]

The predominant religions that co-exist in both India and Pakistan are Islam and Hinduism. By 2018, 80% of India's population was Hindu.[272] By 2015, 90% of the Bangladeshi population was Moslem.[273]

Within the particularly dense and challenging environment at the Kutupalong Refugee Camp, the United Nations International Organisation for Migration (IOM) has helped settlers utilise some new technology to establish food gardens. As it doesn't seem possible to paraphrase an account of their work in a way that highlights its significance in relation to the *Light Garden* model, I have included their description in full below:

> *"IOM, the UN Migration Agency, and the UN Food and Agriculture Organization (FAO) are distributing 50,000 vegetable gardening kits to tackle malnutrition and improve the diet of people affected by the Rohingya refugee crisis in Cox's Bazar, Bangladesh…*
>
> *"Many were already suffering from malnutrition due to poverty and discrimination in Myanmar. Now reliant on basic food rations of rice, lentils, cooking oil and spices distributed by aid agencies every two weeks, the refugees, particularly children under five years old, urgently need to diversify their diet. Local families also need access to more diverse and nutritious food.*

"The micro gardening initiative, which will provide seeds and tools to 50,000 families - 25,000 in the refugee camps and 25,000 in host villages in Ukhiya and Teknaf sub-Districts – is part of a USD 3 million programme to promote home gardening and larger-scale production among local farmers. The initiative is funded by the US State Department's Bureau of Population, Refugees and Migration (PRM). Almost half of the households receiving the kits are female-headed.

"In the coming months, we'll be able to have leaves and vegetables regularly," said 27-year-old Hamida, a young mother living in the Kutupalong- Balukhali mega camp with her husband and two children, who recently received a micro gardening kit. "Now we only eat them when we have money to buy them in the market. Otherwise we just eat rice and lentils or sometimes just rice with some chili and salt," said Hamida.

"The kits mean that they (the refugees) can grow leaves and vegetables on whatever land they have around their shelters. They can also sell the extra produce," said Mohammad Abul Kalam, Commissioner of Bangladesh's Refugee Relief and Repatriation Commission (RRRC) in Cox's Bazar, who handed over the first kits in the Ukhiya sub-district complex. "This will enable people to live better," he added.(11)

"Local day labourer Rashid Ahmed, 48, agreed 'Buying leaves and vegetables regularly from the market isn't possible. But we can have it almost every day if I grow it myself.' said Rashid, who is the only person earning money in his seven-member family. 'It will bring in some money as well. I can earn at least 100 taka (USD 1.19) a week selling the extra produce,' he added.

"As part of the kits, families received red amaranth, high-iron spinach, lady fingers, long yard beans and pumpkin seeds. They also got compost, a spade and a watering can. The kits include a watertight, 60-litre food storage drum to prevent mould and infestation of food stocks, which will be essential in the coming wet season. Local families received a slightly different kit, as most have bigger kitchen garden areas than the refugees. All the beneficiaries received basic training in micro gardening techniques.

"The initiative mainly focuses on providing high quality, nutritious food to improve nutrition at the household level, but also focuses on production capacity and farm-to-market strategies for farmer groups," said Peter Agnew, FAO's Emergency Response Coordinator in Cox's Bazar.

"We're also introducing new technology to the communities, as it's been successful in producing high-nutrition vegetables for the refugee population and providing some income generation for the host community." FAO is implementing a five-year project with Bangladesh's Department of Agricultural Extension (DAE).

"Seven months into the crisis, it's not only the refugees, but also the host community that needs assistance," said Manuel Pereira, IOM's Emergency Coordinator in Cox's Bazar. "The speed of the influx of refugees put huge pressure on local agriculture and the food supply chain.

"There are 400,000 people among the refugees and host communities who currently need nutrition support. This initiative will improve their nutritional status. It will also contribute to mitigating an expected 50,000 metric tonne annual food deficit in Cox's Bazar," he added.[274]

Bangladesh's floating coastal gardens

"…these areas have been repeatedly affected by cyclones, heavy rainfall, flooding, salt damage caused by sea level rise and snow melting from the Himalayas, resulting in extremely low agricultural production."[275]

Such is the plight of many in Bangladesh as climate change takes hold in the 21st century. Approximately 28% of the population of Bangladesh lived in coastal areas in 2020. The total population of Bangladesh in 2020 was reported as 164,689,383 people, of whom approximately 21 million lived in the capital city of Dhaka.

All around the world, people rendered homeless by climate change are not adequately considered under existing legislation and policies for recognition of refugee, or displaced persons status. For example, as coastal lands are inundated, millions of Bangladeshis have been forced to leave behind their rural livelihoods and move to the slums of Dhaka. Despite these omnipresent afflictions, the people who are able to remain in the coastal deltas of Bangladesh have not suffered any loss of the freely available sunshine and light. Utilising that as the energy source, (plus their hard work), they make Dhaps. These are floating, soil-less gardens made from tightly packed hyacinth plants.

Water hyacinth is regarded as a weed and can be extracted from the vast quantities that accumulate in the Ganges delta. It is then labouriously packed onto rafts to make the Dhaps. This work tends to be done by people who do not own land on higher ground. The nutrient rich waters of the Ganges Delta mean fertilisers are not required to grow crops on the dhaps.

As part of their coping strategy and motivation for making dhaps, Bangladeshis have a term for seasonal hunger: *Mongo*.

"Local communities didn't choose the way to conquer this severe environment, but choose the way to cope with the surrounding nature."[276]

Image 30. *Bangladesh's dhaps. The dhap at right includes an enclosure for fish and ducks.*

Fish are harvested from the water before it recedes in the winter. If storms or waves have not destroyed the rafts, they are left in situ or moved to higher ground, where they form compost for winter crops. It is reported that although small farmers face competition from commercial landowners for the best spots to anchor the dhaps, for 60 – 90% of the population, this form of gardening is their primary and best livelihood option.[277]

In 2015, the Food and Agriculture Organization (FAO) declared the floating gardens as one of the world's 34 types of *"Globally Important Agricultural Heritage Systems."* [278]

One million organic homes in Jaipur

As an example of innovation with sunlight and 21st century technology in India, a Jaipur based company has developed an innovative rooftop organic farming system. Six million people live in Jaipur and by 2020, twenty five percent of households in Jaipur were expected to be participating in the system. [279] The government's water management program provides subsidies for drip irrigation systems. The motivation for this government action is to tackle the city's falling water tables and changing climate.

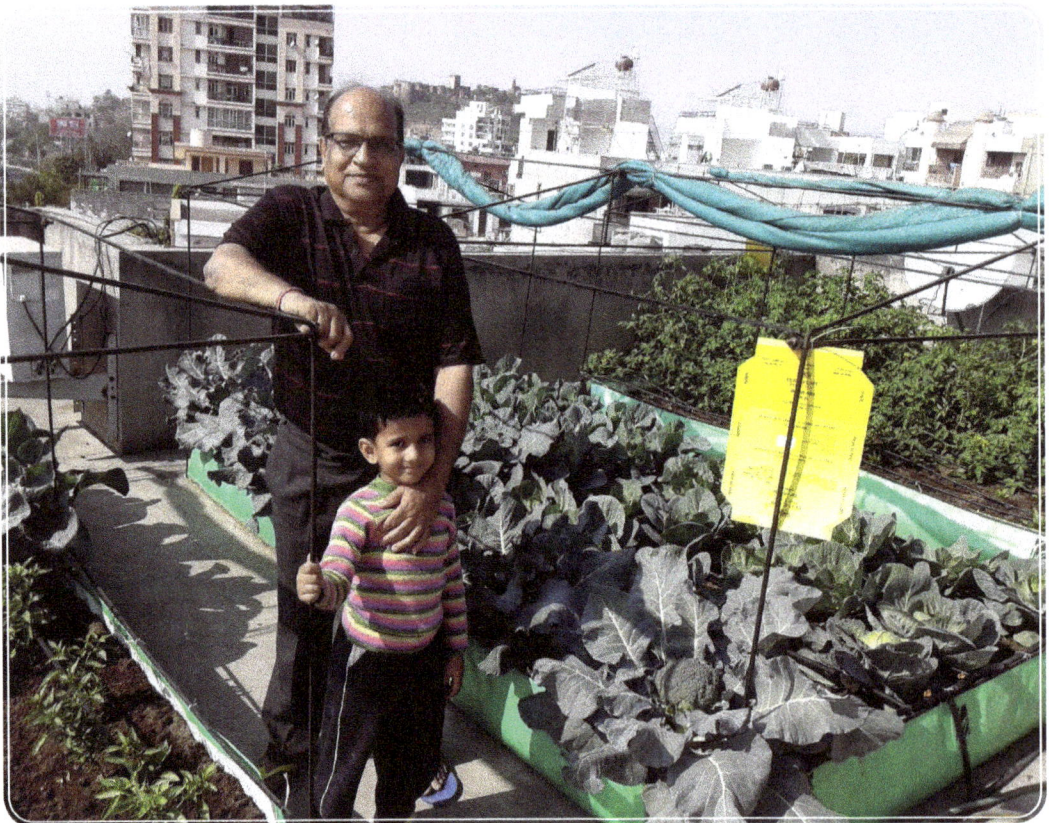

Image 31. *One million organic homes in Jaipur: an alternative to pesticides.*

Image 32. *Jaipur's one million organic homes program*

As an example of India's spreading urban organic movement, one company has set itself three goals to achieve by 2020. Firstly it would create one million organic homes. Secondly, it would cover one million square feet with living green walls. Thirdly it would become the most extensive urban farming company in the world.

The company states that with government subsidies for drip irrigation systems, each household can produce around 100 – 120 kilograms of food per year.[280] As one of the householders who participate in this program said:

> *"It's really very simple. Nature comes back with a force but we just have to give it a little bit of space and a little bit of time…"* [281]

That sentiment is very much in accord with the *Light Garden* model's second principle: allow ecosystems the space & time they need to rejuvenate.

Summary

In the 21st century, many media images depict India's rapidly expanding urban areas, where there are plenty of electric lights but hardly a tree to be seen. However, to imagine that India has ever separated from its farms and gardens - or its celebration of light and colour - would be as unlikely as India ever separating from its rich cultural history. As Dr Vandana Shiva said in 2018:

> *"The Holi Festival is a festival of colours. It has been made toxic. Come to Navdanya and celebrate a toxic free Holi…Make Holi a Festival of the real colors of nature!"* [282]

In recent decades there has been a tendency for toxic, factory-made powders to flood the market in India and supplant these safe, natural alternatives. However, as illustrated below at Navdanya, they have produced the traditional, natural plant based colours used for sprinkling coloured powders at the Holi Festival.[283]

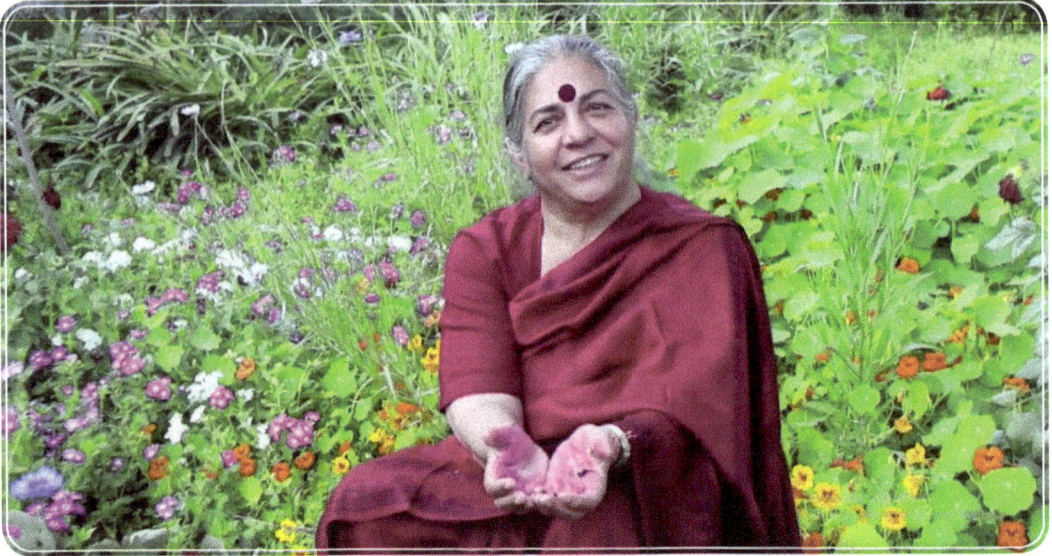

Image 33. *Dr Vandana Shiva, physicist, activist, farmer.*

As part of the broader program at Navdanya, the gardeners and farmers, like millions of others across the nation, are harnessing ancient knowledge, new technology and the power of sunlight to help preserve biodiversity and enact their vision for India to become a modern, biodiverse, organic civilisation. Supporting this vision are the innumerable temple gardens where the flames of faith and pilgrimage burn bright. Irrigated rooftop terrace gardens are greening the cities. Famous gardens such as the Taj Mahal are more popular than ever.

Rivers of refugees pour into Bangladesh. Using micro-garden technology provided in the refugee camps, these people harvest the energy of sunlight to grow food plants in whatever space they have available. They are all part of the non-violent green revolution that continues to evolve in India and Bangladesh during the 21st century.

7

Europe

The whole concept of striving for beauty might be seen as a dualistic contradiction if beauty is conceived of an extraordinary phenomenon, rather than as the natural order of things, where natural environmental processes are allowed to flow and human activity is restrained within the limits of nature.

Europe is a vast and diverse place, where techniques of working with light at the scale of gardens for human use are well developed. The benefits of applying the *Light Garden* principle Number 9 for *Human Use* of natural resources are apparent when considering just a few of these techniques. That principle entails using natural resources in an intelligent, restrained manner. Let us begin by looking at how sunlight floods the simple rural scene shown below.

Image 1. *The extent of the village is restrained within the landscape and the local economy flourishes.*

The people who live in this village and landscape do so with time honoured customs that inherently exercise some restraint on the way in which natural resources, (including light), are used. For example, unlike the urban sprawl of so many new urban settlements, there is a clean-cut edge between the agricultural landscape and the village's urban footprint. This definite edge is a positive sign of a culture that values the natural resources of the land and exercises restraint in how they are used.

Instead of urban sprawl, the reflected light from structures is controlled by a limited colour palette and the limited scale of the building units and fields. These limitations contribute to the creation of a place that attracts visitors. The welcome visitors enhance the wealth of property owners and local residents, who welcome guests but limit the number who can come to share being in this place.

Paris: City of Lights

In recent times, Europe has become somewhat restrained in the use of natural resources and proactive in addressing the global sustainability agenda. This has been achieved through innovations such as making reductions in carbon emissions. To a limited extent, these innovations have ameliorated the global impacts of centuries of European colonialism. Carbon emissions, climate change and the effects of colonialism and globalisation in relation to *Light Gardens* are considered in other chapters of this book. However, the focus at present lies with Paris.

Historians have noted that the design principles used at Versailles were perpetuated for centuries, through to the redesign of Paris in the 19th century. Perhaps in comparing the indulgent 17th century culture of Versailles to the more restrained 21st century Parisian culture, we shall find the presence of more *Light Gardens*!

Regardless of whether an economy is regarded as sustainable or indulgent, *travel and tourism* are classified as a significant sector of the economy. For at least a decade prior to 2020, this sector accounted for about 10% of the global gross domestic product and one in ten jobs globally.[284]

In addition, about 4.4% of jobs in the European Union are in the agricultural sector. This sector includes food gardens, farms, the flower trade and horticultural activity.[285] Thus in Europe, the combined economic importance of agricultural, gardening, horticultural, tourism, landscape management, natural resource management, conservation and similar activities accounts for about 20% of employment. All these occupations rely upon *equitable access to sunlight* as the power source that drives plant growth and creates attractive, liveable places where people want to be. Paris is one of those places!

From the earliest years of the 19th century, Napoleon Bonaparte set the goal of making Paris the most beautiful city in the world.[286] This work continued in the mid 19th Century under Napoleon Bonaparte's nephew, Emperor Napoleon III. He appointed Baron Haussmann to redesign Paris with a new standard of city infrastructure to be constructed in time for the Paris World Expo in 1889. The Eiffel Tower was part of the construction carried out around that time.

Due to its sound engineering, appropriate location and beautiful fractal proportions, the Eiffel Tower was an immediate popular success. It has endured as a centrepiece in the skyline because the citizens of Paris have been willing and able to exercise restraint. They have actively avoided allowing more recent structures to be located where they would block views to the tower. This consensual control for the common good is an example of *Light Garden* Principle 9: Human Use within a culture of intelligent restraint.

Image 2. *In Paris, trees surround the Eiffel Tower and town planning regulations have kept the city high rise buildings clustered some distance away from this landmark.*

As illustrated above, the cluster of high rise buildings in Paris is located at a sufficient distance away from the tower that they do not interfere with views around the tower. The Eiffel Tower is the most visited, paid-entry landmark in the world and draws the endless admiration of some seven million tourists each year. [287]

Baron Haussmann's work in Paris during the 19th century included introducing underground railway stations, which were new technology at the time. They required significant re-design of relevant parts of the city. Streets were redesigned to be wide enough to function as tree lined boulevards which accommodated pedestrians, cyclists and vehicles. The urban design work also included efforts to eliminate the epidemics of disease that had plagued the city for centuries. Such public health goals were addressed by providing a safe and healthy system of underground water, gas and sewerage. [288]

Paris soon became known as the City of Light for several reasons. Although some residents criticised Haussmann's vision because it involved removing old, low-cost housing in poorly drained alleyways where people had lived for centuries, the enlightened approach inherent in the new city design benefited all citizens. Benefits arose by providing features such as illuminated boulevards where all people could walk in safety; new public parks and an integrated water, gas and sewerage system that was safe, clean and available for all.

Image 3. *A light filled, people friendly, tree lined boulevard of Paris*

Image 4. *Paris: City of Lights*

A second reason for Paris becoming known as the City of Lights was that the French Impressionist movement coincided with Haussmann's' work. From 1874, the impressionist artists such as Monet and Degas celebrated and consciously painted light, whether it was in the city or the country.

In 2015 Paris was the host city for the *United Nations Framework Convention on Climate Change,* which led to the signing of the Paris Agreement in 2016. This agreement was an international effort by signatory nations to combat climate change. The importance that the agreement placed on setting targets to limit global warming added another layer of meaning to the term *City of Lights,* (as city lights are often associated with global warming).

Just as the Eiffel Tower in Paris is known throughout the world as a distinctive landmark, so too the horticultural practices of Europe form distinctive landscapes. They illustrate conscious management of the Earth's resources to achieve the combination of light and temperature that people and plants need to flourish. There are many traditions of European sustainable farm, garden and landscape management practices. Bearing that in mind, cultivation of the humble tulip is a fascinating example of a typically European way of managing *Light Gardens* and using plants to harvest light.

Tulips, turnips and Kuekenhof

Thousands of tulips may be closely planted in European gardens such as Keukenhof in Holland. As illustrated in image 5, this takes careful planning and great precision, as well as artistic flair. The Dutch cultural sensitivity lends a sense of free flowing, natural forms in the landscape, rather than the flowers being merely showpieces.

Flowing bands of flowers beside the lake create a feeling of the abundance of nature. The human eye has grown accustomed to seeing green foliage in such views but why is foliage coloured green, whilst flowers come in so many different hues?

That question takes us back to the process of photosynthesis. Plants use sunlight to create food. Of all the wavelengths of sunlight, the green frequency is the least useful to plants in the process of photosynthesis. So the green wavelengths are reflected off the surface of the foliage, rather than absorbed as an energy source for photosynthesis.

Let us now look more closely at Image 5 and the human intervention that has used light in creative ways to structure this garden at Keukenhof. Thousands of tulips have been planted in a band of sunlight beneath the trees. There is consistent, careful attention to the spacing between each plant, so each one obtains suitable sunlight, airflow and nutrients. The nutrients flow first to roots and leaves, before the flowers that bloom. Just as in a mixed vegetable garden, different types of plants not only have different colours, they also grow to different heights. Often, they grow best in combination with certain other plants and organisms, such as the soil mycorrhizae.

By considering these details, we can see that tulip cultivation in Europe embodies several of the *Light Garden* principles outlined in Chapter One. For example, there is careful measurement and sophisticated awareness of human perception in how the bulbs are planted out. This reflects the application of principle number seven: *Measurement and Perception.* There is also restraint exercised in the human use of these gardens, which are open to the public for a limited season each year. *Light Garden* principle number nine refers to *Human Use* that is appropriately constrained. Here it works in partnership with other *Light Garden* principles such as *Context and Environment,* (principle number eight).

Gardeners cultivate the *Context and Environment* conditions in the soil of their gardens over many years to ensure the garden's long-term viability and that of the wider environment in which the garden and all other creatures exist. This occurs not just in Holland but all around the world. Refer for example to the plan of the cultivated area tended by Jorama Onjimbo in Kenya, Africa (Chapter 5), and to the photographs of Bali's biodiverse gardens in Chapter Ten.

In addition to space and light, tulip bulbs need eight to fifteen weeks of chilling at 35 to 55 degrees Fahrenheit, or they will not produce shoots and flowers. There is an optimal temperature for vegetative growth in each plant variety, with growth dropping off as temperatures increase or decrease. Similarly, there is a range of temperatures at which many plants will produce seed. For example, corn will fail to reproduce at temperatures above 95°F (35°C) and soybeans above 102°F, (38.8°C).[289]

The golden stamens of a tulip are protected by translucent petals as they develop. As the petals unfold, the stamens move up towards the sun, then release pollen. Centuries of human intervention and breeding of tulips have not deterred the stamens from this essential task.

A tulip garden may be a thing of beauty to the human eye but to the tulip, it is a chance to produce seeds and propagate with the help of sun, wind and insects. When planning for the preservation of the natural world, we need to bear this in mind. Don't crowd things. Leave space for flowers to catch the light and wave gently in the breeze.

The tulip is an example of *Light Garden* principle number two: allow the space and time that is needed for life processes and ecological systems to coexist. But what is it about a particular flower that means people will pay much money for it, as in the case of tulips and roses? Meanwhile, other flowers similar to a tulip, (such as wild turnips for example), will not catch a second glance.

Image 5. *Skilfully planted tulips at Keukenhof*

Once it reaches the flowering stage, the wild turnip, Brassica rapa ssp sylvestris, is a tall competitive annual weed, capable of causing large reductions in crop yields due to competition for light, nutrients and water.[290] Many cultivated plants and weeds grow in competitive environments. For example, a tulip bulb is similar in appearance to a turnip bulb, which illustrated in Image 6. Not surprisingly, amongst turnip bulbs, there is a difference between the wild turnips and those cultivated as crop species. The cultivated species have larger storage organs (bulbs) than the wild ones.

Here we may have the answer to the question about why tulips are considered beautiful. During a period of hundreds of years, tulips and turnips have been cultivated from wild species to be what humans desire. Turnips have been cultivated as useful food plants. Tulips have been cultivated for their perceived beauty, which not least of all arises from how the flowers interact with light. Tulip petals have a translucent quality that allows sunlight to shine through them. Is this just so that they appear more beautiful when we look at them, or are there other reasons?

Having considered tulip cultivation on the previous pages and how it incorporates several *Light Garden* principles, we can begin to glimpse how it also includes principle number five: *Multiplication effects and Scale*. This is a natural phenomenon that can inspire tulip growers. They plant vast drifts of flowers that capture the human imagination, extending well beyond the beauty of individual flowers.

Tulips and turnips

As we have seen, the form of flower petals is highly relevant to whether we will find two otherwise quite similar flowers, (such as tulips and turnips), either irresistibly attractive or as something to be disregarded.

Millions of people go to gardens each year to experience the tulips. Millions of people do not go to look at turnip flowers each year. However, the same people may be glad to eat turnips rather than tulips. For example, by far the highest per capita annual consumption of turnips in the world occurs in the freezing conditions of Uzbekistan. A tulip souvenir from a visit to a flower garden in Holland would not be a welcome substitute for turnips on a dinner plate!

Turnips cultivated as crop vegetables from wild species are not only hardy; they are amongst the top ten vegetables, in terms of the global annual consumption of vegetables. Available statistics tell us that 42.7 million metric tons of carrots and turnips combined were produced in 2016.[291] This may be compared to the much lower annual global production of about 119 thousand metric tons of tulip bulbs.[292]

Image 6. *A turnip bulb*

Horticultural products, including flower bulbs, are a significant part of the Dutch economy. 77% of bulbs traded internationally come from the Netherlands.[293] According to NASA statistics, The Netherlands is the largest grower of tulip bulbs globally. 4.2 billion bulbs are produced annually in The Netherlands and half of these are exported.[294] So we are talking about big business when it comes to this type of *Light Garden*, powered by the sun and human labour.

We cannot take the space and light needed for gardens and landscapes for granted. Already in the second decade of the 21st century, we are seeing Governments auctioning off the planet's airspace. For example in 2018 the United States Secretary of the Interior announced that the Bureau of Ocean Energy Management was planning to put up for auction the offshore wind farm rights for an area near Massachusetts.[295]

As with all other natural resources on this planet, (such as fresh water and clean air), there will be competition for the resources of light and space, unless we can learn new ways to coexist with the growth of living creatures in *Light Garden* places and landscapes. What is being done to ensure that there *will* be light and space to support the growth of flowers, people, bees and other creatures? One approach is the work of the Intergovernmental Panel on Climate Change (IPCC), which in October 2018

> *"issued its bleakest report yet this week, saying that without drastic changes, the world doesn't have a hope of avoiding uncontrollable climate change. Unless emissions are halved within 12 years and virtually eliminated by 2050, temperature increases will likely exceed 2 degrees Celsius."* [296]

That same IPCC report refers to "tipping points" such as melting of the permafrost. Once tipping points are past, global temperature increases are likely to continue to grow exponentially.[297]

In my native country of Australia, in the summer of 2018 – 19, we officially recorded an average two degree increase in temperature, which is more than the IPCC target of limiting increases to 1.5 degrees Celsius.[298] Such temperature increases have rapid economic impacts. For example, imagine the effect on the Dutch economy if temperatures rose to the extent that winters were not cool enough for tulip bulbs to sprout and artificial chilling was not viable. Keukenhof, a famous garden in Holland, would undoubtedly be affected if this happened. The natural resource of sunlight is skilfully used as part of the design of the garden, which in turn is an integral part of the horticultural, tourism and recreational sectors of the Dutch economy.

Pools of light and shade at Keukenhof

The word Keukenhof translates as 'kitchen garden' but it has become much more than that. Over a million tourists visit during just two months of spring each year. For similar reasons, even larger numbers of tourists visit famous gardens in Asian centres such as Kyoto and Hangzhou. More detail about these North Asian gardens is provided in Chapter Three.

In the Netherlands, Keukenhof gardens cover an area of 32 hectares (79 acres). Each year they are planted with 7 million bulbs.[299] On a bright sunny day in maximum sunlight, up to 100,000 lux of illumination may fall upon a garden as the flowers burst forth. In the shaded parts of the gardens on the same day, the lighting intensity is more likely to be about 20,000 lux.

In contrast, on a cloudy, overcast day, 1,000 – 2,000 lux may be present. During a storm, the illumination may drop to less than 200 lux. One lux is equal to one lumen of visible light, which is otherwise known as *luminous flux*. Illumination measures the intensity of light falling upon a surface.

Hence the intensity of light falling upon a flower in full sun on a bright, clear day (say 100,000 lux) is five times more intense than the intensity of light falling upon a flower growing in the shade on that same day, (say 20,000 lux).[300]

Image 7. *Plan of Keukenhof*

While light intensities are low, the rate of photosynthesis increases proportionately with increases in light intensity. *'The more photons of light that fall on a leaf, the greater the number of chlorophyll molecules that are ionised and the more ATP and NADPH are generated.'* [301] However, above an optimum temperature, the rate of photosynthesis begins to decrease, as the enzymes involved lose their structure and cease to function normally.[302]

Tulip growers and all agriculturalists will thus keep a close eye on the weather while trying to maintain optimal growing conditions for their crops, as they plan to coincide with events such as peak tourist seasons, festivals and big sale orders. In addition to cultivating the flowers, the garden designers at Keukenhof skilfully play with pools of light on the lawns, streams, pools and foliage that thread through the site.

There are many layers of meaning to the concept of 'pools of light' that meander through Keukenhof. For example, compare the greyscale and full colour versions of the same photograph of flower gardens at Keukenhof in Images 8 and 9.

Try also to imagine the photograph of the colourful garden on a cloudy day, when the pools of light would be absent, even though the colours would be still visible. What a difference it would make if there were no bright patches of light upon the lawn and flowers to contrast with the darker shades of trees and shrubs!

Keukenhof is rated consistently amongst the world's top ten most beautiful gardens. The plan illustrates how it has been created with a mixture of some basic geometry to the plan layout, plus many meandering pathways. When one looks at photographs taken by visitors to Keukenhof, it is the views of meandering flowerbeds and water that people overwhelmingly chose as subjects to photograph. The garden pool illustrated on this page is an interesting example, where the shape of the pool introduces a formal geometric element into an otherwise meandering, informal layout.

Pools of light can appear molten, as shown in Image 9. Gentle ripples from the fountains make their way towards the viewer. This feature of the design helps to develop a sense of depth, perspective and tranquillity. Following the light, our eye tends to meander peacefully from the blue, pink and white flowers in the foreground, on to the tree trunks and the thin line of tall red tulips in the background shrubbery.

Designing effective transition zones between sunlight and shadow is a part of landscape and garden design. Looking at the photograph in Image 11, one can see a quite clear-cut edge between the shade of the shelters and the full sun on most of the lawn, without the subtle transitions between vegetation, light and shadow that we have looked at so far at Keukenhof.

Image 8. *A simulated image, under low light conditions such as moonlight at Keukenhof.*

Image 9. *Pools of light in the gardens of Keukenhof*

Image 10. *Plan highlighting geometric vs free flowing shapes in black and white.*

Compared to Image 11, the popular tulip gardens in the flowing lawns of Keukenhof have more dappled light and irregular edges between different areas. In keeping with a common human preference for the shelter of dappled light, the people in the two photographs of Image 12 have chosen picnic tables in nearly full sun when wearing winter jackets and almost full shade when not.

Image 12 shows typical public parkland settings, which have been designed as recreation areas in the contemporary Western style. The combination of lawns and shade tends to attract teachers, parents and grandparents to bring children to a safe, pleasant and convenient setting.

Children growing up without adequate exposure to outdoor light has become an issue in the 21st century. Exposure to sufficient hours of outdoor sunlight each week is particularly important for growing children. Recent research has proved that without this, their eyes grow too long and become short-sighted.

People need sunlight but they also need trees. The aerial photograph in the collage on the following page illustrates how much more tree cover there is on the Keukenhof site than in the surrounding agricultural areas, urban area and car parks. As shown

Image 11. *(Above) There is clear cut transition between sun and shade in this park.*

Image 12. *Upper image in winter sun and lower image in summer shade.*

in the plan inset of Sustainability City included in the lower left part of the collage, thousands of trees have been planted around the perimeter of that site. Perhaps one day the tree canopy cover at *Sustainability City* will grow to be similar to that at Keukenhof. *Sustainability City* is designed with solar panels covering all the car parks and buildings, so shade from trees is not likely to be welcome over much of the site where the panels are located.

Although the Keukenhof gardens feature flowers, the design incorporates many similar principles to food gardens, where intensively planted crops are interspersed with the fallow ground. A mosaic of cultivated areas, within a larger framework of trees, streams and walkways is developed. This is not unlike the concept of the vegetated central waterway at Sustainability City.

In contrast to the tulip gardens of Keukenhof, the 17th century French estates of Vaux - le - Vicomte and Versailles may be considered as expressions of a mindset with virtually infinite resources to command, rather than a *Light Garden* mindset that voluntarily adopts restraint. The philosophy behind Versailles is unlike that of the Korean rulers, who sought to set an example for their citizens at

Image 13. *Comparison of the tree cover around Kuekenhof* (Top and above), *with Sustainability City in Dubai* (Left)

Huwon Palace. Refer to Chapter 3 for more details. The Versailles mindset might be described as one that says all resources, including light, earth, water, air, space and human labour, are unlimited and at the command of the property owner. The landscape designs at Versailles and Vaux-le-Vicomte explore images of infinity, reflected light and vanishing points.

The design at Vaux-le-Vicomte is the mid-17th century work of Landscape Architect Andre le Notre. The collaboration between Architect, Landscape Architect and Interior Designer on this project marked the beginning of what became known as the Louis XIV style.

"To secure the necessary grounds for the elaborate plans for Vaux-le-Vicomte's garden and castle, Fouquet purchased and demolished three villages. The displaced villagers were then employed in the upkeep and maintenance of the gardens. It was said to have employed 18 thousand workers . . ."[303]

Shortly after the construction of Vaux–le-Vicomte, King Louis XIV listened to advisers who spiked his jealously of Fouquet. The king sentenced Fouquet to life imprisonment. He then promptly commissioned Versailles, which was intended to be grander than Vaux–le-Vicomte![304]

Embodying many principles that are regarded as classical European style, gardens such as Versailles continue to attract crowds of tourists. However, the original designs of these sites are in stark contrast to the sustainability agenda of the 21st century. In the 21st century, large, publicly accessible tourist sites are usually supported by a design that embodies sustainable design principles, rather than allowing past practices that dissipated natural resources to continue. More examples of this sustainable design are provided in Chapter 11.

In contrast to the 17th and 18th century monarchs of France, the contemporary Korean Royal Families chose to immerse themselves in gardens within natural settings. Their chosen activities, dedicated to the benefit of the nation, were ritual, study and contemplation. These were conducted around natural streams flowing through the palace grounds.

The aesthetic of such places contrasts strongly with that of Versailles. The natural flow of streams is nowhere to be seen at Versailles. Abstract expressions of light, water, space, vegetation, and matter are patterned to create a sense of the monarch's infinite power.

The whole concept of striving for beauty at sites such as Versailles might be seen as a dualistic contradiction, if beauty is conceived of an extraordinary phenomenon, rather than as a normal phenomenon in the world of Nature. Where natural environmental process are allowed to flow and where human activity is restrained within the limits of nature, beauty often flows too.

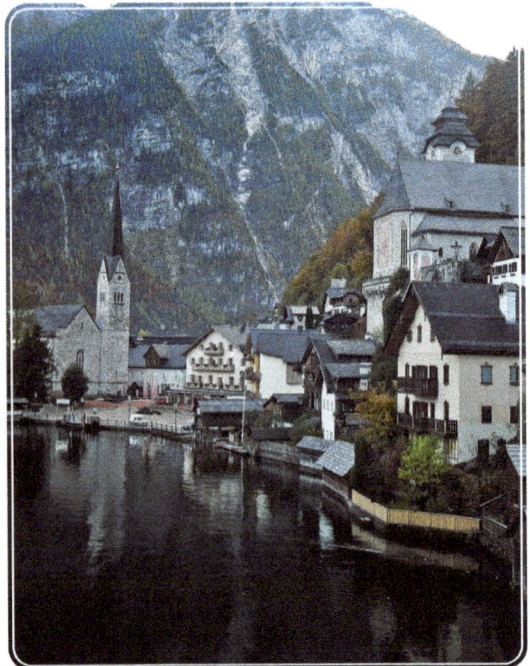

Image 14. (Top and above) *the infinite light of Versailles and Vaux – le –Vicomte, compared to the more restrained settlement pattern in a lakeside village.* (Right)

8

South America

The philosophical base and rallying power underpinning the agricultural movements in South America and Central America cannot be underestimated.

In 1993, farmers' organisations in Central America were among the founders of La Vía Campesina. This group is now recognised by the United Nations as the world's largest family based, sustainable farmers' alliance group. It represents 200 million such groups globally and has been invited to make presentations to the United Nations Human Rights Council and the Food and Agricultural Organisation (FAO).

La Via Campesina has identified "extractivism" as a rampant issue with adverse effects around the globe in the 21st century. Extractivism firstly includes the activity of land grabbing. People who have lived in certain territories for centuries are forcibly removed by the governments of their own countries. Foreign corporations

Image 1. *La Via Campesina*

are then allowed to use or buy the same land from which the people have been removed. This has been the experience of many people in South and Central America. Secondly, extractivism involves the commandeering of access to natural resources such as freshwater, oceans, seeds, soil and biodiversity *away* from local communities. These natural resources are then reallocated for use in large scale infrastructure projects such as dams, mines, large solar power plants, industrial scale farming, livestock raising and fishing.

> *"In many places, the people who defend themselves against and resist this 'development' model face being demonised and criminalised, which in turn leads to prosecutions, imprisonment, violence at the hands of state or private security forces, and even murders. These are not random 'incidents', they are occurrences reported by almost every organisation."* [305]

In 1993 at the Uruguay Round of the General Agreement of Tariffs and Trade (GATT) meeting, the *Trade Related Intellectual Property Rights* document and the World Trade Organisation's *Agreement on Agriculture* document were approved and signed by participating groups.

"These agreements caused backlash from many people around the world for focusing on technical problems rather than the human right to access to food, especially for those living in the Global South. Globalisation was under way at this time, affecting many industries including agriculture." [306]

"In South America, Argentina lost more than one-third of its farms in the two decades from 1988 to 2008. Between 1997 and 2007, Chile lost 15% of its farms with the biggest farms doubling their average size, from 7,000 to 14,000 ha per farm. The United States has lost 30% of its farms in the last 50 years." [307]

South America is a continent of contrasts. Compare for example, the freedom symbolised by the Condor on the Bolivian Coat of Arms to the relative domesticity of a trout farm in Peru. Trout from farms, (rather than wild caught), is now one of the staple foods in the northern regions of South America.

2a

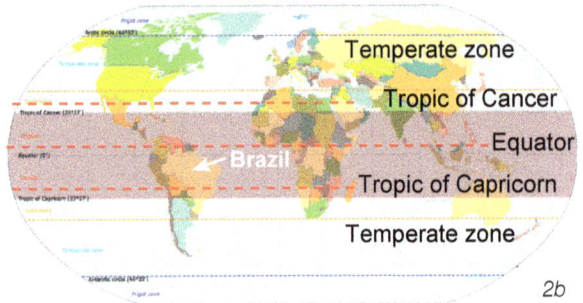

2b

2c

2d

2e

Image 2. *Map and Images of South America*
2a. *There are 12 countries in South America and those mentioned in this chapter are labeled for reference.*
2b. *This map of the globe illustrates how much of South America lies within the (pink) tropical zone.*
2c. *Cerviche is the national dish of Peru. The name comes from the indigenous quechua language word 'siwichi,' which means fresh fish.*
2d. *The Bolivian Coast of Arms on the national flag. It features a condor at the top, plus the sun and an alpaca in the central motif.*
2e. *Trout farms are now an important source of fish in Peru.*

As reported by the United Nations in 2014, small farmers produce 70% of the world's food. However, in recent decades they now have access to less than 25% of the world's available farmland. In addition, climate change is taking hold more rapidly than any collective action to avoid it. The fire of rampant growth in the use and control of the planet's natural resources continues to grow.[308] Access to sunlight is foreseeably developing as one of the next frontiers in this global battle for resources.

With access to sunlight, comes access to food, good health, illumination for daily activities, the ability to move about safely, enjoy outdoor recreation and utilise the natural powerhouse of solar energy production. Like a soft but deadly blanket quietly given to us, the effects of urban smog and smoke from forest fires raging in the Amazon and elsewhere have already made their impacts felt in the atmosphere. As reported in the international media, in August 2019, 2,500 forest fires were burning in the Amazonian region of Brazil. The fires were also mapped independently by satellite imagery. The publication of this imagery appeared to catch off guard the Brazilian government, who continued to announce that the extent of fires, (and fines for illegal forest destruction), were merely incidental.

> *"Official data from Brazil's environment agency shows fines [for illegal forest destruction] from January to 23 August dropped almost a third compared with the same period last year. At the same time, the number of fires burning in Brazil has increased by 84%."* [309]

Are we about to re-enter another late stage of the dinosaurs, when smoke blanketed the Earth? The lush vegetation that had supported the growth of large dinosaurs perished under the blanket of smoke. So too did the giant dinosaurs. Anxious to avoid becoming 'dinosaurs' themselves, corporations, governments, not for profit groups and communities all around the world have all made proposals for the restructuring of growth economies to avoid this type of negative impact. The proposals were yet to make significant impacts as of the year 2020 when global carbon emission levels were still rising.

When the wind changes, a fire does eventually end. The flames are turned back upon themselves, and the smoke abates. Groups such as La Via Campesina in South America are not standing by, wishing and waiting for that to happen. They are empowering the winds of change, as local communities develop the skills and strength in numbers to stand against the fires and be viable alternatives to "extractivism."

Measuring sunlight

A smoke filled atmosphere reminds us of how important it is that sunlight reaches the surface of the Earth. How do we measure sunshine and what exactly do we mean by harvesting it? As illustrated in the graphs below, the intensity of light is measured in units known as lux. Plants harvest the energy of sunlight to grow. The intensity of light at the equator is greater than at distances further away from it. For example, image 3 illustrates how as latitude

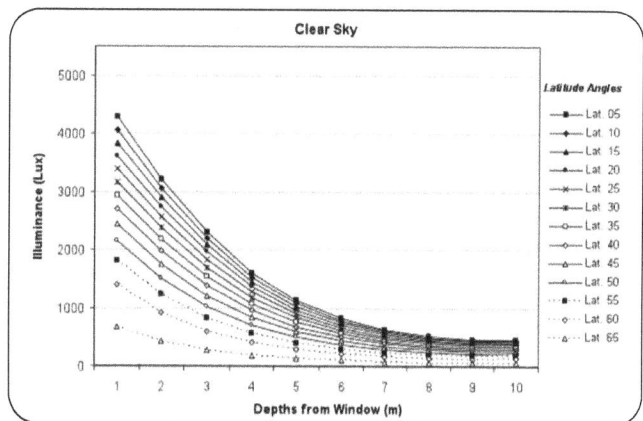

Image 3. *The amount of sunlight decreases as the distance from the equator increases.*

increases, (that is the distance from the equator increases), the amount of sunlight reaching the Earth's surface decreases. The amount of sunlight is measured in lux, as shown by the vertical bar on the left hand side of the graph.

Light, temperature, altitude and latitude all interact to affect the growth of plants. For example, low latitude maize is grown in South American countries such as Peru and as shown in Image 4, it is subject to global

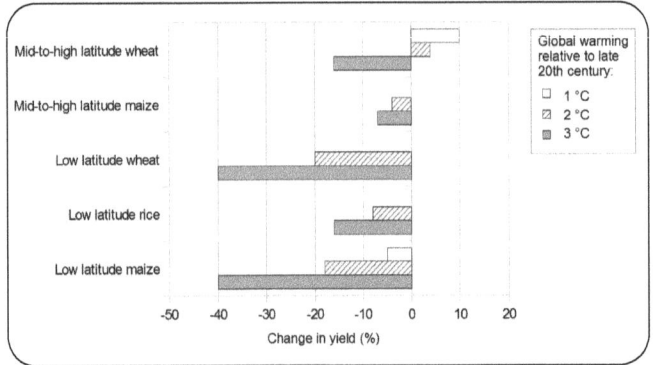

Image 4. *Light, temperature, latitude and altitude all affect the growth of plants*

warming temperate changes. Fortunately, in South America there is a long history of experimenting and developing multiple varies of maize that are adapted to different temperatures. For example, as illustrated later in this chapter, the Incan site at Moray in Peru is one of several sites used for that purpose, dating back to the period of the 13th to the 16th centuries.

Outdoor Lighting Conditions	Illuminance (lux)
Brightest sunlight	120,000
Bright sunlight	111,000
Shade, with light from an entire, clear, blue sky at midday	20,000
Typical overcast day at midday	1,000 – 2,000
Extreme of thickest storm clouds at midday	< 200
Sunrise or sunset on a clear day (ambient illumination)	400
Average general purpose indoor room lighting	40 - 300
Task lighting for close indoor work	>1,000
Fully overcast, sunrise/ sunset	40
Moonlight or extreme thickets of clouds	<1

Image 5. *Illuminance Table*

There is still enough light for human vision to discern things in a moonlit garden, but the intensity of light is much greater during the day. Daylight can provide more than one hundred thousand times the level of illumination that is available in the moonlight. The definition of illuminance is:

"a measure of how much luminous flux is spread over a given area." [310]

"One can think of luminous flux (measured in lumens) as a measure of the total "amount" of visible light present, and the illuminance as a measure of the intensity of illumination on a surface. A given amount of light will illuminate a surface more dimly if it is spread over a larger area, so illuminance is inversely proportional to area when the luminous flux is held constant." [311]

The bright sunshine and natural beauty of the South American landscape is celebrated in the local culture. The Brazilian cotton farmers depicted in Image 6 will join the celebrations once their harvest is done. The sun is a common emblem in several South American cultures. It is found on the coat of arms of Bolivia. It is also part of the coat of arms of Ecuador and the historical flag of Peru. These three countries were part of the Incan Empire.

Image 6. *Farmers harvesting cotton*

Sun Gods

In the Peruvian city of Cusco and many other parts of the continent, *Inti Raymi,* or the Sun Festival is still celebrated each year at the time of Southern Hemisphere Winter Solstice. The festival originally was designed to celebrate the start of a new planting season. With tourism being an important part of Peru's 21st century economy, the festival in Cusco now attracts thousands of tourists each year to this ancient capital of the Incan empire.

The Sun God was the primary God of the Incan empire. Incan rulers symbolised the importance of light to the civilisation. They were believed to be direct descendants of Inti, the Sun God. Particularly in the highland parts of their empire, where the cool climate created more challenging growing conditions, sunlight also was valued because it was believed the heat of the sun caused rain, as well as powering the growth of food crops such as maize.[312]

The Inca dedicated many ceremonies to the Sun to ensure the Sapa Inca's welfare. During the rainy season the sun was hotter and brighter, while during the dry season it was weaker. The Incas would set aside large quantities of natural and human resources throughout the empire for Inti. A Sun Temple would be established in each major province and each conquered province was required to dedicate a third of their lands and herds to Inti.

Crops cultivated across the Inca Empire included maize, coca, beans, grains, potatoes, sweet potatoes, ulluco, oca, mashwa, pepper, tomatoes, peanuts, cashews, squash, cucumber, quinoa, gourd, cotton, talwi, carob, chirimoya, lúcuma, guayabo, and avocado. Livestock was primarily llama and alpaca herds.[313]

> *"Incan priest-scientists experimented with wild vegetable crops to determine which should be disseminated for domestic production to farmers with fields all over the Andean region. Pollen samples found in Moray indicate that a huge variety of crops grew there – perhaps not surprising, since about 60 percent of the world's food crops originated in the Andes, including all known forms of potatoes, the most familiar types of corn, and, of course, the lima bean, named for the Spanish capital that succeeded Cuzco."*[314]

For thousands of years, South American people have known how to grow and weave cotton. However, where the large cotton plantations exist today, there was formerly a mixture of forests and villages. In these areas the indigenous people had previously utilised a diverse range of traditional fibres, including cotton. The Indigenous people also harvested foods such as cassava, nuts and fruits. These foods added to the fish and other wildlife in the diet.

From 1500 onwards, Europeans started taking control of the land in South America. The abundant sunshine and local population were harnessed with forced labour to establish cash crop plantations.

The pace of change in Brazil slowed during the period 1970 to 2006 but the number of large commercial farms still increased. The average size of farms in Brazil grew from 60 to 67 hectares during this period. However, the number of small farms decreased, with the exception of gardens of less than one hectare in size.

Since 2006 the trend to larger commercial farms has been balanced to some extent by many smallholders in Brazil and other South American countries choosing to join an international sustainable farming alliance. This alliance has a five year strategic plan based around four themes: good practices, sustainable landscapes, robust infrastructure and enabling policy environments.[315]

Timeline for light harvesting and cotton harvesting in Brazil			
> 4,000 years BC	1500 AD	Mid nineteenth century	2017
The Incas, Brazilians and the Egyptians knew how to grow and weave cotton	The Portuguese arrive in Brazil. By 1530 they begin trading with local people to cut trees.	Cotton growing in north east Brazil becomes more widespread.	An international alliance of family based farmers, (including Brazilians), work with Solidaridad, the World Wildlife Fund and The Pesticide Action Network UK to launch the Sustainable Cotton Ranking Index. Many companies assessed with this Index were found to be in need of more sustainable practices.

Image 7. *Timeline for cotton growing*

Turning now to a famous historical Peruvian site that in many ways was the antithesis of smallholder farming, let us consider Machu Pichu. One of several places where Sun Temples were constructed, Machu Pichu is world renowned for its dramatic mountain top impact. As illustrated on the following page, beams of sunlight still step down the terraces at this Incan site. Let us consider how it rates as part of the *Light Garden* concept.

Machu Pichu rates relatively highly in terms of two *Light Garden* principles. These are Number Six: Entanglement and Focal Points, plus Number Seven: Perception and Measurement. However, as described in Image 10, Machu Pichu is rated as barely 2.5 out of 5 when considered against the criteria of being a *Light Garden* site that enhances rejuvenation of Earth's life systems.

Consistent with that relatively low rating, the historical records tell us that Machu Pichu was abandoned only one hundred years after it was constructed. It was never resettled. In contrast to that, another terraced, hillside, World Heritage-listed site, (the Rice Terraces of Bali), has remained in production and human habitation for centuries. Refer to Images 10 and 11 in this chapter to compare these sites in terms of all the *Light Garden* principles.

In that context, it is interesting to see why the Balinese site rates highly in terms of *Light Garden* principles. It has demonstrated a capacity for sustainable human use over a long period. The Machu Pichu site rated less highly when used as an Incan Temple. However, as historical records indicate that local tribes used the area before the Incas arrived, it could be interesting to consider that time period, if more information was available.

The UNESCO World Heritage listing for Machu Pichu captures some of the mystique of the site in the following comments about its enduring aesthetic appeal:

"The historic monuments and features in the Historic Sanctuary of Machu Picchu are embedded within a dramatic mountain landscape of exceptional scenic and geomorphological beauty thereby providing an outstanding example of a longstanding harmonious and aesthetically stunning relationship between human culture and nature." [318]

Image 8. *Rays of sunlight at Machu Pichu.*

The Incas: comparison to Bali

To better appreciate how the *Light Garden* concept directly applies to human management of natural resources, a detailed comparison of how the *Light Garden* model applies to Machu Pichu and the Rice Terraces of Bali is interesting.

A rating of 1 – 5, from low to high, is given in the right hand column of each of the images overleaf. This rating indicates the extent to which each site reflects the *Light Garden* principles.

As can be seen by comparing the ratings for these two sites, the Balinese rice terraces rate far more highly as an example of applied Light Garden principles.

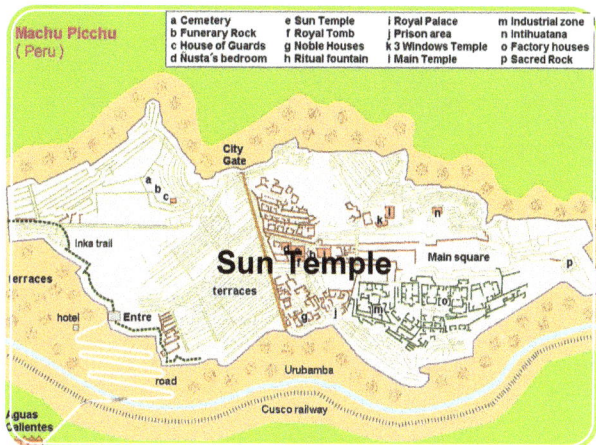

Image 9. *Plan of the Sun Temple at Machu Pichu.*

Incan site of Machu Pichu

Light Garden Principles 1 – 10.	Rating 1 – 5
1 ENERGY: *(summary rating of the extent to which the site reflects Light Garden principles): To some extent.* The Incas had a highly developed knowledge of the movement of the sun and the site was a Sun Temple. The energy of the sun was used to grow food to sustain the population at Machu Pichu. However, that proved difficult at the high altitude location.	2.5
2 SPACE and TIME: *Probably not.* Although multiple theories have been developed as to the purpose of Machu Pichu, many scholars consider that it was built as a retreat for Inca rulers. Whilst the site is undeniably dramatic and suited to a temple, it was not operated as a place where the space and time supported the flourishing of life or a 'Light Garden'. Indeed the settlement was abandoned about 100 years after the herculean effort of establishing it.	1
3. WAVES and PARTICLES: *No.* To me the site is primarily symbolic of a wave of religious devotion, in which the individual particles, (the individual people who lived and worked there), were subordinated to the wave. I would not say that the site reflects the quantum theory that light behaves as both a wave and a particle.	1
4. LINES, PATTERNS and PROBABILITIES: *Mostly not.* Although this site demonstrates a mastery of stonework and solar astronomy which could be said to reflect patterns and probabilities within those realms, the decision to occupy this site was not based on the probability that ecosystems would endure and be rejuvenated. To the contrary, this site was a challenge to such concepts!	1
5. MULTIPLICATION: *Partially.* To the Inca mind this site probably rated very highly in terms of being a focal point for worship that was necessary to create religious multiplication effects for ongoing maintenance of life systems. Today we are unaware of how ecologically sound their broader system of management was, but we do know that the site was abandoned.	2.5
6. FOCAL POINTS: *Partially.* Partially. As for item (5) in terms of creating a focal point for expression of Inca belief systems that included concepts of positive entanglement for ongoing maintenance of life systems, as well as other negative concepts such as human sacrifices to the Gods.	4
7. MEASUREMENT and PERCEPTION: *Substantially.* This site functioned as a Sun Temple with ancillary activities, demonstrating a culture that valued non-locality and aesthetics in Perception. By non-locality, I mean the belief in the ritual role of religion in bringing about and maintaining the ongoing order and welfare of the empire. In addition, this site was certainly based on a culture of careful measurement and perception of astrological events, of stone masonry and of meticulously planned agriculture, in what was a physically steep and challenging environment.	4
8. CONTEXT: *Partially.* This settlement definitely considered the broader context in which it was established. It was concerned with rejuvenation of the living, biological aspects of the society and environment, through the role that religion played in those processes.	3
9. HUMAN USE: *Partially*. This site was and is a challenge to human use of natural resources within the culture of restraint that is part of the 'Light Garden" principles. It is not planned around the carrying capacity of the planet's living systems but around more inert concepts.	1
10. STORAGE of Information: *Partially*. The story of this site has been preserved in the stones.	2.5

Image 10. *The Light Garden model used to assess the Incan site of Machu Pichu*

Comparative rating for the Rice Terraces of Bali

Light Garden Principles 1 – 10.	Rating 1 – 5
1 ENERGY: *Yes.* The Balinese have an integrated religious, social and agricultural system, including daily religious practices. *Lempuyang*, a temple to 'the Light of God,' is located on the eastern tip of Bali. The energy of the sun is used to grow food to sustain the population. The way the land is managed to achieve this includes responsible, sustainable stewardship of the island environment.	4.5
2 SPACE and TIME: Yes. The traditional Balinese culture with the *Tri Hita Karana* philosophy includes a system of governance and organisation derived from the philosophy and a landscape scale approach to natural resource management. This culture consciously values space and time not only for agriculture but also for many other purposes such as for religious rituals, strategically places shrines, decision making based on participatory democracy, an inclusive approach to the production of artwork and music by all members of the society and conscious management of resources such as water, soil and forests.	4.5
3. WAVES and PARTICLES: Yes. This landscape results from adherence to the *wave* of the *Tri Hita Karana* philosophy, plus the efforts and expertise of individual people, or *particles*.	4.5
4. LINES, PATTERNS and PROBABILITIES: Yes. This site demonstrates mastery of irrigated agricultural techniques that follow traditional patterns. It also reflects a culture in which the probability of sustaining the ecological viability of whole landscape ecosystem is high, provided that adverse 21st century outside influences can be overcome and managed well.	4.5
5. MULTIPLICATION: Yes. The rice terraces landscape demonstrates the multiplication effects that arise in particular structures such as stone terraces and thatched shrines. It also reflects the multiplication effects that occur in the form of social and environmental benefits. These benefits arise when the *Tri Hita Karana* philosophy manifests as a cohesive society, that is not prone to intertribal violence. It also has a system for natural resource management that is sustainable.	4.5
6. FOCAL POINTS: Yes. For example, water temples within the rice paddies act as focal points for religious and agricultural activity within the broader patterns of daily life. This spiritual and agricultural activity demonstrates the principle of entanglement.	4.5
7. MEASUREMENT and PERCEPTION: Yes. This site demonstrates careful measurement of features such as irrigated rice terraces and shrines. It also reflects a culture that values the quantum biophysics concept of non-locality in perception, through the daily rituals. These rituals display the role of religion in maintaining the ongoing order and cohesion between society and nature.	4.5
8. CONTEXT: Yes. Management of this landscape was concerned with rejuvenating and maintaining the living, biological health of the society and environment, as described above.	4.5
9. HUMAN USE: *Yes.* This site is managed within the culture of restraint and *Light Garden* principles.	4.5
10. STORAGE of Information: *Yes.* Cultural knowledge and religious rituals have been refined and passed down from one generation to the next for centuries.	4.5

Image 11. *Light Garden comparison between Machu Pichu in Peru and the Rice Terraces of Bali*

More drama in the landscape

Like the principles behind the construction of Machu Pichu, Brazilian government intervention in forest management currently bears little resemblance to the Tri Hita Karana system described above for Bali. In recent decades, the forests of Brazil have attracted much international attention. In earlier years, the sentiment was different. For example, in 2012 the British Broadcasting Corporation, (BBC), portrayed the ethos of South America in an evocative narrative:

> *"South America's 13 countries are home to dramatic landscapes, archaeological splendours from the past and a dizzying variety of wildlife. For the sheer awe factor, it is hard to top seeing the snow- covered peaks of the Andes, the world's longest continental mountain range, which stretches for nearly 8,000km from Venezuela to southern Patagonia."* [319]

Despite this awe factor, how rare it is to find foregrounds to views of wild landscapes that reflect the inspiration of the natural panorama beyond. Juan Grimm, South America's most accomplished Landscape Architect of the early 21st century, has attained this rare achievement. He is known for his expertise in integrating the vivacity and unique character of wild native South American native plants into the structure of his landscape designs. Refer for example, to the illustration below of his work at Los Vilos, Chile. All good visual dramatists work with lighting as one of their design tools, as can be seen here.

In Spain, the Alhambra also offers a good example of the inspiring integration of foreground details with distant panoramas. This was illustrated and described in Chapter 4.

Image 12. *A garden by Landscape Architect Juan Grimm in Los Vilos*

Reflection and absorption of light

The conscious use of lighting in the detailed design of a garden also can be considered by comparing two similar landscapes. This comparison can help to highlight the particular qualities of the light in each landscape. In the example depicted below, the light in a South American garden is compared to an Australian scene.

The garden depicted in Image 13 A below is found on the outskirts of Los Vilos in Chile, near the eastern shores of the Pacific Ocean. The Image 13 B garden depicted below is located at a similar latitude on the other side of the Pacific Ocean, at Bodalla on the East Coast of Australia.

Bodalla has a latitude of 36 degrees south, whilst Los Vilos has a latitude of 32 degrees south. Bodalla is a small coastal village at a similar latitude to Australia's national capital of Canberra. So the qualities of the sunlight reaching these two coastal gardens should be reasonably similar.

Light reflection

The light-reflective qualities of the tree canopies in gardens (A) and (B) are different. In Chile, the dark, dense, pointed forms of the pine tree canopies *absorb* much light. In Australia, the paler, more open, olive green clumps of foliage in the Eucalypt trees *reflect* much light. The shrubs in both gardens are mostly pruned into rounded, clumping shapes. In the Chilean garden, these shrubs tend to be darker and denser than the lighter foliaged shrubs of the Australian garden. In both gardens, the paving provides a pale coloured, hard surface which contrasts with the surrounding foliage.

Pools or lines of light

There is a bright pool of light at the centre of the Australian garden (B). This pool is highlighted by the white oval shape superimposed over the photograph below right. The pool of light is emphasised with a Xanthorrhoea clump growing as a focal point in the centre of the circular driveway.

In the Chilean garden below left, there is also a pool of light in the centre of this view of the garden. In this view, the light from the central area meanders off into the distance. It moves through a landscape which has a definite structure provided by walls and hills. In garden (B), the landscape has a softer, less well-defined structure and a softer, less defined contrast of light and dark in the landscape. The eye tends to move in several directions, rather than along a well-defined path, as in the Chilean garden.

Image 14. *Australian garden (B)*

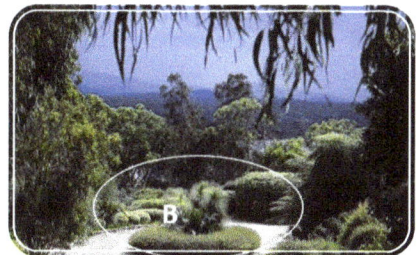

Image 13. *Garden (A) in Chile*

Colour, light and outline

Let us now consider how sunlight, plus the man–made garden design elements of walls, waterways and plants are incorporated in another South American *Light Garden*. In the view of the garden depicted below, the dark background foliage contrasts with the light reflecting off the meandering waterway and lawn terraces. One can imagine the water flowing down from the mountains then on through the garden. Tracing one route that the water might take, a white zigzag line has been drawn. Complementing this zigzag route are the rounded shapes of mountains and the carefully chosen native plants in the foreground. These are hardy native shrubs that thrive in the high altitudes of Peru. Here they have been planted in an urban garden.

Image 15. *A garden in Urumbina, with flowing lines leading down from the hills and through the garden.*

In the centre of the design, a white oval shape has been added around a group of shrubs. These shrubs act as a soft visual foil for the more dramatic pattern of light and dark shapes in the landscape. Imagine if masses of bright orange flowers had been planted here, instead of these simple pale green shrubs. The whole focus of the view would change, as the bright colours would draw attention away from the meandering lines linking the foreground and the mountains. This garden is an example of applying the *Light Garden* principle for considering *Environment and Context*.

A passionate heritage and contemporary examples

Pablo Neruda's poetry leads us further down the path of thinking about the gardens, landscapes and places of South America in the local languages and sentiments. Neruda is of Chilean nationality. When translated into English, his "Canto General" poem reads:

'The Wide Ocean'

"Ocean, if you were to give a measure, a ferment, a fruit
of your gifts and destructions, into my hand,
choose your far-off repose, your contour of steel,
your vigilant spaces of air and darkness,
and the power of your white tongue,
that shatters and overthrows columns,
breaking them down to your proper purity.
Not the final breaker, heavy with brine,
that thunders onshore, and creates
the silence of sand, that encircles the world,
but the inner spaces of force,
the naked power of the waters,

the immoveable solitude, brimming with lives,
It is Time perhaps, or the vessel filled
with all motion, pure Oneness,
that death cannot touch, the visceral green
of consuming totality." [320]

With such a passionate heritage as portrayed in Pablo Neruda's poem, it is little wonder that both ancient and modern sites in South America have become world renowned for their dramatic impact. These creative works enhance human appreciation of the drama of natural landscapes and our connection with the underlying character of the natural world. Within the set of ten *Light Garden* principles proposed in this book, this type of appreciation is included within principle number seven: perception and measurement.

While some people have called Chile the land of poets, Chilean academic Oscar Galindo has noted that the concept of Chile as "a land of poets" is largely a foreign one that has been assigned to his native country.[321]

Chile has a population of 17 million people. It is one of three South American nations that stretch along the Pacific Ocean coastline of this continent: Chile, Bolivia and Peru.

Sensing this heritage seeping through the landscape today, many visitors to the site of Moray in the Cusco Sacred Valley of Peru remark upon the mystique of this Incan site. It sits as an amphitheatre within the surrounding flowing forms of the landscape. It has a quality they cannot quite explain.

Image 16. *Moray in Peru – an example of careful measurement and perception in a Light Garden.*

Image 17. *The Wide Ocean as seen from another of Juan Grimm's Landscape Architectural designs at Los Vilos in Chile.*

As well as a highly developed sense of perception, a great deal of careful measurement would have been needed to translate the perceived design for this concentric stone terraced site into the actual built form. Renowned for horticultural innovation as well as aesthetics, the site is thought to have been an agricultural experimentation station dating from the 13th to the 16th centuries. It is located at an elevation of 3,500 metres. The circular depression is 30 metres deep, creating temperature differentials that are significant to the growth of different crop species within it. Incan priests were often responsible for organising crop breeding experimentation at such sites, indicating the high status accorded to the role.

The fate of small farmers in South America is a tragic counterweight to the wealth and expertise that has supported the construction of gardens such as many of Juan Grimm's fine works. This fate has been described in a well-documented report published in 2014:

> *"The single most important factor in the drive to push small farmers onto ever smaller parcels of land is the worldwide expansion of industrial commodity crop farms. The land area occupied by just four crops – soybean, oil palm, rapeseed and sugar cane – has quadrupled over the past 50 years."* [322]

The land area involved in this process is approximately the same as the total area of farmland in the European Union.[323]

This process of pushing small farmers onto ever smaller parcels of land is continuing to occur in America on a vast scale in the 21st century. Meanwhile, the invaluable forests of the Amazon burn in the ineffectual spotlight of mainstream media attention.

Image 18. *Urban farming in Cuba*

Having suffered food shortages and decimation of the economy for decades, the residents of Havana in Cuba chose a different path than continuing to push smallholder farmers off the land. The government and the urban population came together and worked out a better plan. Relying upon community-organised horticultural skills, innovative recycling and well respected teams of workers, the government provided initial support for people to become self-sufficient in the production of vegetables and livestock.[324] They have chosen to continue on this path ever since and enjoy near self-sufficiency for their basic food needs.

In another positive 21st century example that runs counter to what is happening in the Amazonian forests, Kris and Doug Tompkins began in the early 1990s to buy hundreds of thousands of acres in the wild Patagonia region of Chile. Their goal was to:

> *"buy and restore as much land as they could, improve and protect it, and then return it to people as public, national parks."* [325]

After two decades Kris and Doug had acquired 2.2 million acres. In 2018 the Chilean government accepted a gift of one million acres of this land to be managed as National Park. Before the land was handed over, infrastructure such as paths and cabins had been built. Regeneration of native ecosystems was also well underway in the new National Parks and on adjoining lands.[326]

9

North America

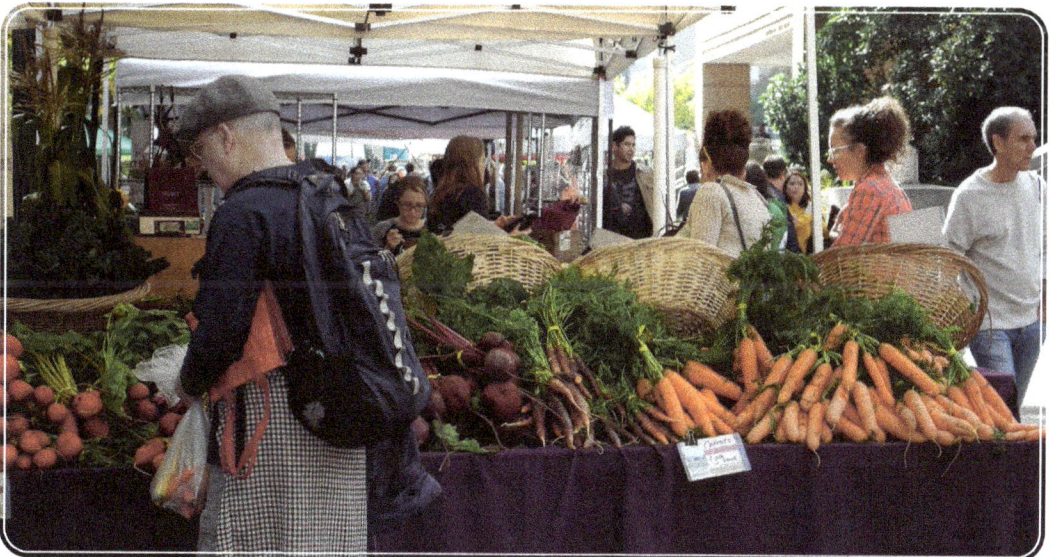

Image 1. *Markets have been a popular part of the resurgence of organic farming in the 21st century*

North American culture has included many frontiers and milestones. The ongoing use and appreciation of sunlight have been part of the cultural evolution. Several themes emerge when milestones in the historical tableau are reviewed. For example, there is an undercurrent of organic farming and food production that continues into the 21st century through the realms of urban farming and space travel.

The development of farming practices, settlements, conservation reserves, and technology have been features of North American life. Efforts to preserve nature have been juxtaposed against a series of technological breakthroughs. These include 20th century milestones such as mass urban development with airconditioned and glass-walled buildings.

Changes in the conscious, sustainable management of light and other natural resources can be traced through actions such as the integration of Amish communities since the early 18th century; the construction of Central Park in the mid 19th century; the declaration of North America's first National Park in 1890 and the emergence of a comprehensive approach to environmental planning in the early 1970s.

After describing each of the milestones listed below through the course of this chapter, they are then considered in terms of how well they rate as *Light Gardens*. Some, such as the farming communities of the Amish, rate well as *Light Gardens*. Others operate in a more constrained context. For example, the famous floral displays of Butchart Gardens on Vancouver Island are considered beautiful by many visitors. However, the site as a whole achieves a moderate rating in terms of *Light Garden* principles.

- Circa 10,000 BCE Native American culture begins
- 1730's to the present day: the Amish in Pennsylvania
- 1858 Central Park in New York by Landscape Architect Frederick Law Olmstead
- 1890 Yosemite National Park in California
- 1904 Butchart Gardens on Vancouver Island by Jenny Butchart
- 1914 Longwood Gardens in Pennsylvania, begun by Pierre du Pont, then continued by others
- 1935 Fallingwater by Architect Frank Lloyd Wright
- 1969 "Design with Nature" by Landscape Architect Ian McHarg
- 1970's communities: such as Arcosanti, begun by Architect Paolo Soleri
- 2012 Detroit urban renewal gardens by thousands of city residents
- 2016 Edible gardens in space by NASA

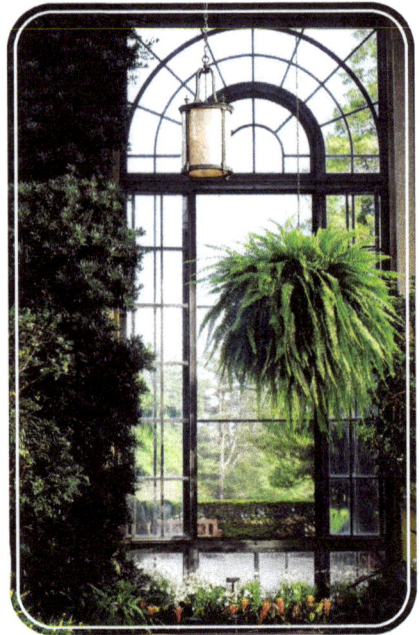

Image 2. *Longwood Gardens. The glasshouse: this structure was opened in 1921. As Longwood's second and largest conservatory, it is considered one of the world's great greenhouse structures.*

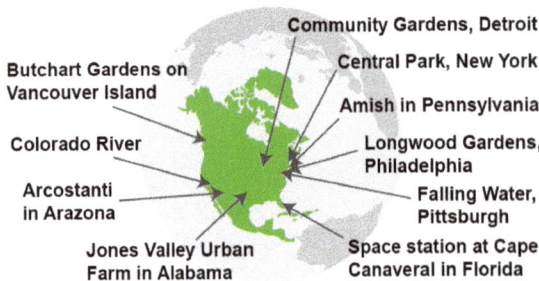

Image 3. *Location Map of sites in the timeline on page 2.*

The Image 3 map shows the location of North American sites discussed in this chapter. There are many types of *Light Garden* subcultures in evidence on this continent. For example, The Amish could be considered one of these subcultures, due to factors which allow their community to disconnect

"from the strings that bind most of us to modern-day corporate, capitalist society ... The Amish communities live a sustainable life in large part because of their traditional agricultural practices, economic freedom and alternative healthcare practices." [327]

10,000 BCE: Native American

Native Americans have given a significant gift to the world because 60% of the current world's cultivated garden and farm food supply species originated in the Americas. These plants include wild species of corn, rice, beans, nuts, berries, tomatoes and potatoes.[328] [329] The Native American peoples engaged in patient cultivation of these plants from wild varieties over thousands of years.

During the last ice age, around 10,000 BCE, these peoples migrated eastwards across the Bering Strait land bridge. As described by Park et al.:

> *The people quickly adapted to local food sources and developed gardens where corn, beans and squash formed the three basic inter-planted food species. Gardens and food sources included many other cultivated and wild plant foods and medicines, plus fish, wild game, berries and nuts.[330]*

Multiple tribes of people developed, and over five hundred Native American Tribes are recognised in the United States alone. The territories of some of the well-known tribes are illustrated on the map below. Fish formed a significant part of the diet for many tribes. Food gardens were made typically but not exclusively of mounds of soil, raised about 300mm above intervening irrigation channels. Proximity to water sources and arable soil was thus a common feature of settlement patterns.

Locally adapted varieties of corn were grown by hand at all latitudes from southern Canada to Central America. Nutrient rich organic fertilisers, including rotting fish, were used to meet the soil's nutritional requirements for growing corn.

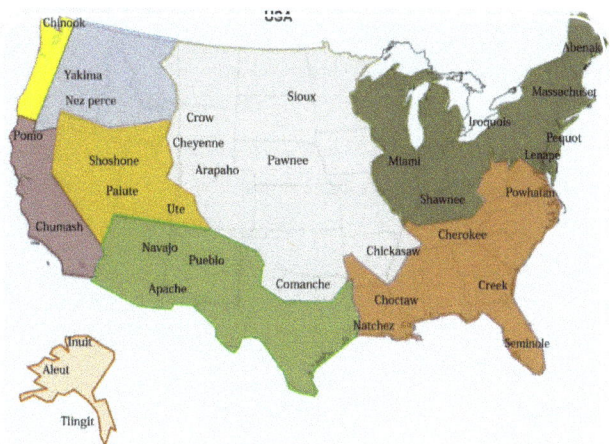

Image 4.
(Top left) *Photograph of Geronimo*
(Below right) *A map of tribal areas in the USA.*
(Below left) *some of the many varieties of corn cultivated by the Native Americans*

A famous Native American named Geronimo was born into a tribe in Arizona in the year 1829. He spoke of the significance of light in the gardens and landscape of North America when he said:

> *"I was born…Where the wind blew free and there was nothing to break the light of the sun…"[331]*

Painting a picture of Native American life in the early 19th century, Geronimo described how he started growing food with his parents when he was a child. Fields were about two acres in size. They broke the ground with wooden hoes and planted corn in straight rows. Beans, melons and pumpkins were interplanted in the same fields and allowed to spread across the land. Various organic fertilisers were used.

Geronimo described how melons were eaten as soon as they were gathered but pumpkins, beans and corn were stored for use in winter. His tribe had ponies to help carry loads of corn from the fields but they had no cattle. Thus all the energy for the villages came from open access to sunlight.[332]

> *The fields were never fenced. It was common for many families to cultivate land in the same valley and share the burden of protecting the growing crops from destruction by the ponies of the tribe, or by deer and other wild animals.*[333]

Thus, Geronimo's tribe had what would be described in the 21st century as a zero carbon economy. They had free access to the energy of sunlight and shared access to other natural resources such as space, water, land, and living organisms. They harvested the sun's energy by converting it to food energy that humans could eat in the short term, or store away for winter. Thus we see historical precedence for managing the natural resources of North America under the *Light Garden* concept.

The three realms of the *spirit, human and natural worlds* are present in Native American cultures. These realms have similarities to the Balinese *Tri Hita Karana* philosophy described in the following chapter. The connection between people, sunlight and the cosmos was also celebrated in Native American chants such as the following one. It is attributed to the Sioux:

> *Kuate, leno leno, mahote.*
>
> *Hyano, hyano, hyano*
>
> *(We are one with the infinite sun. Forever and ever and ever).* [334]

By the 21st century, this chant had been taken up by many other groups in North America and around the world. These groups also felt and celebrated their connection with the sun and the divine order.

Although most languages have a word for the concept of beauty, the traditional Navaho people of North America did not. To the Navaho, *Nizhoni* is their closest concept to beauty - and that word can refer to something that is both *good* and *attractive*. Beauty is a *sense of being* that must be felt as an internal harmony and balance.

That sense of being is as true for a whole person, as it is for a whole garden and the whole natural world order. The essence of the Navaho philosophy - which encompasses beauty, harmony, order and balance – has quietly persisted in North American culture. How that has occurred will now be considered with reference to a series of historically significant milestone events and sites.

These include the Amish settlements in North America from 1730; the construction of Central Park in New York in the mid 19th century and the rise of the National Parks movement from the late 19th century. These examples are followed by descriptions of several famous gardens constructed in the early 20th century and the ongoing development of environmental awareness, as it continues into the 21st century.

1730 to the present day: the Amish in Pennsylvania

"If you admire our faith -- strengthen yours. If you admire our sense of commitment -- deepen yours. If you admire our community spirit -- build your own. If you admire the simple life -- cut back. If you admire deep character and enduring values -- live them yourself." [335]

The first Amish arrived in Pennsylvania in the 1730's, having departed Europe to escape persecution. As illustrated below, 21st century Amish gardens, farms and buildings have an air of being built in traditional styles that may well be very similar to those brought from Europe some 300 years ago.

In an interesting turn of events, the Amish's time-honoured organic farming practices have become profitable sources of off-farm income for the Amish in the 21st century. Knowledge of the benefits of organically grown food has spread more widely through the North American community. The Amish religion permits interaction of the Amish with the broader community through the sale of homegrown organic produce at road-side stalls.

The traditional farming practices used by the Amish are based on their understanding of Biblical scriptures. Tilling the soil has religious significance. A large proportion of the population, from children to the elderly, are engaged in working on the land, using horse drawn machinery and human labour.

Farming, stewardship of the Earth and food production are also vital means by which the Amish seek to live in accordance with their philosophy of local, self-sufficient and sustainable communities. They choose to turn away from influences of the outside world that would lead them away from this philosophy.

For example, Amish predominantly use their own alternative health care practices, rather than purchase healthcare insurance, or use the mainstream health care system. However, if it is decided that a member of an Amish community does require mainstream healthcare treatment, members of the community will pool together and donate the funds required to obtain the treatment.

An impression of the Amish way of life is also stamped upon the public consciousness in North America by the image of their black horse-drawn carriages travelling along country roads. The Amish do not own cars but instead use horse drawn carriages with metal wheels. When the need arises, the Amish will accept transport in cars and taxis owned by other people.[336]

Image 5. *An Amish Farm in 21st century North America*

An Amish Barn raising event – reviewed as a potential Light Garden event

Notes 1 to 10 in the example below describe the extent to which the ten *Light Garden* parameters identified in Chapter 1 are present in a traditional Amish barn raising event.

1. **Energy.** The sun is the energy source for the Amish, as they live in self-sufficient farming communities and only drive horse-drawn buggies.

2. **Space.** The bright red barn encloses a readily recognisable, purpose-built space.

3. **Waves and particles.** Waves of Amish men work together to place the roof tiles.

4. **Lines, Patterns and probabilities.** The barn's design and the work clothes the men wear are highly probable to be the same as buildings and garments in other Amish settlements.

5. **Multiplication effects.** The recognisable style of Amish buildings when clustered together creates multiplication effects.

6. **Entanglement and Focal Point.** The roof's peak is a focal point in the farm landscape, as illustrated more clearly in the photograph on the previous page. In addition, psychological entanglement within the community is demonstrated by the deep sense of security that the Amish have in knowing that the community they are part of will return such barn-building favours if they ever find themselves in need.

7. **Perception and Measurement.** The people involved in this project applied careful measurements and human mindsets appreciative of the cultural significance of what was being built.

8. **Context.** The building materials in Amish settlements do not necessarily come from the surrounding landscape. They are one example of the Amish's need to interact with the wider community to obtain materials for activities such as barn construction.

9. **Human use.** Barn raisings are an example of what the Amish term "frolics." Barns have more than a utilitarian use!

10. **Storage and sharing of information.** The design of this barn and the lives the people who use it are based on information stored in the Biblical scriptures, the Amish traditions and the people's minds. Barn raisings are supervised and planned by master Amish engineers. They organise the free labour to build the barns and they employ centuries-old building techniques.

An Amish man described his satisfaction in participating in a barn raising event as follows:

I "take pleasure from participating in joint cooperative work projects—both from the social aspect as well as from the deeper sense of satisfaction in seeing tangible results of one's labor". [337]

Image 6. *An Amish barn raising with Light Garden numbers added to match the description above*

1858: Central Park, New York by Frederick Law Olmstead

Although it may be difficult to imagine in the 21st century, by the time the famous Native American Geronimo was thirty years of age, the design and construction of Central Park in New York were underway.

Thus, it is not so incongruous in the historical context that we find that Frederick Law Olmstead, the Landscape Architect who designed Central Park, had many values in common with Geronimo.

Olmstead is regarded as the father of Landscape Architectural profession in the United States and he was the originator of the term "landscape architect." That term was subsequently adopted as the profession grew in countries all around the world.

As described below, Olmsted's philosophy was formed in his early years. Although he does not specifically refer to light, he does refer to "cultivating susceptibility to the power of scenery."

> *"The root of all my good work is an early respect for, regard and enjoyment of scenery and extraordinary opportunities for cultivating susceptibility to the power of scenery."* [338]

Describing this influence in more detail, an observer noted:

> *"…his father set him on a pillow in front of his saddle and took his son through the countryside around their home in Hartford, Connecticut. These short rides expanded to become annual tours in search of the picturesque that took Olmsted, by the age of sixteen, through the Connecticut Valley and White Mountains, up the Hudson River, and westward to the Adirondacks, Lake George and Niagara Falls."* [339]

Central Park is located in the densely populated CBD of New York City. It probably rests beside the Statue of Liberty and the New York Public Library as one the city's three best known icons. Olmstead designed Central Park to heighten people's psychological sense of connection with nature.

He did this by including walkways between trees and lakes, whilst being aware of the most robust human response to the power of scenery that would prevail in particular places within the design. He insisted that design elements that would distract from this primary purpose would not be permitted.

Image 7. *Central Park in New York City*

"He vigilantly guarded against distracting elements that would intrude on the consciousness of the observer. In the process, he simplified the scene, clearing and planting to clarify the "leading motive" of the natural site and heighten the effect of a particular quality of nature." [340]

As described in Chapter Ten, Jorn Utzon included a similar stipulation in the Sydney Opera House's design guidelines. He insisted that white café umbrellas would not be permitted on the harbour-side outdoor podium of the Opera House. This was because white umbrellas would detract from the building's white roof sails as the dominant and uncluttered statement on the site, in contrast to the darker blues, browns and greys of the surrounding harbour-side setting.

Although profound, Olmstead's philosophy has rarely been allowed to prevail by clients who could not fully embrace his comprehension of the connection between nature, light, the human soul and society. However, there are some happy examples of this philosophy capturing the public imagination in later projects by other North American designers. Not least among these were Ian McHarg and Frank Lloyd Wright.

Continuing the reference to the light and open spaces of the prairies that Geronimo cited, it has been said that Frank Lloyd Wright

"liked the sense of shelter in the look of the building" yet he "loved the prairie by instinct as a great simplicity — the trees, flowers, sky itself, thrilling by contrast." [341]

Nearly eighty years after the construction of Central Park, in 1935 Frank Lloyd Wright designed one of his most famous projects: *Fallingwater.* As with all his projects, he designed the colours, forms, lines, massing and play of light and shade to reflect his philosophy of creating organic forms that blend with nature.

Although it may take some imagination, by referring to the photographs overleaf, one can compare the towering cliffs, waters, and forest of Yosemite to Manhattan's towering buildings, with Central park in their midst. Through this process, one may come to some appreciation of the Western concept of bringing the rejuvenating qualities of Nature and "a green lung" into the city, through projects such as Central Park.

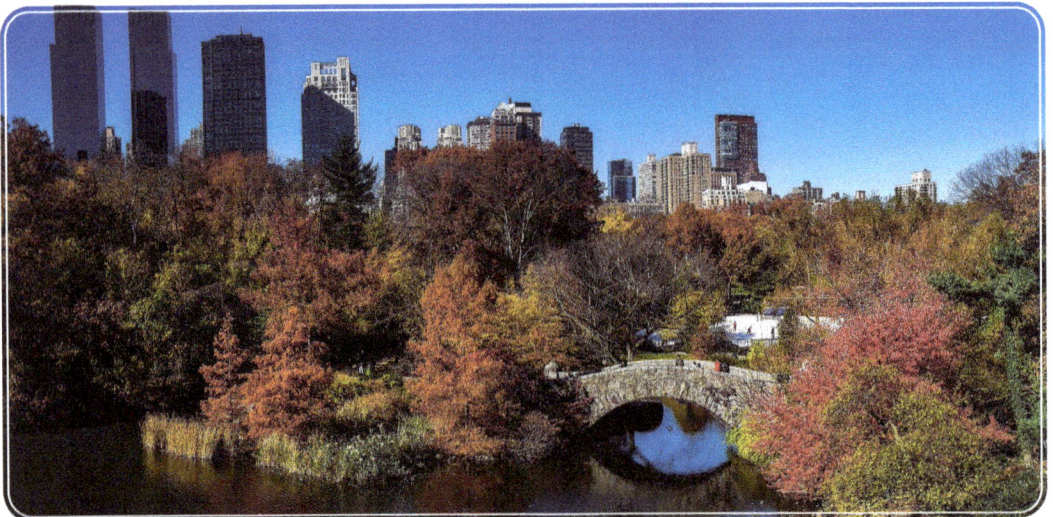

Image 8. *Central Park with towers and trees reminiscent of the forests and cliffs of Yosemite.*

Image 9. *Yosemite*

1890 Yosemite National Park

Illustrating the rapid development of the movement for the preservation of wilderness at the same time as urban development was occurring in many parts of North America, Yellowstone was declared as North America's first National Park in 1870. This declaration occurred only ten years after the construction of Central Park in New York. The world's first National Park had been declared almost a century earlier by the Mongolian Government at Khan Uul in 1783.[342]

Yos.s.e'meti (from the Central Miwok Native American language), originally referred to the Indian tribe that lived in Yosemite Valley.[343] Few people are aware that Yosemite translates as *"those who kill"*.[344] However, in 1851, some forty years before the declaration of Yosemite National Park, the Native American tribe of the area was largely killed themselves. Survivors were forced to relocate to a distant Indian reservation.

Prior to this event, the County Sherriff had been found *"unequal to the task"* [345] of eradicating the local Native American population. There are various accounts of whether it was the Sheriff, or Dr Bunnell, who wished to honour, rather than kill the tribe when making the following note concerning the naming of Yosemite National Park:

> *As I did not take a fancy to any of the names proposed, I remarked that "an American name would be the most Appropriate;…American scenery—the grandest that had ever yet been looked upon. That it would be better to give it an Indian name than to import a strange and inexpressive one; that the name of the tribe who had occupied it, would be more appropriate than any I had heard suggested." [346]*

After California became a state in 1850, the US federal government tried to persuade or force tribes in the Sierra Nevada region, (including the Yosemite tribe), to move to reservations in California's Central Valley. Unconvinced, most tribes fought to stay where they were.

In 1851 a state-sanctioned militia, mostly made up of prospectors and miners calling themselves the Mariposa Battalion,

> *"invaded...the group razed and set fire to the village of the Ahwahneechee, forcing the tribespeople onto reservations down in the Central Valley and capturing their leader, Chief Tenaya."* [347]

Chief Tenaya later escaped from the reservation and managed to spend his last days at Yosemite and thereabouts.[348] Conservationists later persuaded President Abraham Lincoln to declare Yosemite Valley, (and the land where a grove of giant sequoia trees stood), as a public trust of the State of California in 1864. This declaration was the first time that land had been protected for public enjoyment by the US government. In 1890, Yosemite National Park was declared. It was the third National Park to be declared in the United States.

1904 Butchart Gardens

Butchart Gardens in Canada is consistently rated by visitors as one of the world's top ten most beautiful gardens.[349] Nevertheless, it is doubtful that Frederick Law Olmstead, Chief Tenaya, Frank Lloyd Wright or Ian McHarg would agree with all the principles behind the construction of the colourful floral displays on this site. The golden yellow tulips depicted in Image 10 are part of these floral displays that draw one million visitors to the gardens each year. If one were to think: "I should learn more about what makes this garden beautiful because there is money to be made in such things," it would not be an original idea.

Before the boom and bust cycle of tulip mania in Holland ended in the 17th century, prized tulip bulbs were worth their weight in gold. The Butchart family, originally planning to make a garden from a disused quarry on their property, certainly also discovered a way of making money from sharing the beauty of tulips and flowers.

Butchart Gardens remains a family run business that must make a profit to survive. In 1907, while the family's quarry was still in operation, Japanese designer Isaburo Kishida of Yokohama was commissioned to design a garden. It was constructed thereafter but it is the garden that Jenny Butchart designed and planted once quarry operations ceased that made Butchart Gardens famous.

Jenny had shown artistic talent from a young age and had intended to travel to Europe to study art before marrying Robert Butchart. After marriage, she became involved in his limestone quarry and cement plant business in Canada. The following extract from an article by Steve Whysall in the *Vancouver Sun* describes how the garden grew from this:

> *"It is not too big a reach to see the parallel between Jennie's restoration of the old limestone quarry with the reconciliation and renewal of her own personal passion for artistic expression".* [350]

Perhaps, like Olmstead, Jenny also had a passion for connecting people and nature. However, she was not designing a park on public land, so she simply set about planting the steep quarry banks, while also planning the floral displays that now bloom in the rich soil in the base of the quarry below.

Image 10. *Tulips under a tree at Butchart Gardens*

Olmstead wanted his designs to remain true to the character of their natural surroundings, and not to clash with them. The frequent failure of flower bedding and specimen planting of hybrids to follow this premise was one of his chief reasons for differentiating his profession of landscape architecture from that of gardening.

In this respect, as in many others, Olmstead kept alive the teachings of eighteenth-century English writers on landscape design. The prevalence of conifer trees and shrubs

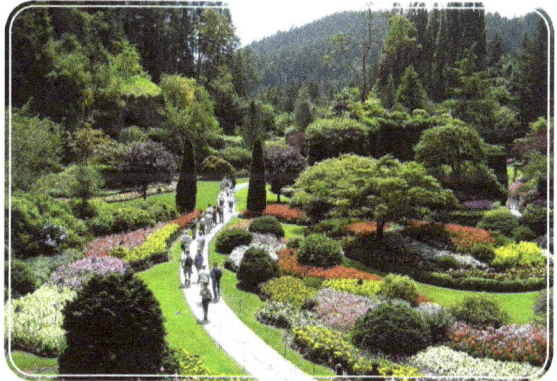

Image 11. *Flowers and trees blend with the surrounding landscape at Butchart Gardens on Vancouver Island.*

in the foreground, middle ground and background of the view through the garden depicted in Image 11 provides a subtle framework for the flowers that feature in the centre of the garden. It was this type of flower beds and hybrids that Olmstead warned can clash with the natural character of a site. Nevertheless, after a close look at this view, it is apparent that people can enjoy moving through the garden, admiring the flowers and feeling connected with the site's natural setting. In accordance with Olmstead's principles, the trees on the site

> *"remain true to the character of their natural surroundings and [do] not…clash with them".* [351]

Quarry revegetation projects in the 21st century generally seek to recreate natural plant communities but Butchart Gardens was not conceived of in that manner. Beginning in 1904, Jenny Butchart used her ideal vision of a grand and beautiful garden as her guiding light for the design. To keep Butchart Gardens as an economically viable, internationally renowned visitor destination, succeeding generations of the Butchart family have added to the original gardens with more attractions, such as a large fountain in a pond.

1914 Longwood Gardens

Unequivocally designed to harvest light and create delight, the conservatories at Longwood Gardens attract over one million visitors per year. They were built under the patronage of Pierre du Pont. At the age of 36, Pierre was inspired by a desire to save the trees on the Longwood Gardens site from logging. He purchased the 436 hectare site in 1906 and subsequently enlarged the farm homestead and built the gardens.

The first glasshouse was built in 1914. The second and largest conservatory at Longwood Gardens is regarded as one of the world's great glasshouses. Opened in 1921, it houses 4,600 types of plants and trees.[352] A photograph of that glasshouse may be seen in Image 2 at the beginning of this chapter.

As well as the glasshouses, there are outdoor mass displays of colourful flowers and formal gardens with fountains at Longwood Gardens. The floral displays have been compared to Eastern style gardens, such as found in China and Japan. Young North American gardeners James Rockwell and Timothy Heslop have observed that in Eastern cultures, beauty is often seen as arising from unique details that give something its particular character.

Image 12. *Light streams through a conservatory at Longwood Gardens*

This concept of beauty is associated with what they described as the Japanese focus on the expression of the individual. They have described Longwood Gardens as perhaps the epitome of the Western tendency to see beauty not as something individual but as something created with a massed display of flowers:

"There is something awe-inspiring in the large drifts of color strewn across a living canvas." [353]

1914 – 2014: Glass and Light

Glasshouses may be the epitome of designs intended to inspire awe through the beauty of space, light and plants. The reflective flooring and arched shapes of huge conservatory windows at Longwood Gardens complement each other to create a light-filled, spacious and inspiring experience for visitors. Several world famous glasshouses were constructed in the early 20th century to house exotic plants and entrance visitors. In many ways, these glasshouses were harbingers of the atriums and air-conditioned buildings that have proliferated since that time.

The first modern electrical air conditioning unit was invented in 1902 by Willis Carrier in New York. By 1904, the public had been exposed to the concept of air-conditioned buildings at the St Louis World Fair. By the 1920s, air conditioning had become common, not in homes or offices, but in the newly constructed movie theatres of the USA.[354]

Returning to the story of glass walled, light filled, air-conditioned buildings that house plants, the first atrium in a modern building in the USA was constructed thirty years later in 1957.[355]

By the early 21st century, indoor gardens and the exterior walls of buildings had started transmogrifying into what came to be known as *Green Walls*. The Green Wall, (or *Botanical Brick*), concept had been patented in 1938 by Professor Stanley Hart White of the University of Illinois. However, his work did not receive much public attention. Some fifty years later, the talented French Botanist Patrick Blanc started to modernise, popularise and promote the aesthetic appeal and feasibility of the concept, with notable success in many cities around the world.[356]

Image 13. *An atrium in a 21st century building*

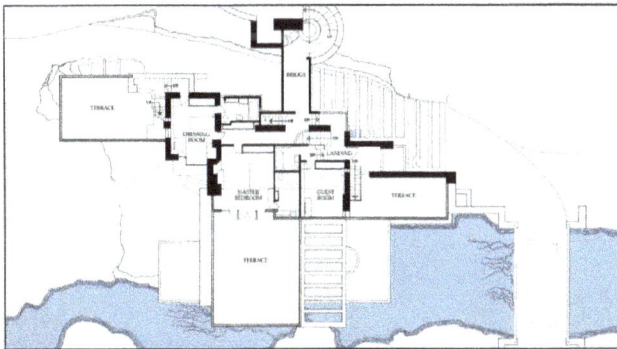

1935 Fallingwater and falling light capture the imagination

Frank Lloyd Wright achieved similar brilliant success with his *Fallingwater* project in 1935. Probably the most remarkable feature of the design of *Fallingwater* is the juxtaposition of the structure against its forest setting. After an eventful but professionally unsatisfying life, Frank Lloyd Wright was 67 years old by the time he achieved a turning point in his career with the design of the country house *Fallingwater* near Pittsburgh in the USA.[357]

> *"Almost from the day of its completion, "Fallingwater" was celebrated around the world. The house and its architect were featured in major publications including the cover of Time Magazine. Over the years its fame has only increased."* [358]

FALLINGWATER   SECOND FLOOR PLAN

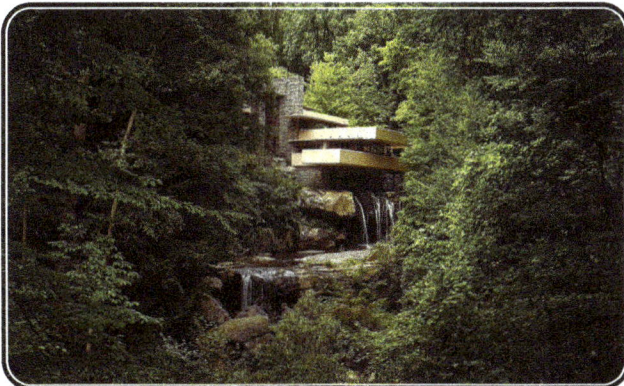

The visual impact of *Fallingwater* relies heavily upon a beam of sunlight that streams through the surrounding forest onto the house. It highlights the dramatic concrete form of balconies that overhang a forest waterfall.

One may wonder about the apparent disparity between the espoused American dream of living in harmony with nature, and the 21st century reality that the USA virtually has the largest ecological footprint of any nation on Earth. The similarly large ecological footprints of several other countries also contribute disproportionately to the depletion of Earth's natural resources. This process can be only partly explained by reference to the historical examples given in this book.

Image 14. *Fallingwater: Plan above and photograph below*

1969 'Design with Nature'

Far less publicised in the media and much less well known to the general public than Frank Lloyd Wright, Ian McHarg was a Professor at the University of Pennsylvania and a practitioner in Landscape Architecture. He went into far greater detail than Frank Lloyd Wright to develop systems to make the American dream of living in harmony with nature more of a reality.

Ian McHarg's book *'Design with Nature'* sets a wider agenda than anything before it for environmental planning in the USA. It was acknowledged as a pioneer in the worldwide movement towards sound environmental planning.[359] The book was published in 1969, just over a century after the design of Central Park. It set forth principles and practices for how to go about designing cities and whole regions in a systematic and ecologically sustainable process. I was young at that time and had started reading books about society and the environment. By the time I was a university student, the principles of *Design with Nature* had been brought to my native country of Australia. There was excitement amongst the academic and student community when opportunities arose to apply these principles to natural resource management and design.

In 1971, Mc Harg delivered an address to the North American Wildlife and Natural Resources Conference in Portland, Oregon. At that time, he publicly warned that the human species may not survive if it continued on the economic globalisation path, or the path of killing and plundering the planet's living systems. Almost forty years later in 2018, naturalist David Attenborough gave a similar address in the United Kingdom, focusing on climate change and biodiversity conservation.

Both these issues were encompassed within the broader Landscape Architectural and Planning processes that McHarg's team established. In the 1960s, Mc Harg used the term *biosphere* to refer to the planet's living systems. Since the "Earth Summit" in 1972, the United Nations has also used that term. Flowing from this, by the year 2020, a worldwide network of approximately five hundred biosphere reserves had been established. Integrated management of economic, social, educational, environmental, cultural and aesthetic factors is encouraged in these reserves.

Image 15. *An eagle soars, hunting over a protected area of forest.*

The value of this integrated approach to management is briefly described in Chapter Ten with reference to the World Heritage listing of the *'Cultural Landscape of Bali Province: the Subak System as a Manifestation of the Tri Hita Karana Philosophy'.* The limited value of including a site on the World Heritage Register without adequate comprehensive planning of the type encouraged under the Biosphere reserve program has been apparent in Bali. Notwithstanding, on-going efforts will seek to address this problem gradually. As with many things, time is of the essence with this process, before the older farmers die and with them, the opportunity to pass on their agricultural skills to the next generation. The need for timely action in such cultures highlights the value of *Light Garden* principle number two: Allow the time and space needed for ecosystems, (and cultures), to regenerate.

1970 Arcosanti

In many ways but not all, *'Arcosanti'* was the antithesis of Ian McHarg's work. Established from 1970 onwards as an artisans' community, Arcosanti proclaimed that one of its goals was to be environmentally sustainable. Fifty years later, although buildings and a swimming pool had been constructed, the revegetation and other site works that would align with *Light Garden* principles had lagged behind. Although the Arcosanti community has been promoted as a remote desert experience, it is quite close to a State Highway, as illustrated below.

One of the original strengths of the Arcosanti vision was that people who lived in the community would utilise their artisan and artistic skills to become self-sufficient. In the 21st century, the Arcosanti community manufactures and sells large metal bells, receives visitors and hosts students. These activities provide revenue sources to support the residents whilst also allowing visitors to learn from their experiences.

Image 16. *Arcosanti in Google Earth aerial views.*

21st century urban farms: Alabama and Detroit

Helena Norberg-Hodge, writing of rural Chinese villages in the last years of the 20th century, said:

"the people I encountered were able to meet most of their basic needs locally, using their own labor and ingenious small-scale technologies. We were greeted with spontaneous laughter and humor." [360]

Such accounts of the value and happiness of cooperative village life have inspired many 21st century ventures in the USA. For example, Jones Valley Urban Farm is located on a five acre property in the downtown area of Birmingham, a city of just over 200,000 people in the state of Alabama, USA. This not-for-profit organisation runs educational programs about healthy food and grows organic produce and flowers. These are marketed in the local community.

During the late 19th century, Birmingham had developed as an industrial city where relatively cheap, non-unionised labour could be sourced. Even so, since the mid 20th century, those enterprises have declined.

In the city's post-industrial era, sizable inner city sites have become available for urban farms and gardens, attracting the attention of government support agencies with funding available for community group projects. Local people have moved in and established urban farming enterprises.[361]

Oko Farms is the catchy name of another local community project. It is an aquaponic farming business set up in Brooklyn, New York and it has brought affordable, healthy, fresh food to people in the neighbourhood. Residents have been pleased to find it provides other benefits as well, such as being a safe place to meet other people or enjoy some time sitting outdoors, amidst greenery and gardens in their dense urban neighbourhood.[362]

Gandhi knew that in India he needed to promote small scale, local businesses as an important part of empowering local communities to speak up for their rights in the more extensive democratic system. So too in Brooklyn, the Oko Farms project has begun to function in that way, under a capable leadership team that includes a nutritionist and mental health worker.

Image 17. *Gandhi, Jones Valley and Oko: all empowering communities through local enterprise*

2012 Detroit and vertical gardens

Moving from New York to Detroit, we find that in 2012, Detroit was considered the most dangerous city in the USA. It had a murder rate ten times that of New York City. In the 1950 census, the city of Detroit reached its peak population of 1.5 million people. During the next 65 years, it lost well over half its population, leaving vast areas of the inner city derelict.[363]

Urban farming has been one of the most successful ventures supporting residents to rise out of this inner city dereliction in Detroit. As of 2019, there were approximately 200 urban farming and community gardening enterprises in the city. Visitors book tours to see them and the city has announced its goal of becoming a food sovereign city for all the fruits and vegetables that are consumed.[364]

By 2012 vertical gardens for food production started to appear in high rise buildings in various countries around the world. Lighting for the gardens is an important factor in any cost-benefit analysis of these enterprises. Although lighting can be sourced from sunlight or LEDs, full spectrum light is not required for plant growth. Red, blue or purple light can be used and generated at a lower cost, with less electricity, than full spectrum light. In 2018, commercial LEDs were about 28% energy efficient, but two years later, research had demonstrated that LEDs could be made with a significantly increased energy efficiency of 68%.

The world's first commercial vertical farm was opened in Singapore in 2012. In 2018 the United States Department of Agriculture and the Department of Energy held a workshop focused on vertical agriculture and sustainable urban ecosystems, citing opportunities to address the nation's food security.[365]

Around this same time, a Chinese Academy of Agricultural Sciences speaker presented data about extensive research into vertical farms in China. One of the advantages he was reported as describing was that due to climate variabilities in China, their vertical farms *"need to be capable of producing food in winter in temperatures as low as -55 degrees centigrade."* [366]

Image 18. *Detroit*

2016: Light Gardens in Orbit and the Quakers Light of God

By the 21st century, gardens began to proliferate as hybrid offspring of initiatives aimed primarily at other things such as solar energy production, carbon sequestration, waste management, water conservation, biodiversity conservation, economic localisation, sustainability, organic farming, hydroponics, aquaculture and so on.

The first *Light Gardens* in orbit around Earth have now launched. Space stations and rockets often contain solar panels and they can now house units for production of food plants grown under artificial lights.

As illustrated below, gardens can now be grown onboard the International Space Station. In 2016, astronauts had their first taste of lettuce they had grown on board during their flight. Specially designed red, green and blue LED lights were used to simulate Earth's natural lighting conditions for the growth of plants.[367]

This innovation opens up the question of growing plants on Mars. Now that water has been found on Mars and we know there is light on Mars, how long will it be before plants are grown in special containers on Mars? Maybe plants will come from planet Earth, or from seeds found somewhere else but whatever the horticultural outcome, awareness of the value of access to life-giving sunlight will increase.

Taking a more low risk approach to daily life and planning for the future, when asked about how they share their lives together back on planet Earth, some North American Quakers replied:

> *"We eat together at least once a week, we garden together, we delight in each other's children, and we care for this land and its non- human inhabitants together. We work together to care for and maintain our common house "*[368]

Quakers believe the light of God exists within each person. Following on from this belief, Quakers were prominent and successful in the social movements in North America for both the abolition of slavery and the granting of equal voting rights for women.

Light from the heavens is a common symbolic analogy in many religious groups found in contemporary North American society. In the past and going forward, these groups exercise considerable influence, as the historical example of the Quakers has shown.

Image 19. *Light shining on plants in the International Space Station and from the face of Mother Mary.*

Review: 1730 – 2030

In the 21st century, the USA is acknowledged as placing higher importance upon religion than many other comparable Western, or globalised, non-indigenous cultures. The relevance of this to *Light Garden* culture in North America is considered in a brief review that follows. The chapter summary on the following page also provides a little more comment on that subject.

According to 2015 survey data, about 55% of American citizens say religion is very important in their lives. The importance of religion was much lower in comparable countries such as Canada (27%), Germany (21%), Russia (19%), Australia (18%), Japan (5%) and China (3%). [369]

Among Western cultures, the prevalence of gardening does not correlate with this data about religion. In a 2015 survey, it was found *"that Australia has the highest level (45%) of daily or weekly gardening among all the countries measured. China came in second (36%), followed by Mexico, the US, and Germany – all of which had levels of over one-third."* [370]

How have these patterns of participation in religion and gardening influenced the gardening, farming and environmental movements in North America? By looking at some of the oldest and some of the newest gardens in America, we may find some answers to that question.

For example, as described earlier in this chapter, the Amish first settled in Pennsylvania in 1730. They brought with them a religion developed in Switzerland during the 17th century. Some three hundred years later, they still live in self-contained rural communities following the original religious precepts.

Tilling the Earth through farming and gardening has religious significance to the Amish, as described in their biblical texts. In contrast to the longevity of the Amish communities, the innovative artisan community of Arcosanti has struggled to stay focused on its values and goals since it was established in 1970 by the charismatic leader Paolo Soleri.

Soleri's vision was for an ecologically sound, medium density, urban settlement of artisans working together as a community. Revenue to support the ambitious Arcosanti building project has been generated on site. However, religion was not part of the vision. Gardens have not blossomed on the site either. As of 2017, neither the terraced gardens nor the fields included on the original plans for the site had been constructed.[371]

In contrast to Amish communities, which are intentionally self-reliant and self-contained, Arcosanti proactively seeks to attract up to 40,000 visitors annually. It tends to have between fifty and one hundred and fifty residents at one time. Many of these are architectural students who stay for a while to assist with building work and learn about life on the ten hectare site.

Based on a different set of principles, Amish communities are planned around families that work together from early childhood to old age. Their farming principles are based on adherence to centuries old traditions. Contrasting with this, Arcosanti was conceived of as a bold new adventure to create a community on the edge of the desert, with easy vehicle access to a State Route highway only one kilometre away.

Chapter summary

Each event identified on the timeline below has been assigned a rating based on the more detailed discussion earlier in this chapter and the *Light Garden* model set out in Chapter One. The ratings are somewhat arbitrary and space does not permit a full explanation of the reasons behind them. Please read them with a sense of critical review and note the projects most relevant to addressing 21st century issues.

For example, the age old practices of the Amish are quite well aligned with the *Light Garden* concept, so they have been rated as 4.5 out of 5 on the timeline diagram below.

Yosemite National Park and "Design with Nature" are also rated highly because of the comprehensive manner in which they address *Light Garden* principles. All the milestones on the timeline are historically significant. They are quite positive examples of the application of *Light Garden* principles but some, such as Butchart Gardens and Arcosanti, have been assigned three star ratings for various reasons.

These reasons include factors such as the energy use on the site may not reflect best practice for sustainability. There may be few examples of *Light Garden* quantum biophysics entanglement and multiplication effects in the designs. Alternatively, the site's use may not be planned in a restrained manner that reflects a wider agenda to contribute towards the rejuvenation of natural resources of the planet.

These comments are not to be taken as failings of the projects but rather as a way of charting how the historical development of thought and priorities for such projects has occurred.

Ratings for examples of North American Milestones in the use of Light	
Ratings assigned from **5 (highest)** to **1 (lowest)**	
4.5	Circa 10,000 BCE to the current day: Native American culture
4.5	1730's to the present day: the Amish in Pennsylvania
3	1858 Central Park in New York by Landscape Architect Frederick Law Olmstead
4.5	1890 Yosemite National Park in California
3	1904 Butchart Gardens on Vancouver Island by Jenny Butchart
3	1914 Longwood Gardens in Pennsylvania, begun by Pierre du Pont, then others continued
3	1935 Fallingwater by Architect Frank Lloyd Wright
4.5	1969 "Design with Nature" by Landscape Architect Ian McHarg
3	1970's communities: such as Arcosanti, begun by Architect Paolo Soleri
4	2012 Detroit urban renewal gardens, built by thousands of city residents
3	2016 Edible gardens in space by NASA

10

South East Asia

In Indonesia during the period 2015 – 2050 there could be a projected net gain of 41% forest cover, or a net loss of 47% forest cover.

Examples of work from five South East Asian countries are referred to in this chapter: Malaysia, Bali, Papua, The Philippines and Vietnam. The countries of the South East Asian region are shown in dark green colour on the map below. The focus of this chapter is as a broad 21st century example of how it is possible to achieve three of the *Light Garden* concepts introduced in Chapter One:

(i) Apply the principles of Light Gardens at the regional, national and local scales.

(ii) Achieve the goal of managing half the planet's land and water areas as nature reserves and

(iii) Rapidly address climate change at the global and regional scales as necessary to achieve effective results.

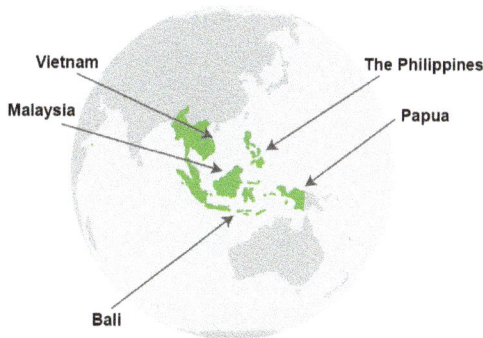

Image 1. *South East Asia*

Image 2. *A forest dweller in South East Asia - an Orangutan.*

In Malaysia, during the period 2015 – 2050, there could plausibly be either be a net gain of 14% forest cover, or an equivalent net loss of forest cover.[372] This may come as a surprise to many people who have developed an attitude that there is nothing that realistically can be done to reverse the trend of recent decades, where the worldwide loss of tropical forests has occurred at unprecedented rates.[373]

However there is much than can and is being done for reforestation of the planet and South East Asia provides examples of this. In 2016 Biologist Edward O. Wilson proposed that half the planet's land and water areas be set aside as nature reserves. In support of this proposal he set out the scientific basis for calculations that 80% of existing living species could be preserved by such action.[374]

In that species conservation context, the *Light Garden* theme of this book gains significance because it points to a future in which the healthy growth of living organisms - and the Life processes themselves - are at the centre of the next wave of our local and international cooperative and scientific efforts, rather than diverting funds away from living systems and into non-living technology, such as ever faster spacecraft, mobile phones or geoengineering.

This next wave of cooperative efforts includes the sphere of nature conservation, in conjunction with work towards local socio- economic stability. Some of the successful cooperative cultures and forest management practices of South East Asia provide an insight into how aspects of the *Light Garden* concept are already being put into practice in several South East Asian countries. The transferability of these practices to other locations will also be considered.

While they were once considered a moderate sink for atmospheric carbon, by 2019 research studies had shown that the carbon balance of tropical forests has tilted towards being a net source of carbon emissions, due to extensive deforestation and a reduction in carbon density.[375]

Although it may at first seem an unattainable goal to set aside half the planet's land and water areas as nature reserves, vast areas of the planet's land masses are already covered by forests. Map Image 4 in this chapter illustrates this. For example, in Russia and North America, 30 – 47% of the land is forested, whilst in the Amazon, Central Africa and South East Asia, forest cover extends over 47 – 54% of the land area. This does not mean all of this land has no human habitation, or that it is not used for commercial purposes, food production or other purposes. It does not mean all of this land is of high biodiversity conversation value. It does not mean that other biomes in the oceans, swamps, peat lands, tundras and grass lands of the Earth do not also contribute to nature conservation, ecosystem functioning or carbon sequestration.

However it does mean that about half the Earth's surface is already covered by forest of some type. This provides a living fabric of natural resources that can be managed to support nature conservation as well as other purposes. It also provides a living baseplate for restoration of forests at a scale that will help with carbon drawdown, in the race to develop effective global practices for climate management.

As an edited collection of scientific research published in 2019 states, there is still a chance for humanity to act collectively to avoid decimation of the human population through climate change. A new climate model published by Springer Nature in early 2019, "Achieving the Paris Climate Agreement Goals", shows that we can only meet the target of remaining below 1.5 degrees C in average global temperature rise by:

> "…ending the conversion of forest and other natural lands by 2030, effectively placing half of the Earth's lands under protection.

> "This major conservation effort would need to be coupled with a forest restoration effort and other natural climate solutions to draw down carbon from the atmosphere (providing 'negative emissions') alongside a rapid transition to carbon free energy, like wind and solar power, by 2050." [376]

Shared socio-economic pathways forest management

By the end of the second decade in the 21st century, tropical deforestation was responsible for around one-tenth of total anthropogenic carbon emissions.[377] For example, replacement of tropical rainforest with palm oil plantations

> "may still show on satellite surveys as forest cover, but the plantations lack the biomass, biodiversity and carbon sequestration capacity of the rainforests." [378]

A palm oil plantation will thus have a lower carbon density than rainforest that was knocked down to make space and light to establish the plantation. By the year 2019, despite being known for high rates of deforestation in recent decades, South East Asia contained about 15% of the planet's tropical forests and forests covered 33% of South East Asian land.

In addition, 56.68% of land in South East Asia was used for agricultural purposes in 2015, according to the World Bank collection of development indicators. The area of land used for urban purposes in South East Asia increased by 22% between 2000 and 2010 to approximately 10% of the land mass.[379]

Meanwhile, by the year 2019, forests covered about 31 percent of total land area of the globe, or just over 4 billion hectares (ha).[380] South East Asia lost about 80 million ha of total forest cover between 2005 and 2015.

A best practice study published in 2019 examined five scenarios for future forest management in South East Asia. Of these five scenarios, or *"shared socioeconomic pathways,"* the best-case outcome indicated that one quarter of this 80 million ha loss of forest could be regained by intelligent resource management during the next thirty years to the year 2050.[381]

The *"shared socioeconomic pathways"* (SSP) scenario study generated useful outcomes, showing plausible ways to achieve a net increase in forest carbon stores, given associated socioeconomic considerations. Under the worst case SSP scenario to the year 2050, a further loss of another 5.2 million ha of forest in South East Asia would occur.[382] As described in the SSP study:

> *"Considering the multiple interacting uncertainties and the dynamics of socioeconomic systems, charting the path of the region's forest future [through the SSP approach] is a challenge, and requires exploratory scenario-based analyses…Scenario analysis is a structured process of exploring and evaluating alternatives aimed at providing insights regarding plausible rather than probable futures.."* [383]

The further loss of 5 million ha in the decades from 2015 to 2050 might at first glance appear comparatively insignificant compared to the loss of 80 million ha during the ten years between 2005 and 2015. However the further loss of forest in South East Asia is particularly significant at the global scale.

This is because tropical forests cover only 7% of the Earth's land surface but account for 68% of the global carbon stock. Thus any further loss of tropical forests, (in South East Asia or elsewhere), leads to a relatively significant loss in the global carbon stock.[384]

This is a significant issue in the global challenge to manage climate change and natural resources because carbon stocks must be increased, not reduced, as part of a multi- factorial approach to climate and natural resource management. Tropical forests also generate rainfall in countries all around the world, through the water that is transpired into the atmosphere by the forests.

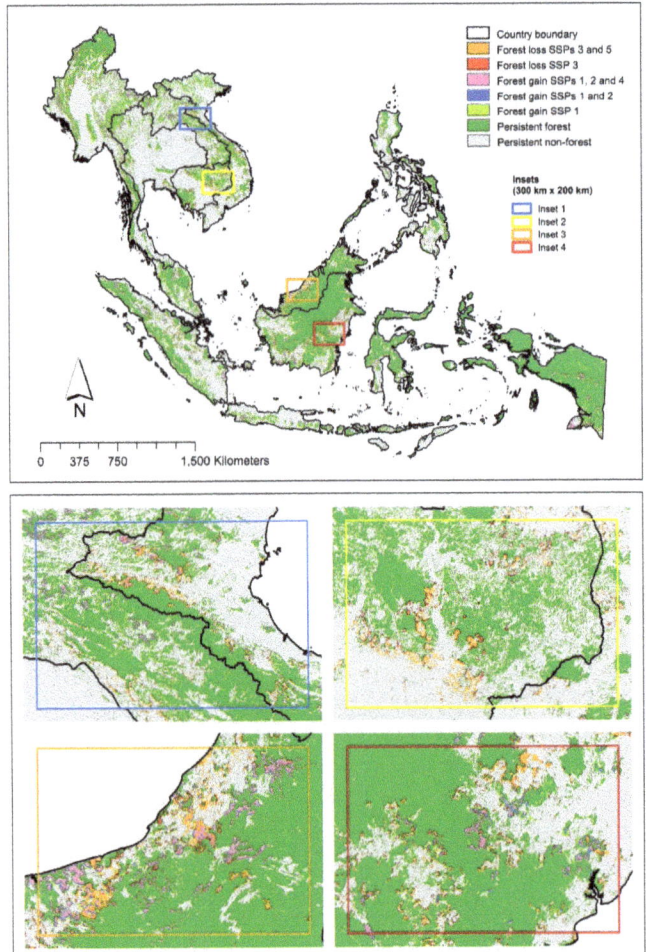

Image 3. *Outcomes of forest management in South East Asia can vary radically according to the goals adopted.*

The "shared socioeconomic pathways" approach adopted in the 2019 study is acknowledged as being a significant advance over previous resource scenario frameworks, particularly the *Intergovernmental Panel on Climate Change (IPCC) Special Report on Emissions Scenarios (SRES)*. As noted by independent research published in *Nature Geoscience* by Zeng et al:

> *"the actual area of forest loss in South East Asia represents 57 percent more loss than current estimations of deforestation made by the IPCC."* [385]

The Image 3 maps are based on satellite data collection and scientific modelling from 2015 - 2019. They illustrate how forest cover can be lost or gained under different management strategies. They highlight how the continued loss of forest cover is not an inevitable process.

The SSP study is considered an example of significant advances over previous resource scenario frameworks because it was able to prepare rigorously documented alternative scenarios for addressing the numerous uncertainties and socioeconomic realities that natural resource management has to correlate and coexist with.

The need for a capacity to prepare alternative scenarios given these uncertainties also correlates with the need for adoption of quantum biophysics principles. Such principles underpin practical ways to work with uncertainty and multiplication effects, as described in Chapter One. The "*Earth as a Light Garden*" model is proposed in that context to meet the resource management challenges of the 21st century.

The need to work with quantum biophysics principles such as "uncertainties" is also apparent once one moves from consideration of forests at the regional and global scale to forests in a particular landscape or place.

For example, as described in a well-balanced review of the implementation and management of the UNESCO World Heritage listed Cultural Landscape of the Bali Province, adequate consideration of uncertainties and socioeconomic factors for the local residents was identified as sorely lacking in this project. This report was published by the Stockholm Environment Institute in 2015.[386] Discussion of this Balinese Cultural Landscape is included later in this chapter.

Forest cover for Light Gardens

South East Asia is one of the three main areas of the world where the sum of the *forest* cover is reported to reach 47 – 54% of the land area. These three areas are highlighted by the white oval shapes on the map in Image 4. South East Asia also contains one of the world's three largest areas of *tropical rainforest* cover.

The dollar value of planting forests is still questioned by some, despite all the evidence. Let's look at this subject from the other side of the coin: no-

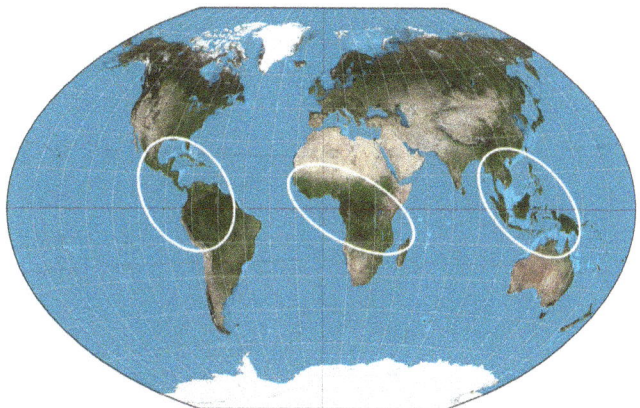

Image 4. *Forest cover is reported to be 47 - 54% of the land area in three regions of the world.*

one disputes the adverse effects of knocking down trees, or of unseasonal droughts. Already there are calls for legislation to retain and manage forests so that rain will fall in other parts of the globe.

For example, Egypt and Ethiopia have been negotiating for many years on how to equitably manage water from the Nile.[387] However efforts to equitably share water will be to no avail if deforestation in the Congo basin of Central Africa means rains do not fall in the Ethiopian highlands. Rain is needed for native plants to grow the forests, which generate the rain and stabilise ecosystems. There are voices saying:

> *"Processes such as moisture recycling…can, and ought, to be governed."* [388]

Similarly, as we move from considering access to *water* to considering *sunlight*, another frontier emerges. This time it is about access to sunlight.

Examples of positive forest management in Malaysia and the Philippines

As illustrated earlier in the Image 3 mapping of South East Asian forests, Malaysia was one of several South East Asian countries that participated in a study published in 2019. That study presented detailed data and modelling to create alternative scenarios for future management of forests. In each country, five different socioeconomic scenarios were used for modelling. The model developed was designed to also inform climate management decisions at the global scale.

The detailed maps produced in the study showing areas of projected changes to forest cover highlighted the important contribution that every patch of forest makes as part of the dynamic global balance between loss and gain of forests. Sometimes the attitude is voiced that what happens in one patch of forest does not matter, given the huge scale of issues involved. These issues include soil carbon conservation, biodiversity and climate management.

However by careful management, Malaysia alone could make a difference of 25% between the best and worst case scenarios likely to be achieved within only a few years, using their existing forest resources.

The difference for Indonesia is even greater. There the difference in outcomes is 88%. There could be a projected net gain of 41% forest cover, or a net loss of 47% forest cover. Applying multiplier effects to those figures for all countries at the global scale, it is immediately apparent that there are huge gains to be made in forest cover and associated climate management factors such as moisture recycling, carbon sequestration and temperature control, if appropriate management is adopted.

In The Philippines, the *National Greening Program* was commenced in 2011. It was recently expanded to cover the period 2016 – 2028. Within that twelve year period, the aim is to reforest all the nation's degraded, unproductive and denuded forestlands. This comprises an area of 7.1 million hectares. The original program that began in 2011 aimed to plant 1.5 billion trees by 2016 on 1.5 million hectares. Building on that experience, the prospect of planting 7.1 million hectares in a twelve year period to 2028 appears quite feasible.

From its inception the program was designed to

> *"reduce poverty, promote food security, environmental stability and biodiversity conservation, and enhance climate change mitigation and adaptation."* [389]

Bali as a Light Garden

While I was immersed in reading about the kaleidoscope of South East Asian cultures, Dr John Tyman's account of living with local people in a Balinese village came to light.[390] He captured a moment in time that provides an entry point to describing traditional and contemporary *Light Gardens* in South East Asia.

Reading his account of village life under the Subak system in Bali we see a living *Light Garden* culture. It is easy to see that the concept of *Light Gardens* isn't something that only exists with reference to 21st century concepts of quantum biophysics. At the time when Dr Tyman was in Bali, the *Light Garden* culture was alive and well. It wasn't an abstract, unattainable idea.

Image 5. *The way of life of the Balinese people includes managing the forests that protect the water supply and the farming terraces and villages through which the water flows.*

The concept of the *Light Garden* principles needs to be feasible in a variety of cultures and locations all around the world. That could mean existing in the lush tropical environment of Bali, or in more arid areas such as African desert fringes. What can be learnt from how the *Light Garden* concept works in the Subak system of Bali then transferred to management of natural resources in other locations? The reasons documented by UNESCO for listing the rice terraces of central Bali as a World Heritage site provide a good starting point to consider in relation to that question.

World Heritage listing for the Cultural Landscape of Bali Province

UNESCO did not list just one or two rice paddies in Bali as typical examples of farming practice. They named the World Heritage Listing as the *"Cultural Landscape of Bali Province: the Subak System as a Manifestation of the Tri Hita Karana Philosophy."* [391] Inherent in this naming is recognition of the need for management of natural resources, including the land, water and light that are needed to grow rice. The Tri Hita Karana Philosophy is based around three interdependent factors:

1. A philosophy to underpin management of natural resources *(The Tri Hita Karana Philosophy)*.
2. An effective system of governance and organisation that is derived from the philosophy. *(The Subak System)*.
3. A landscape scale approach to natural resource management. The listing covers an area of 19,500 hectares. It refers to the *cultural landscape of Bali Province*. Five rice terrace sites with their associated water temples are specifically mentioned within this area. The full area is shown on the Image 6 map.

Water temples are a key way in which the philosophy of *Tri Hita Karana* is literally transplanted to the grass roots level of daily farming practice. Water from springs and canals flows through a multitude of temples into terraced rice paddies. Offerings are made at the temples and a collective respect for the divine symbolic connection between the three *Tri Hita Karana* realms of the spirit, human and natural worlds is maintained.[392]

Image 6. *Map of some temple sites in Bali.*

Water temples in Bali have drawn inspiration from several ancient religious traditions, including Saivasiddhanta and Samkhyā Hinduism, Vajrayana Buddhism and Austronesian cosmology.[393] As illustrated above, different types of temples are located throughout Bali. These include the "Light of God", *Lempuyang Luhar* temple, which is located at the eastern tip of the island, where the morning rays of the sun first reach the island as the Earth rotates.[394] Thus we begin to see how the three elements of the Tri Hita Karana philosophy manifests as the *Light Gardens* of Bali.

Individual farmers are not at liberty to use water as they wish. Decisions about access to water and distribution of water are made through the *Subak* system. Unlike the caste system of India, the Balinese Subak system is based on an egalitarian and democratic decision making process that includes farmers.

The value of this approach has been reiterated during the 21st century as Bali seeks to control the adverse impacts of tourism in the rural areas. These impacts have included water being diverted away from agriculture for tourist use. Farmers have received tempting offers to sell their traditional farming land for tourist redevelopment, thus taking labour and agricultural land out of production. The Subak decision makers have countered this by requesting fees for tourists to visit farming areas. However much progress remains to be made. If tourist fees are to benefit farmers and support continuation of the Subak system, they need to be diverted away from multiple layers of bureaucracy that can intervene. Without the skills and commitment of the farming families who built the Balinese World Heritage site, its ongoing maintenance will run adrift and the site will fall into disrepair.[395]

Light, temples and shrines

In Balinese cosmogony, Lempuyang Luhur is considered the sacred temple of the East and the abode of God Iswara, keeper of the peace. The meaning of the word *Lempuyang* has long been debated but is said to be derived from the words "lampu" (light) and "hyang" (God). Thus the word "lempuyang" means the "Light of God."[396] Another meaning of the word "lempuyang" is derived from the word "emong or empu" that means "guardian." Lempuyang is one of the six major Hindu Temples in Bali and is relatively small in size. The other five main temples are Andakasa Temple, Uluwatu Temple, Watukaru Temple, Ulun Danu Batur Temple and Besakih Temple. Lempuyang has shrines to padmasana and shares a single foundation dedicated to Hyang Gnijaya.[397]

Part of the Ulan Datu Beratan Temple at Lake Beratan is depicted in Image 7. The taller shrine with eleven roofs is for Shiva and the one with three roofs is for the Rice Goddess. Such temples have become popular international tourist destinations during the 21st century, allowing wider appreciation of their sacred religious significance.

Image 7. *Ulan Beratan Temple*

As the rays of dawn strike the high volcanic peaks of Bali, they are reflected in the waters of the sacred crater lakes.

Set at a cool tropical altitude of just over 1,200 metres, Lake Beratan is one of the main crater lakes. Water has flowed south from the lake for centuries, though some forty kilometers of rice terrace landscape. The whole island of Bali is about seventy kilometers wide at this point.

Image 8. *Looking through Lempuyang Ulan towards Mt Agung.*

Despite thousands of water temples being located throughout this landscape, in the 21st century crater lakes are being drained and rice terrace hillsides left dry and barren. This is a poignant reminder of the need to adhere to the traditional Tri Hita Karana system of governance and water allocation. The *Light Garden* principles are available to assist in reinstating an appropriate system of natural resource management on the island, as not all people of influence now follow the Tri Hita Karana philosophy. The *Light Garden* principles respect the traditional Tri Hita Karana system and offer a means of working with it, as well as drawing support from a 21st century scientific approach that may be more familiar to some stakeholders. All the *Light Garden* principles need to be applied if they are to support reinstatement of the Tri Hita Karana system. As highlighted by the observations of Cole and Browne below, not least among these principles is the tenth one: Storage and Sharing of Information:

> *"In particular, user groups are highly diverse, transient and stratified, thereby inhibiting communication and knowledge sharing. This, in combination with weak governance systems and the economic power of the tourism industry, interact to affect declining water resources and the iniquitous impact of this."* [398]

Mount Agung heavily influences that rainfall pattern of the island of Bali and is believed to be home to Mahadewa, the supreme manifestation of Lord Shiva. Shiva is considered by many Hindus as the supreme god. Balinese shrines are located so that they face towards Mt Agung. An illustration of one such shrine is included in Image 2 of the first chapter of this book and Dr Tyman's work provides further illustrations. [399]

> *"Mount Meru is a sacred cosmological mountain that bears heaven on its summit and is considered to be the centre of all universes; physical, metaphysical, and spiritual…Some people believe that [Mt Agung] was first a part of Mount Meru brought to Bali by the first Hindus."* [400]

In addition to the mountains and temples, there is no understanding Bali without the trees, shrines and rice terraces. Inundated by the temptations of Western culture to forego their traditional ways, the villagers have never forgotten how pleasant and sensible it is to live in villages where trees provide shelter of every form.

Image 9. *Shrines within a Balinese family village compound*

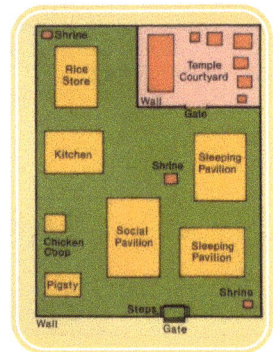

Image 10. *Plan and photos of a typical Balinese family compound in the Subak system village. The photographs are not all taken from the same site.*

Image 11. *Notes 1 - 10 below describe the extent to which the ten Light Garden parameters are present in this traditional Balinese village shrine.*

1. **Energy.** The sun is the energy source in this village.

2. **Space.** The shrine courtyard has a central 'light garden' space for activities.

3. **Waves and particles.** Waves of devotees come and go through the shine.

4. **Lines, Patterns and Probabilities.** The thatched roofs of the shrine follow traditional patterns and the design is highly probable to be the same as other village buildings.

5. **Multiplication effects.** This courtyard is framed by a series of thatched roofs which together create a multiplication effect.

6. **Entanglement and focal points.** The shrine is a focal point. It also relies for its significance upon the courtyard in which it is located. This is an example of entanglement.

7. **Perception and Measurement.** Careful measurements and human mindsets appreciative of the cultural significance of what was built were used to construct this devotional shrine

8. **Context and Environment.** The materials in this village come from the forest and trees that enclose it. The scale of the construction fits within the spaces between the coconut palms and other the trees. These factors help to provide a comfortable and ecologically sound framework for life.

9. **Human use.** "Visitors from the "developed world" sometimes write off Balinese beliefs as "superstition": but if the purpose of religion is to help people live in harmony…with one another and with their environment…it certainly works in Bali, and works well." [401]

10. **Storage and sharing of information.** The design of this village and the lives of the people are based on information stored in the minds of the people and Hindu traditions.

A Light garden landscape

Although it is the terraced Balinese rice paddies that tend to catch the attention of visitors, in reality there is a complex land use relationship between forests, rice paddies and gardens around dwellings. For example Dr John Tyman described one property as: "a tropical garden of 2,000 square metres...a rice growing area of 3,000 square metres - and not least of all, a lily pond where they raised fish, frogs and lily roots to add to the diet." [402]

Dr Tyman's description is a good illustration of the *Light Garden* concept where, light is harvested for a complex series of interdependent uses. The intensive Balinese agricultural system is acknowledged as likely to be the most productive in South East Asia.

The area of land actually devoted to rice paddies in full sunlight is roughly equivalent to the land area managed with more tree cover. Land with tree cover includes forest water catchments, plus trees and gardens around and within the rice paddies and dwellings.

The Balinese fish pond in Image 15 below tells the tale of a culture where religion is reflected in the way daily activities are carried out. The lotus is a symbolic, sacred flower that grows unsullied out of the mud as it reaches for the light. Its leaves shelter aquatic life and its roots are also edible, making the harvesting of light in the Balinese fish pond much more diversified and ecologically stable than in a modern trout farm, for example. Chickens roam the gardens around the pond, while geese chase frogs in the rice paddies and cattle assist with the ploughing.

Image 12. (Top left) *Ducks feed happily around the rice paddies during daylight hours.*

Image 13. (Top right) *The Balinese rice terrace landscape.*

Image 14. (Bottom left) *Fish, frogs and lily roots from the pond all add to the diet.*

Image 15. (Bottom right) *A Balinese lily pond*

Light Gardens: living in harmony

"In Bali people don't just talk about religion, they live it." [403]

Making music for the village, the older village residents depicted below are playing in a local gamelan (orchestra). The same men are likely to also be seen ploughing their rice paddies. The music and the farm work has artistic and religious significance, so not surprisingly, the artwork depicted below right includes a shrine amidst the rice paddies. These shrines are a common sight in Bali.

Meanwhile, a woman quietly draws water from the village stream that flows past a stone paved courtyard. A venerated Tulsi plant grows behind her. This plant is worshipped by Hindus in the morning and in the evening.

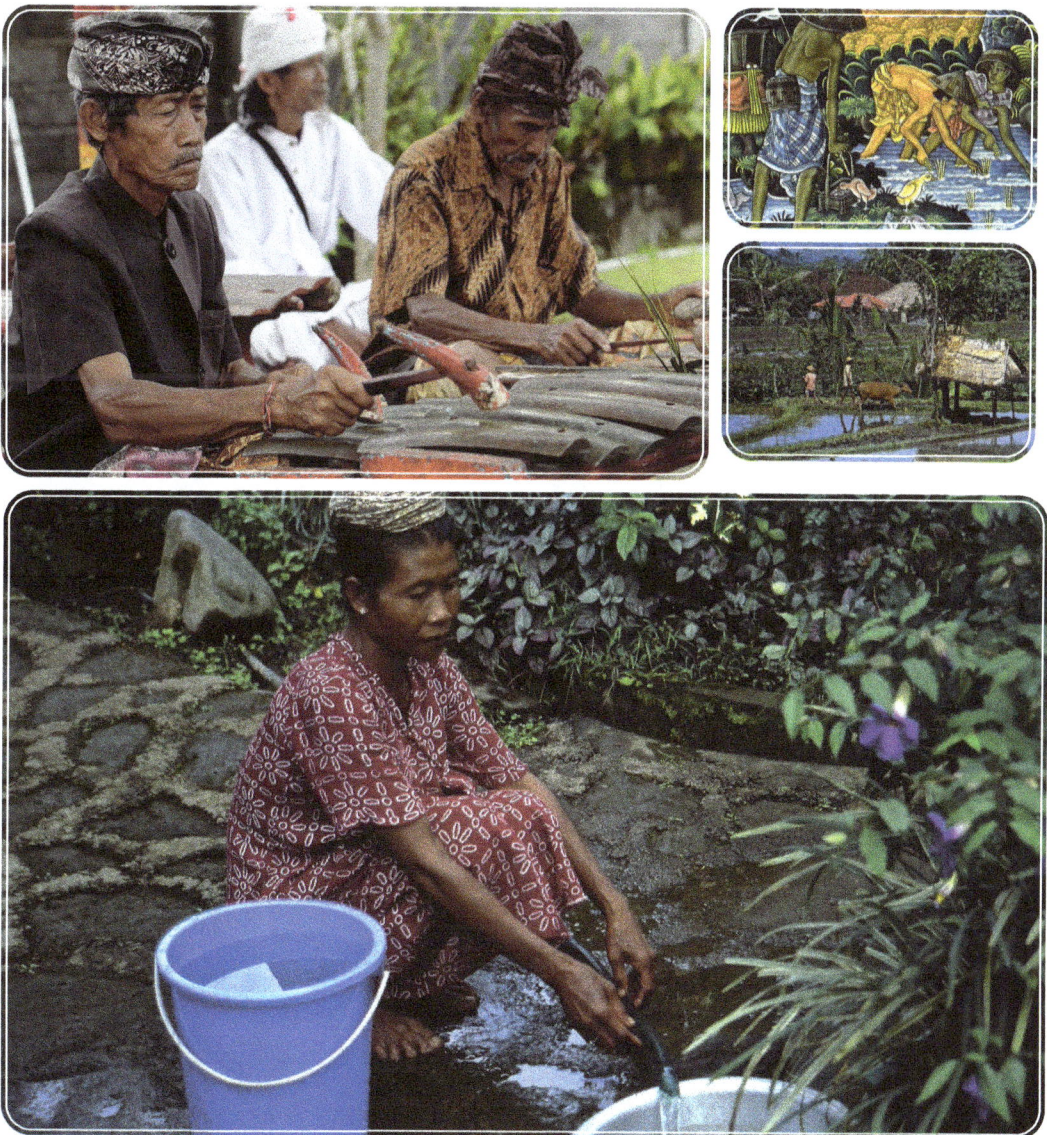

Image 16. *A collage of Balinese life under the subak system.*

"Visitors from the "developed world" sometimes write off Balinese beliefs as "superstition": but if the purpose of religion is to help people live in harmony...with one another and with their environment...it certainly works in Bali, and works well. Christian missionaries were sent here long ago but were unable to make any converts." [404]

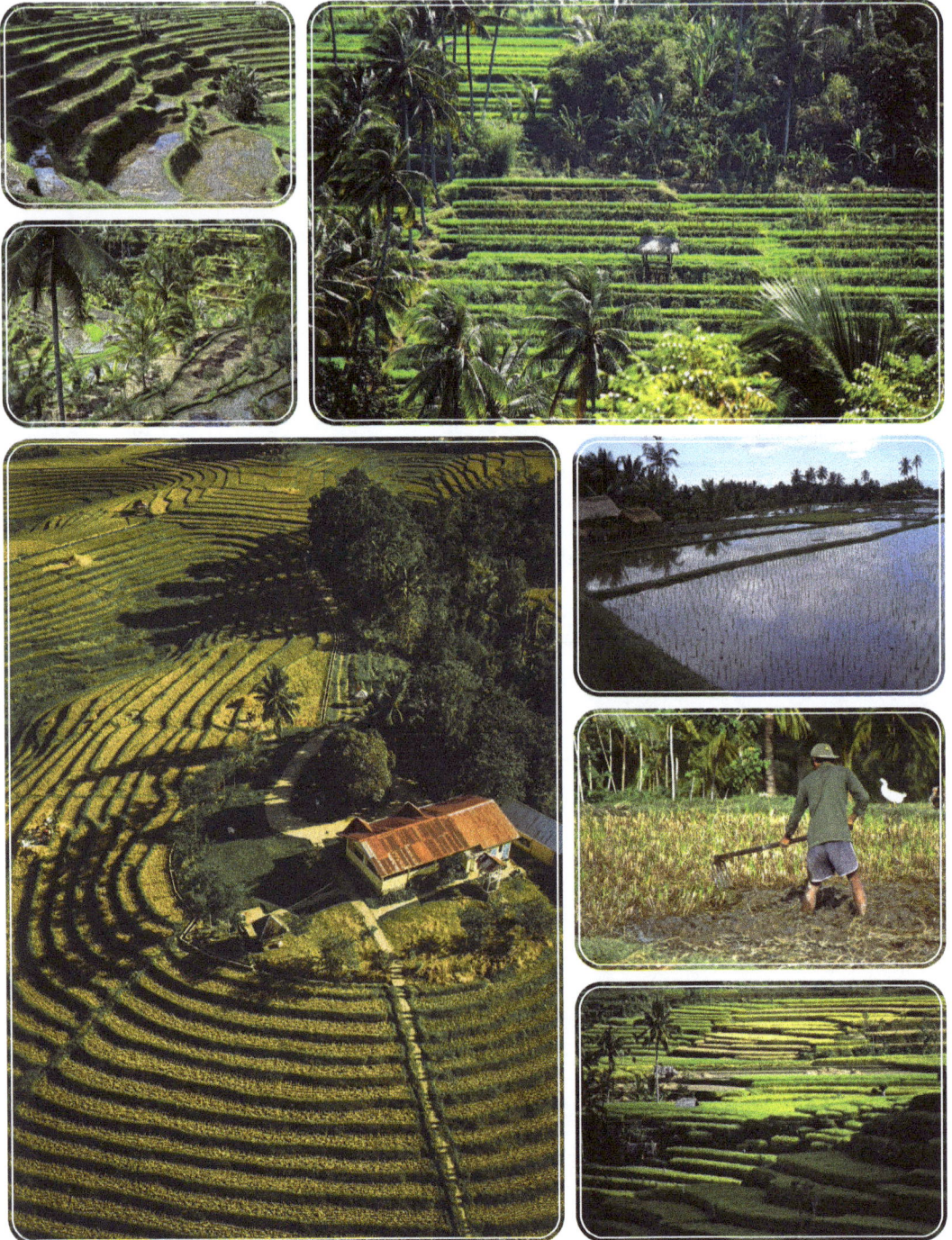

Image 17. *A collage of images from the rice terrace landscape of Bali*

11

The Light Garden in the 21st Century

In the 21st century, the term dysbiosis has been used to describe both an unbalanced internal human gut biome and unbalanced ecosystems that threaten to collapse.

In the 21st century, regenerative farming, agroecology, carbon farming, seaweed farming, fisheries and similar progressive agricultural, forestry and resource management movements are starting to make a big difference to the direction in which climate change and natural resource management are heading. Combined with proven traditional techniques, these movements also are well within reach of making a net positive contribution to global climate change management.

Food production and food security on land and water

As well as making net positive contributions to the management of global climate change and use of natural resources, some food producers are also helping to redefine our consciousness about what human food production entails. Giving an excellent example of this when she spoke in 2020, seaweed farmer Pia Winberg said:

> *"And so that's why this seaweed is really exciting because we can include it as a core ingredient and it's a core new crop for Australia, it's not just a novel little gourmet side, it can actually have a big impact because all of the carbon in this product that is now in the seaweed is much more efficient production of food, and so we can really eat our way to better health and sustainability."* [405]

Pia is a research fellow at the University of Wollongong and head of PhycoHealth, a company that farms and processes seaweed in Australia. During the fifty years prior to 2020, the annual global production of seaweed rose to become the world's second largest aquaculture product. It was second only to the fish in terms of the volume of production.[406] In countries such as China and Japan, seaweed can provide up to 10% of the total human diet.

Pia Winberg was speaking about the multiple benefits of her seaweed farming enterprise. Although these include the efficient production of food, other benefits to the economy, community, human health and the broader environment are just as important. This approach to food production heralds the rejuvenated 21st century awareness of the role of food producers as land and water managers. They work with a team of other people in the wider community. Under the *Light Garden* model, these food producers are paid by the broader community for any net positive contributions they make to global climate change management and resource management, as well as for the food they produce!

Commenting upon Pia's achievements in revitalising a whole network of local industries which literally flow into and out of her seaweed farm, Robyn Williams exclaimed:

> *"…if you were to have told ten years ago…make seaweed the basis for a major set of industries, would they have been amazed?"* [407]

This network of local industries is an exciting example of *Light Garden* principles in action. Decisions are based on criteria such as managing energy flows to stop carbon emissions and seeking positive entanglement between different industries and components to rejuvenate living systems. How the ten *Light Garden* principles are translated into a set of decision making criteria is summarised in Image 2 of Chapter 12.

One *Light Garden* decision making criteria that is relevant to Pia's PhycoHealth's seaweed enterprise is: *Manage energy flows to stop carbon emissions.* Healthy seaweed traps dissolved carbon dioxide. Seaweed has been reported as being more efficient at trapping carbon dioxide than terrestrial forests. Seaweed is not subject to wildfires either! Nevertheless, seaweed grown under aquaculture conditions is quite susceptible to disease and predation by creatures such as sea urchins.

A 2016 study estimated that about 11% of global macroalgae is permanently sequestered in the ocean. The bulk of that, (about 90%), is deposited in the deep sea, while the rest sinks into coastal marine sediments.[408] So it is difficult for scientists to be specific about how much carbon is sequestered by seaweed. PhycoHealth's seaweed farm also contributes in other more easily quantified ways to natural resource management.

It is co-located with a wheat processing plant so that the ethanol and nutrient by-products of the wheat processing plant become renewable energy inputs to the seaweed farm. These are combined with fresh seawater and sunshine to power the growth of highly nutritious, edible microalgae, (which is otherwise known as seaweed).[409] Microalgae have been described as probably the most nutrient dense plants on the planet:

> *"amazing food-grade phytoplankton whole food products that basically have an amazing array of nutrients, we are talking omega-3 long-chain fatty acids, proteins, carotenoids, vitamins, minerals. Single cell microalgae are probably the most nutrient dense plants on the planet and that's because they are primordial food, they are some of the first living cells on the planet and the start of biology on planet Earth."* [410]

Food security is another major concept within food production chains at the local and global scales. In a similar way to how the role of food producers can be expanded to include the role of paid natural resource managers, our concept of what food security entails can be expanded when utilising *Light Garden* principles. For example, Associate Professor Hamish Quantin, a world fisheries expert, said in 2020:

> *"We tend to think of food security as being about agriculture. Whereas if you are in Indonesia, the Pacific, Asia and many other places, food security is what you can pull out of the ocean and then you can supplement with other stuff off the land."* [411]

In these countries, fish provides 50% of the protein in the human diet. At the global scale, fish is the primary protein source for 35% for the world's population.[412] At a time when United Nations statistics show that 90% of the world's fish stocks are over fished, fully fished or fully depleted, this is of great concern.[413] As sea levels rise during the coming decades, the extent of wetlands may increase. The role of wetlands in sequestering carbon and food production may become more widely appreciated and more actively managed during this period.[414]

Food security often entails supporting many related factors such as localization of the economy; vigorous enforcement of legislation to protect natural resources such as fish stocks; building up local biodiversity and planning for resilience to cope in times of stress. Refer to Chapters One and Twelve for more detail on that subject. Food security forms an integral part of the United Nations Food and Agricultural Organisation's (FAO's) work. Their work is described in further detail in Image 2 of this chapter. This image includes an interesting comparison of the FAO's *Agroecology Principles* with the *Light Garden* principles. The comparison reveals that there is much in common between these two sets of principles.

Regenerative Farming, organic farming, Agroecology, Forestry and Human Health

"Livestock grazing is the single largest land use on the planet, occupying about a quarter of Earth's landscape." [415]

An estimated 14 percent of global greenhouse gas emissions arise from agriculture.[416] In New Zealand, where agricultural production is a significant part of the economy, 34 percent of the nation's greenhouses gases are emitted by livestock such as sheep and cattle.[417] Additional greenhouse gas emissions arise as agricultural produce is transported using fossil fuels. At the global scale, approximately 30% of greenhouse gas emissions arise from the food system, which transfers food from fields and oceans into the hands of those who eat it. An important factor to remember here is that smallholder farmers produce 70% of the world's food, and ten percent of food is foraged. For further details, please refer to earlier chapters with detailed examples in Africa and India.

Within this larger picture, the world's first fully organic state has been declared in Sikkim, which is a northern Himalayan State of India. Here government legislation supports 100% of farms to be organic. In comparison, approximately one percent of farms in the USA were certified organic by the year 2020.[418] The role of the government has been vital in Sikkim. In the USA, the Marin Agricultural Land Trust provides a good example of what is being done at the regional scale to produce food, reduce carbon emissions, sequester carbon and support healthy living ecosystems.

The Marin Agricultural Land Trust does extensive monitoring and research in partnership with farmers and many regional government agencies. Positive contributions to support living systems have been made on agricultural land, and the whole regional land management process has become more efficient. This has been possible because of scalable resource management solutions that extend beyond the farm gate. As one participant said:

> **"Small changes in management practices can yield big results**. *The Marin Carbon Project has shown that a single application of compost can sequester carbon in soils, increase plant production, and if scaled to 5% of California's rangelands could offset up to 10% of the commercial and residential energy sector."* [419]

The work of the Marin Agricultural Land Trust's, scalable compost management protocols shows

> *"...compost applications not only directly benefit rangeland managers through increased productivity, but also remove agricultural waste from the waste stream. By working with dairy farms to capture and process liquid manure, land applications of unstable compost can be avoided in favor of green-waste enriched solid compost, keeping costs to apply industrial fertilizers down."* [420]

Here we see an example of making decisions based on all the *Light Garden* criteria. For example

- Criteria Number six - Proactively seek positive entanglement to rejuvenate life systems.
- Criteria Number one - Manage energy flows to stop carbon emissions and support life.
- Criteria Number five - Make decisions based on quantum biophysics multiplier effects.

With reports of one acre of farmland being paved over every minute in the USA these Marin Agricultural Land Trust solutions counter that trend by increasing the economic viability of using land and water for agriculture. Benefits arise for individual landowners and the wider community because more people are becoming aware of regenerative agriculture's multipurpose benefits. The benefits are also apparent of planning urban areas, (which produce waste), in partnership with farmland, (where it can potentially be utilised as stable compost if appropriate technology is utilised). These concepts have been applied in the Localisation movement to develop organic urban farming projects in the 21st century. Some examples of these projects in North America and India were discussed in earlier chapters.

The non-opioid hemp plant provides another example of regenerative farming practices that have multiple associated benefits. As reported by Ellen Brown,

> *"Industrial hemp has been proven to absorb more CO2 per hectare than any forest or commercial crop, making it the ideal carbon sink. It can be grown on a wide scale on nutrient poor soils with very small amounts of water and no fertilizers."* [421]

A whole farm planted with hemp would not support local biodiversity but used in moderation, hemp crops can be managed in conjunction with the goal of creating carbon sinks. Hemp plants also have a long taproot, which helps to stabilize and regenerate the soil. As well as the excellent carbon sequestration properties of hemp, Ellen also describes its extensive range of uses. These include the production of biofuels and biodegradable replacements for many plastics. Her account of how Henry Ford designed his first car to run on ethanol produced from hemp is interesting. Ford was later forced to amend the design of his car so that it ran on fossil fuels.

In other parts of the USA, instead of regenerative farming that builds up the soil, tons of soil have been lost from the nation's most productive farming areas. For example, in Iowa during the course of the 20th Century, the average topsoil depth on farms decreased by one half, from around 35-45cm to 15-20cm.[422] Blown away by the wind, washed away by rain, compacted by farm vehicles, acidified by inappropriate use of fertilisers...the causes for this loss have been well documented. Recent planting of prairie strips and trees on cropland has proved to be effective in reversing this unsustainable loss in topsoil quality and quantity.

Similarly, attempts have been made to slow the desertification of vast areas in North America, Central Asia, Africa and other parts of the planet by similar means. Nonetheless, much remains to be done. The scale of this work has many similarities and a common purpose with planting 1.2 trillion native trees to combat climate change. This extent of tree planting was identified as the most feasible, immediate way to combat global climate change in an international 2019 research project described earlier on page 41.

Regenerative Agriculture has become a growing international movement in the 21st century and seeks to address the issues that have impacted Bali, Ukraine, and many other places. It has recognised the pressures on farmers that arise due to the consequences of activities such as international trade treaties and tourism. Instead of being able to focus on maintaining and regenerating soil health, many

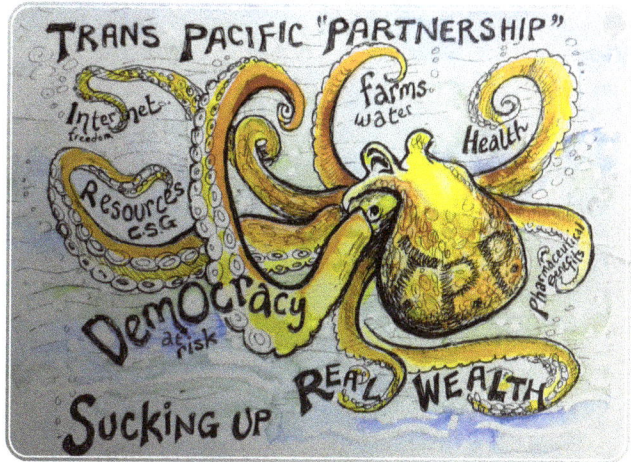

Image 1. *Regenerative agricultural groups have joined with others in seeking fair, not exploitative deals for water, farms, trade, democracy and natural resource management. Cartoon by Dr Liz Elliott.*

farmers feel economic pressures to produce the highest possible short term yields from their farms; to sell their farms or abandon them.

Regenerative agricultural groups are demonstrating that there is another way for farms to remain viable. They focus on partnerships with other businesses and government where their contributions to the public realm are valued and rewarded. They do things such as provide employment; sequester carbon in soils; enrich soils through livestock management; access solar energy and regenerate local biodiversity.

These activities directly align with the first of the *Light Garden* decision making criteria: manage energy flows to support living systems and stop carbon emissions. Similarly, regenerative agriculture aligns with *Light Garden* decision making criteria number four: make decisions based on the probability that ecosystems will endure. At the local scale, Polyface Farms in the USA has some good solutions for how to plan budgets, manage the environment, and create a harmonious society with meaningful work for all. These solutions are completely in accordance with *Light Garden* principles. As the owner of Polyface Farms has said:

> *"A business that can't or won't hire its neighbors due to poor working conditions, low pay, repetitive motion sickness, or anything else, is not neighbor friendly. Redesigning the business to fit, to nest into the local ecology takes innovation, but anything less will create social, environmental, and pathogenic upheavals."* [423]

The integration of agricultural practices with the local workforce and community is a big issue in Europe. Every year the European Union allocates billions of euros towards agricultural production. How this is done has come under the public spotlight in recent decades for many reasons, including outbreaks of diseases such as mad cow disease and the covid 19 pandemic.

> *"One of the biggest obstacles to the roll-out of agroecology in Europe, is the EU Common Agricultural Policy, the CAP. The CAP distributes roughly €60 billion per year, or around 36% of the entire EU budget, to agricultural businesses and farmers."* [424]

Agroecology & Light Garden Comparison

FAO Agroecology Principles

Light Garden Principles

Diversity
Diversity
Diversification is key to agroecological transitions to ensure food security and nutrition while conserving, protecting and enhancing natural resources.

None of the *Light Garden* principles specifically articulate this FAO element, although all of them support it. Diversification is a "key component of agroecology to promote and can contribute to food security and nutrition while conserving, protecting and enhancing natural resources."

Co-creation and sharing of knowledge
Storage and Sharing of Information
Agricultural innovations respond better to local challenges when they are co-created through participatory processes.

This FAO element is more comprehensive than the *Light Garden* principle of Storage and Sharing of Information. The FAO approach emphasizes the value of stakeholder participation and "knowledge" not information.

Synergies
Multiplication Effects
Building Synergies enhances key functions across food systems, supporting production and multiple ecosystem services.

This FAO element is quite similar to the *Light Garden* principle of the *Multiplication Effects*. The emphasis in the FAO synergies is in design of agroecology properties; the use of natural resources and development of multi-stakeholder partnerships.

Efficiency
Energy (as in free abundant forms)
Innovative agroecological practices produce more using less external resources.

The FAO notes that Agroecological systems improve the efficiency in the use of natural resources and advocates to... and to turn to those that are abundant and free, such as solar radiation, atmospheric carbon and nitrogen. Energy from sunlight, one of the *free abundant forms* of energy, is a focus of the *Light Garden* approach.

Recycling
Entanglement and Focal Points
More recycling means agricultural production with lower economic and environmental costs.

Although none of the *Light Garden* principles focus on recycling, the principle of *Entanglement and Focal Points* is relevant. This is because biological recycling tends to draw materials for recycling into focal points, where they can be efficiently processed.

Resilience
Lines, Patterns and Probabilities
Enhanced resilience of people, communities and ecosystems is key to sustainable food and agricultural systems.

Light Garden principles support resilience because they prioritize patterns and probabilities for rejuvenation of living systems. This is similar to Agroecological practices that "aim to work with the biological complexity of agricultural systems to allow the ecosystem to self regulate.

Human and Social Values
Waves and Particles
Protecting and improving rural livelihoods, equity and social well-being is essential for sustainable food and agricultural systems

The FAO emphasis is on improving livelihoods, including income generation and equity. The *Light Garden* principle of *Waves and Particles* supports this through communities acting in groups as Waves - and as individuals working as "particles."

Culture and Food Traditions
Allow Space and Time
By supporting healthy, diversified and culturally appropriate diets, agroecology contributes to food security and nutrition while maintaining the health of ecosystems.

The methodology of the Light Garden book looked at different cultures and considered the feasibility of applying the *Light Garden* model in a diverse range of cultures and allow the space and time for living systems to rejuvenate. This is compatible with the FAO principles.

Responsible Governance
Human Use (Restrained)
Sustainable food and agriculture requires responsible and effective governance mechanisms at different scales - from local to national to global.

The *Light Garden* model includes the concept of restrained human use of natural resources, within the capacity of the Earth's natural systems to support it. Responsible governance is a key requirement to achieve this.

Circular and Solidarity Economy
Multiplication Effects
Circular and solidarity economies that reconnect producers and consumers provide innovative solutions for living within our planetary boundaries while ensuring the social foundation for inclusive and sustainable development.

The FAO emphasis is one strengthening connections in localised economies between food producers and the people who eat the food. The *Light Garden* approach supports this but also aims for a net positive rejuvenation of resources.

Image 2. *FAO Agroecology principles and comparable Light Garden principles.*

In one of many studies, researchers at University College London have identified agricultural practices as one of the primary drivers of the worldwide trend towards degraded habitats.[425] The population of soil microorganisms often sharply dives when land is placed under industrial agriculture.

Individual species exist under stressful conditions in such habitats. Stress makes them less able to contribute to a self-regulating, stable ecosystem and more likely to carry viruses.

Stress also affects the human body in a similar way. However, in addition to that, humans and other species are losing the protective framework that comes from living in self-regulating ecosystems. When shocks ripple through self-regulating ecosystems, often they can be absorbed like ripples in a pond. Harking to the principles of quantum biophysics which inspired the *Light Garden* model, every part of the biological field interacts with the whole field. An analogy for this was described and illustrated in Chapter Two: touch one part of an innerspring mattress and the ripple effect spreads through the whole.

As described in Chapter Two, life forms communicate through the universal field. The genes of fungi, bacteria and protozoa, (many of which live in soil), vastly outnumber other life forms. Viruses have long dispersed their vital genetic information throughout the planet via air and water currents. The connection is immediately apparent between the health of microorganisms in soil, air, water, and in larger creatures such as humans. Millions of microorganisms work together to maintain stable, biodiverse ecosystems inside our bodies and outside them in the wider world as well.

In the 21st century, the term dysbiosis has been used to describe both an unbalanced internal human gut biome and unbalanced ecosystems that threaten to collapse. Thus in order for healthy, self-regulating ecosystems to continue to provide a protective framework for individual species, (including people), there is a need for proactive action. For example, a significant percentage of the annual European Union budget for agricultural production needs to be directed towards the rejuvenation of healthy ecosystems, including healthy soils. The *Light Garden* model provides one tool for this purpose.

"Although the CAP [the Common Agricultural Policy of the European Union], has integrated some environmental concerns over the years, strong voices from science, civil society and thinktanks sharply criticise the policy's failure to shift EU agriculture towards true sustainability.

"The way the many billion euros are distributed is currently under negotiation, as European Ministers of Agriculture and MEPs [Members of the European Parliament] are discussing a reform of the CAP for the period 2021-2027." [426]

At the global scale, the United Nations Food and Agriculture Organisation (FAO) released its innovative Agroecology principles in 2019.[427] These ten principles have many similarities with *Light Garden* principles, as described in the diagram on the previous page..

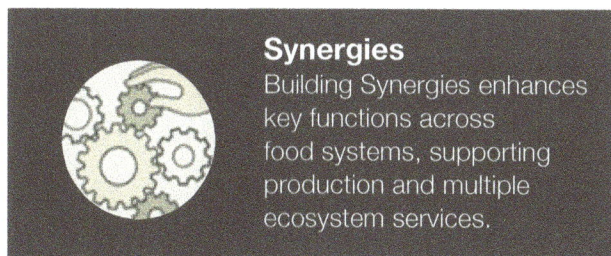

Synergies
Building Synergies enhances key functions across food systems, supporting production and multiple ecosystem services.

Image 3. *An example of similarities between the FAO Agroecology principles and Light Garden principles. This Agroecology principle is quite similar to the Light Garden principle of the Multiplication Effects that arise in natural systems where the whole is greater than the sum of the parts. The emphasis in the Agroecology synergies is in design of agroecology properties; the use of natural resources and development of multi-stakeholder partnerships.*

LIVING SOIL VS. DEAD SOIL
WHY SOIL MATTERS TO FARMERS AND THE ENVIRONMENT

CANBERRA CITY FARM

5 Core Principles of Regenerative Agriculture

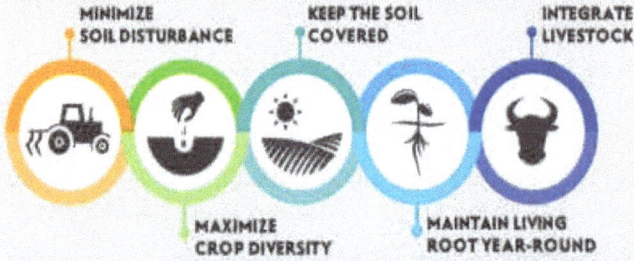

MINIMIZE SOIL DISTURBANCE

KEEP THE SOIL COVERED

INTEGRATE LIVESTOCK

MAXIMIZE CROP DIVERSITY

MAINTAIN LIVING ROOT YEAR-ROUND

3 Key Outcomes

Improve soil health

Foster biodiversity

Promote economic resilience in farming communities

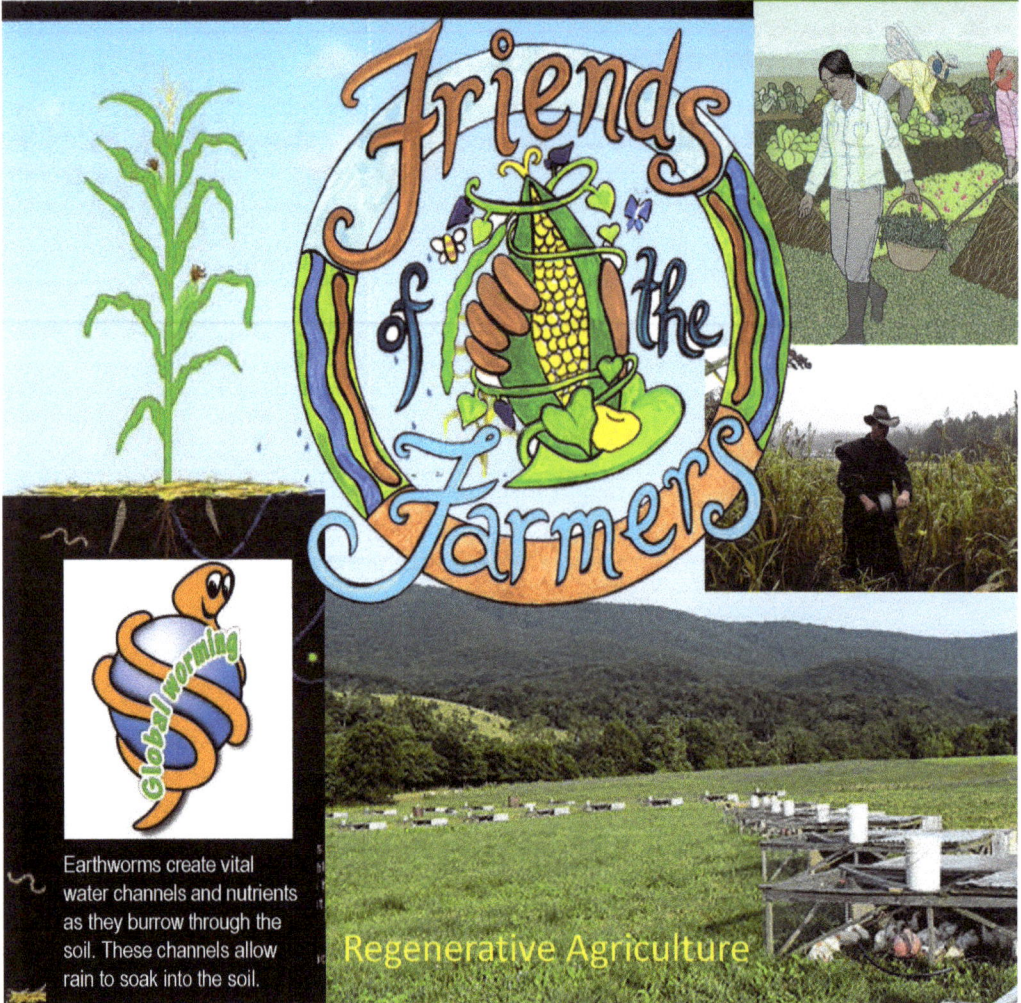

Global warning

Earthworms create vital water channels and nutrients as they burrow through the soil. These channels allow rain to soak into the soil.

Regenerative Agriculture

Image 4. *Regenerative agriculture*

Managing fire, wetlands and water

Wetlands are crucial components of ecosystems for many reasons, including carbon sequestration and water regulation. Speaking about the interaction between planning for the use of fire, water, land and sunlight, Andrew Noble, former director of the Water, Land and Ecosystems project in Sri Lanka, described a nexus between water and solar power:

> *"Solar buyback provisions have tremendous potential to support aquifer health and address the 'energy- water nexus' in the developing world. "I feel this is potentially a 'game changer' in addressing the challenge of over-extraction of groundwater, a challenge that not only India is facing."* [428]

Over-extraction of groundwater is just one of multiple issues that can be addressed more effectively by applying the combined set of decision making criteria in the *Light Garden* model. Mulloon Creek near Canberra in Australia offers a contemporary example of another model being developed to address this problem holistically. It is funded by the Australian Federal Government under the United Nations Sustainable Development Solutions Network (SDSN). In 2020 it was one of five long term case study projects in this global network. The network aims to develop guidelines for sustainable, profitable and productive farming.

The flow of water through the landscape at Mulloon Creek is a primary determinant of the activity that takes place, just as it is in the Balinese Rice Terrace landscape that was described in Chapter Ten:

> *"Central to the system is slowing flow in the creek with "leaky weirs". These force water back into the bed and banks of the creek, which rehydrates the floodplain. This rehydrated floodplain is then said to be more productive and…"* [429]

Image 5. *A Wetland*

Instead of slowing the flow of water through the landscape, far too often wetlands and peatlands have been drained for agriculture, urban development and other land uses. Draining these areas has occurred at the expense of the comprehensive ecological benefits these areas formerly provided. Wetlands can be good carbon sinks, for example. The scientific findings in the aftermath of the devastating wildfire in 2016 at Fort McMurray in Alberta, Canada have words of warning:

> *"Where mossy wetlands (also called peatlands) had been converted by humans into stands of tall black spruce trees, the fire burned with a higher intensity and deep into the ground. Huge stocks of carbon that had been sequestered in the wetlands over thousands of years were lost in the inferno."* [430]

The significance of converting mossy wetlands into forest plantations was that the wetlands were first drained. As the plantation trees grew year by year, their roots penetrated more deeply into the ground and drained more moisture from the wetlands. The groundwater table was lowered and the original, spongy, water-retentive wetland peat species died out. It was replaced by a dry, flammable species of peat. In what has been recorded as Canada's most costly disaster, a subsequent wildfire in 2016 raced through 1.5 million acres and caused US $7.4 billion of damage.

In Bali, trees, shrines and gardens are woven intricately throughout the landscape. In the different European climate context, agroforestry is gaining momentum as an agricultural practice that also consciously weaves trees through the landscape. Tree crops are cultivated with interplanting of smaller plants and grazed pastures. For example, corn might be planted under walnut trees, or sheep gazed around cork trees. With these practices gaining momentum during the early 21st century, the European Agroforestry Federation has become quite active. The scope of their work overlaps with traditional agriculture, forestry and agroecology. In such multiple land use landscape mosaics, management can appear to be more complicated. However, the set of *Light Garden* principles provides a simple ten step process for navigating through that diversity and towards rejuvenated biodiversity and sustainable human resource use within a culture of restraint.

Urban and urban-fringe environments

Bearing in mind that 55% of the world's population lived in urban areas by the year 2018, the remainder of the chapter is devoted to examples of urban and urban fringe projects that demonstrate management of the Earth's natural resources in accordance with *Light Garden* principles.

a) The first project considers the application of *Light Garden* principles in the design of the city of Canberra in Australia.

b) Secondly, examples of trends in the construction of translucent, *Light Garden* projects during the 20th and 21st centuries are considered. These include iconic projects such as the Sky Domes in Singapore.

c) The third part of this chapter traces the rise of multipurpose, sizeable inner city sites with visions for sustainability during the 20th and 21st century.

d) The fourth set of projects focuses on trees and sunlight as part of opportunities for urban renewal and addressing urban blight.

a) Urban: An example of Light Garden principles in the design of the city of Canberra

A century after the construction of Canberra began, wild kangaroos are still frequently seen in the grasslands of public open space in the city. Retreating to nearby hillside bushland to rest, these are protected, wild creatures. They forage freely in the road verges, quieter parklands and larger institutional sites, such as the Australian War Memorial, which adjoins the Mt Ainslie bushland reserve in central Canberra.

For reasons such as this, there is value in looking more closely at the history of how the city of Canberra came into existence and to what extent *Light Garden* principles are reflected in that process. Certainly, principle number eight, *consider context and environment,* is apparent in how the human population of the city co-exists with wild native creatures.

The formerly self-governing British colonies of Australian States become one national federation in the year 1901. The newly formed government of the Commonwealth of

Image 6. *An Australian road sign depicting a wild kangaroo.*

Australia selected an inland sheep station as the site for construction of a new national capital. An international competition for the design of the city was then announced. The winning entry for the competition was prepared by Landscape Architect Walter Burley Griffin and his wife, Marion Mahoney Griffin. Resonating with the Australian fondness for native vegetation and landscape, Walter said:

> *"I am what may be termed a naturalist in architecture. I do not believe in any school of architecture. I believe in architecture that is the logical outgrowth of the environment in which the building in mind is to be located."* [431]

Walter and Marion had both worked in the preeminent American Architect Frank Lloyd Wright's office before winning this competition, so their talent and dedication must have been apparent from the early stages of their careers. In 1911, Marion prepared superb watercolour illustrations of their design for Canberra. As illustrated in Image 7, the watercolours bear a striking resemblance to photographs of the city taken just over a century later in 2018. For example, the watercolour proportions for the design of the proposed new Australian Parliament House align almost perfectly with the current building, where it sits against a backdrop of forested hills. Here we see a keen appreciation by the Griffins of the relevance of *Light Garden* principle number seven, which considers human perception and measurement.

The quantum biophysics principle of entanglement in perception and measurement, (where one phenomenon cannot be perceived or measured separately from another,) is also apparent. As one looks down Anzac Avenue towards Parliament House, Lake Burley Griffin is seen in the mid-ground of the view. Parliament House was placed at a suitable height above the lake so that it would be seen as a building sitting above the lake within a broader, vegetated landscape. Each of these elements in the landscape contributes to the overall balance and none are perceived or measured separately.

Canberra's street layout design is illustrated in a watercolour image included in Image 12. The curving, trees lined boulevards of inner Canberra and the nodes of urban activity have been compared to the Parisian style of street layout. Other observers have commented that the inner city of Canberra has an Art Nouveau feel to the design. This is not surprising, given that in the years preceding 1911, the Art Nouveau movement was at its peak.

Some have criticised the city of Canberra for not feeling as though it has grown organically, in the manner of beautiful old towns that developed over centuries in Europe and elsewhere. Given that Canberra has existed for less than one hundred years, and now includes far greater biological diversity than the sheep station that preceded it, this lack of historical depth to the urban fabric might be forgiven.

Lively medium density precincts were part of the original design for Canberra. However, they were one of many features erased from the original plan by city officials whose priorities lay with the construction of expansive bungalow suburbs that spread outwards from the city centre. This less dense form of urban development could be interpreted as providing more *space and time* for ecosystems to regenerate, in accordance with *Light Garden* principle number two.

However one of the key messages of the *Light Garden* model is restraint in human use of natural resources. Many 21st century observers would comment that restraint has not been exercised in how the new bungalow suburbs have spread across the rolling landscape that enfolds the city's perimeter. Medium density urban development may well be the most appropriate urban form to achieve appropriate restraint in the use of natural resources in Canberra, after a more thorough analysis utilising all the *Light Garden* principles.

Construction of the city of Canberra commenced in 1914. Since then, the space and time needed for the city to develop also have been impacted by *Light Garden* principle number 9: *Human Perception and Measurement.* For example, after an intervening period of over forty years during which Australia participated in the First and Second World Wars, construction of Lake Burley Griffin commenced in 1957. The lake is a central feature of the cultural landscape of the city. It was built along the Molonglo River, a small watercourse that flowed through the site before construction of the city began.

The Australian Prime Minister of the time, Sir Robert Menzies, named the new lake *Lake Burley Griffin*. Menzies declined proposals that the lake be named after himself. The Griffins were under-appreciated during their time in Australia before construction of the lake began. This later gesture by the Prime Minister indicated that public recognition for the quality of their Landscape Architectural design had grown during the decades since 1911 when their winning design was initially chosen.

One of the reasons for the growing appreciation of the design was that its intent has become more apparent to the general public with time. Another reason is that the nexus between the city and the bush has never been lost in Australia's national mythology. Urban development has continued at a steady pace, whilst the original network of native vegetation reserves, public open space, landforms, and watercourses has been largely preserved. There are opportunities to supplement this network by further application of *Light Garden* principles in the 21st century. Hopefully, those opportunities will come to fruition in due course.

Image 7. *An example of Light Garden principles in the design of the city of Canberra. Humanity has great capacity to plan for and live in harmony with nature and share the sunlight, food, water and energy with other living creatures. (Top left) View to the flagpole on Parliament House, Canberra, 2018 (Top right & Bottom left) Watercolour illustrations for the design of the new city of Canberra. City design and illustrations prepared by Landscape Architect Walter Burley Griffin and his wife, Marion Mahoney Griffin. (Bottom centre) Google Earth aerial photograph image of central Canberra in 2018 (Bottom right) A wild kangaroo in the open space grasslands of Canberra*

There have been calls to apply the lessons learnt in Canberra's planning to other areas that suffer from urban blight. Rather than attempting to illustrate a wide range of examples of urban renewal using the *Light Garden* principles, trends in a particular type of development, (which I have called *light garden* buildings), are now described.

The literature on the subject of urban renewal is vast and beyond the scope of this book to review. However, one vital message of the *Light Garden* model is that the quantum principle of coherence applies at all scales from the tiny to the urban to the global.

b) Urban: Trends in the construction of light garden buildings during the 20th and 21st centuries.

Where possible throughout this book, historical and contemporary examples of projects that support Life on Earth to transition to the future *post carbon* era have been described. Many of the examples are not city based, not large scale and not drawn from Western culture. A brief review of trends towards building multipurpose, city enterprises that include visions for sustainability in the 20th and 21st century now follows. The relevance of *Light Garden* principles to those visions is noted where applicable.

Since the golden age of large greenhouses, many domes, pyramids and futuristic translucent structures have continued to be developed as part of light-conscious gardens during the 20th and 21st centuries. Where is this trend headed?

In 1957, the Sydney Opera House's winning design was conceived of as a building that would be a spectacular landmark on the shores of Sydney Harbour. Unlike the more recent concept for the enormous domes at Singapore's Gardens by the Bay site, the Sydney Opera House was to be set apart from the nearby greenery in Sydney's Botanic Gardens. It sits upon an extensive concrete podium that rises from the harbour. Its arching concrete roof form drew inspiration from the white sails of boats upon the harbour. Like them, it contrasts with the dark fluidity of the waters below.

Image 8. *Sydney Opera House.*
(Above) *The translucent sky domes at Singapore's Gardens by the Bay is set amidst trees.*
(Right Top) *The concrete shell sails of the Sydney Opera House contrast with the waters of Sydney Harbour.*
(Right Bottom) *Detail of the intricately designed white tiles on the roof of the Sydney Opera House.*

Fifty five years after his winning design was selected for the construction of the Sydney Opera House, Architect Jorn Utzon was invited to review the site. In 2012 he was asked to prepare a document setting out principles to safeguard the heritage significance of the site. Some years earlier, the Sydney Opera House had been listed on the World Heritage Register.

Utzon's set of principles was to be a benchmark against which the validity of proposals for future work around the opera house could be assessed. One design principle that Utzon emphasized was that the roof of the Opera House should remain as the primary iconic feature of the site.

One way of achieving this was to maintain the contrast of the white roof sails against the broader, darker, harbour setting. During the project's design and construction phases, Jorn Utzon's team went into great detail to achieve the durable, white, reflective finish of the purpose-made tiles that line the roof shells of the Opera House. These are illustrated in Image 8. In another example illustrating Utzon's sensitivity to light as part of the design, he said that white café umbrellas on the building's podium were not appropriate. This was because they would detract from the large white roof sails of the Opera House as the main light-reflecting structure on the site.[432]

Urban forests, green walls, sustainability agendas and *Light Garden* principles were not part of the Opera House's design. Since then, design visions for public buildings have evolved and many large translucent structures have been built. For example, since its construction in 1980, the new glass pyramid erected as part of renovations to the entry of The Louvre has been a controversial landmark in the city of Paris.

Image 9. *Trends in the construction of translucent Light Garden buildings during the late 20th and early 21st centuries. (Top) The translucent Sky Domes at Gardens by the Bay in Singapore. (Bottom) The glass pyramid over an entry to The Louvre in Paris was added in 1980.*

Image 10. *Comparison between domes at Sustainability City in Dubai and Gardens by the Bay in Singapore. Biodomes are used for food production in the 2018 stage of the Sustainability City project in Dubai. Residents live in the nearby medium density dwellings which have solar panels on the roof. Solar powered electric vehicles and pedestrian spines provide access around the site.*

Like the Opera House, the glass pyramid at The Louvre was intended as a city icon. Unlike the *Gardens by the Bay* project in Singapore, this glass structure was not built to house plants. Nor was it promoted as a flagship for a new sustainability model for the city of Paris. The trees that line the boulevards of Paris are noticeably absent around it.

Singapore's Gardens by the Bay includes the Flower Dome, the Sky Dome and the Super Trees, which are numbered 1, 2 and 3 respectively in Image 10 above.

These were designed as giant glasshouses to trap and control light; generate electricity and recycle water and nutrients. They also showcase to the public a new way forward for sustainable city living.

Gardens by the Bay was designed to showcase how trees, light, people and cities may grow in the 21st century. "Super Tree" towers linked by an elevated walkway were constructed above the canopy of live tropical trees.

The Super Trees are an illustration of the concept that photonics are to the 21st century what electronics were to the 20th century. The Sky Domes and Super Trees have a translucent quality, and are illuminated by bright colours. Reminiscent of petals, trees and domes, they reach for the sky, by day and by night.

The Singapore Gardens by the Bay project is an example of a modern free - form design that aims to raise "the quality of life through enhancing the greenery and flora in the city." This project was announced as a major step forward and a role model for "transforming Singapore from a Garden City to a City in a Garden." [433]

The use of large translucent structures is a feature of Singapore's Gardens by the Bay project. In many ways, this project embodies the *Light Garden* model. It is evident that Singapore is experimenting with the *Light Garden* principle of *Consider* Context *and Environment.* The community is seeking to find new pathways to sustainable city living in the tropics. The *Light Garden* principle of *Storage and Sharing of Information* is also a well recognised dimension of this project, as it showcases a new role model for urban living in the tropics.

Gardens by the Bay is not a techno dream but is firmly focused on harmonious living amongst an urban forest of real, living trees in a tropical climate. Singapore has a strong track record of planting trees in public spaces and is seeking to expand the environmental scope and relevance of this to managing climate change. Similarly, as illustrated in Image 10 above, the Biodomes at Sustainability City in Dubai are new ventures in a world where no one knows exactly how climate change impacts will unfold. The government and citizens of Singapore and Dubai are experimenting and investing in solutions that will help them explore, adapt and develop liveable cities for the future.

c) Urban: The rise of multipurpose, large inner city sites with visions for sustainability

The biodomes at *Sustainability City* in Dubai represent a sizable transition in concept and scale from the glass pyramid at The Louvre. The trends in recent decades for domes and translucent structures have been to include more plants and more mechanisms for carbon sequestration; local recycling of nutrients and water; citizen participation in activities and less reliance on fossil fuels for energy generation, transport and other purposes.

Provision for outdoor pedestrian access and exercise has also been an important factor in the *Sustainability City* project. This is part of another trend for construction of large, multipurpose city sites with visions for sustainability. The *Light Garden* model does not have a relevant principle that specifically addresses this phenomenon, but many other aspects of this trend are consistent with

Light Garden principles. For example, visitors to sites such as Gardens by the Bay frequently comment that they like to get exercise walking around in pleasant surroundings with views, flowers and fragrance.

This comment could equally well epitomise the appeal of walking at Southbank in Brisbane, or in many other places, where the universal appeal of flowers is apparent.

Although this brief commentary was prepared based on very limited access to examples of 21st century projects in China and other non-

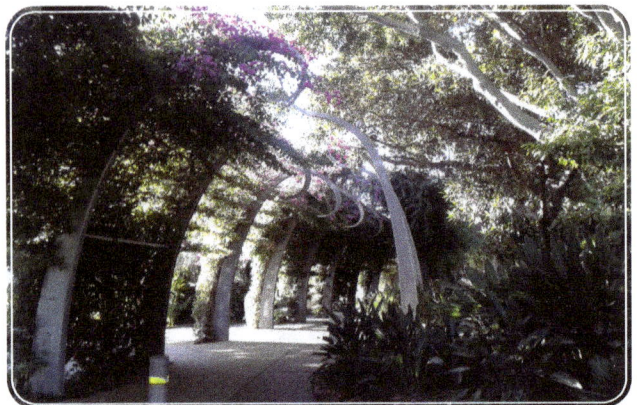

Image 11. *Southbank is an example of cities and urban fringe areas investing in public health through provision of safe, shaded and attractive outdoor spaces for walking and exercise.*

English speaking countries, the Symantec Chengdu Campus in Chengdu provides one example of trends there. This project includes an outdoor recreational walkway, as illustrated below.

The Symantec Chengdu Campus is an example of a contemporary interpretation of the term *Light Garden* in China. The Chengdu garden is set amidst a group of reflective, glass walled buildings. Describing a quite different rural Chinese setting in the last years of the 20th century, Helena Norberg-Hodge, has said:

Image 12. *The interaction between glass walls and vegetation has a unique character at this Symantec office courtyard site in the city of Chengdu, China.*

The combination of light and water at the Symantec Chengdu Campus in the city of Chengdu, China is quite different from that at the Sydney Opera House. Workers who walk through this garden report a welcome sense of retreat as they pass though this patch of vegetation. It was incorporated into the one hectare site that houses the office and research centre of the Symantec company in China.

Surrounded by glass-walled buildings which give off myriads of reflected light, this garden was designed by Landscape Architects SWA and completed in 2009. The vegetation includes conifer and bamboo species, which were chosen because they are native woodland species from the south west region of China where Chengdu is located.

As illustrated in the left hand photograph of Image 12, although this garden does not look like a traditional Chinese garden, it has some features in common with traditional designs, including the elements of water, stone, timber and plants. The stones in the garden are not natural looking stones but as depicted, they are large, white, sculpted forms that contrast with the grey gravel in which they are placed.

As illustrated in the central photograph of Image 12, the water in this garden is not in the form of a pond or stream but flows as a "water mirror": a thin sheet of water only a few centimetres deep beside the path. As illustrated in the right hand photograph of Image 12, LED lights set into the timber path through the garden are an appealing feature. The raised timber path has a practical purpose that could not be achieved by a ground level concrete path, as this garden forms part of the stormwater harvesting and dispersal system for the whole Symantec Campus.

> *"the people I encountered were able to meet most of their basic needs locally, using their own labor and ingenious small-scale technologies. In the villages, we were greeted with spontaneous laughter and humor, simple but delicious food…"* [434]

Helena then compared the changes that she had seen in China and the North American city of Detroit during the fifteen years preceding 2010. On the one hand, many people in China had moved rapidly from village life to high rise, city life. On the other side of the Pacific, the people of Detroit had moved in the opposite direction.

In Detroit, Helena found a grassroots revolution underway, as nearly two hundred community gardens had sprung up amidst the crumbling houses and abandoned factories of the inner city. These gardens provided a focal point for people to gather. There they could enjoy working cooperatively on a worthwhile project and experience a link with the wider world of nature and plants.[435]

Branching out from this example to a broader discussion of the trend towards including gardens and farms as part of creating liveable cities and landscapes in the 21st century, Helena noted:

> *"Around the world, two opposing forces are contending to define our future. On one side are those working for a new economy—one that is more equitable, decentralized, and attuned to the needs of people and nature. On the other are the forces behind corporate globalization and its consolidation of political and economic power."* [436]

Detroit is taking the decentralised approach and the city is moving with a much lower budget than Singapore to become another type of *City in a Garden*. Helena's comments also raise the question of whether allowing rapid expansion of cities is the best way forward for the 21st century. A policy

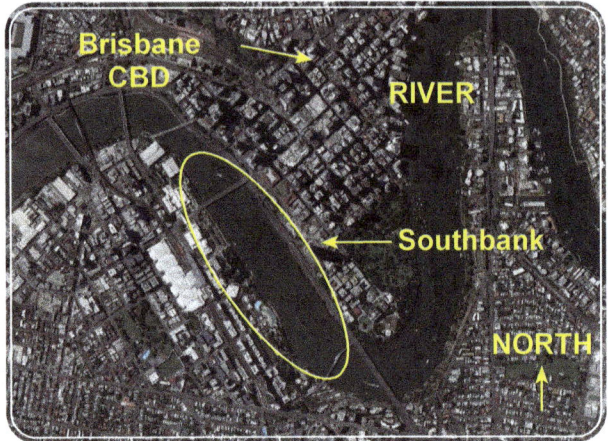

Image 13. *Southbank.*

(Left) *The central pedestran spine through the site. The Southbank site in Brisbane was never envisaged in quite the same way as the Gardens by the Bay project in Singapore but it fulfils some similar roles within the urban fabric. It is immensely popular and receives over 11 million visitors annually.*

(Right) *Aerial view of Southbank, courtesy of Google Earth 2019. The site occupies over one kilometre of inner city riverfrontage.*

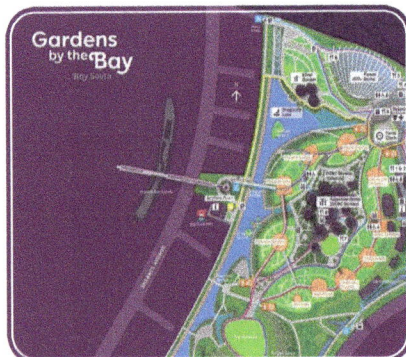

Image 14. *Map of Gardens by the Bay in Singapore*

of decentralisation, localisation and attunement of human settlements to the local ecology and culture may be more appropriate.

In recent decades global demographic trends have run counter to this. By 2014, for the first time in human history, more than half the world's population lived in urban areas. The proportion of the population living in urban areas increased more than exponentially between 1900 and 2014. In 1900, seven percent of the population lived in urban areas. Before the year 1600, the estimated percentage of people living in urban areas was less than five percent.[437] [438]

Designed to cater for an expanding, city based population, *Sustainability City* in Dubai provides an example of a purpose built, 21st century settlement that could be adapted to more decentralised styles of living. Like the city of Singapore, Dubai is investing in, exploring and testing alternative ways of building sustainable settlements for the future. Many of the principles evident at *Sustainability City* support decentralisation, localisation and attunement to the local ecology and culture. To explain why this is so in two sentences is a challenge. Firstly it is possible because *Sustainability City* effectively offers state of the art technology in an intensively managed oasis where the role of trees is valued. Secondly, the solutions developed are scalable for larger and smaller populations.

Within the context of the *Light Garden* model, decentralization entails principles for restrained human use of natural resources, allowing ecosystems the space and time they need to regenerate, and so on. As part of the *Light Garden* vision, programs to manage refugee settlements and climate change through labour intensive, global scale forest expansion, natural resource management and low ecological footprint lifestyles will be organised as part of a global network of decentralized settlements. An example of this was provided in Chapter 6 with reference to the Rohingya refugee settlement in Bangladesh.

In Chapter Five, the violence that has caused many people in Africa to flee the villages where they formerly lived with low ecological footprints was considered. This provides a sharp reminder of what can happen without responsible governance to plan for change. As an alternative to the continued expansion of megacities, safe, viable, long term options are required for people to live close to where the living systems of the planet need their stewardship and labour input for rejuvenation. There is more than enough money, knowledge and global resources for this if resources are not dissipated through activities such as greed, domination, coercion, warfare and violence. It is beyond the scope of the *Light Garden* principles to specifically recommend ways of changing this type of negative human behaviour. What the *Light Garden* vision offers to humanity is a tool to help achieve an effective and humane transition to coexistence. This tool can be utilised by individuals, groups, or on more complex projects such as Southbank in Brisbane.

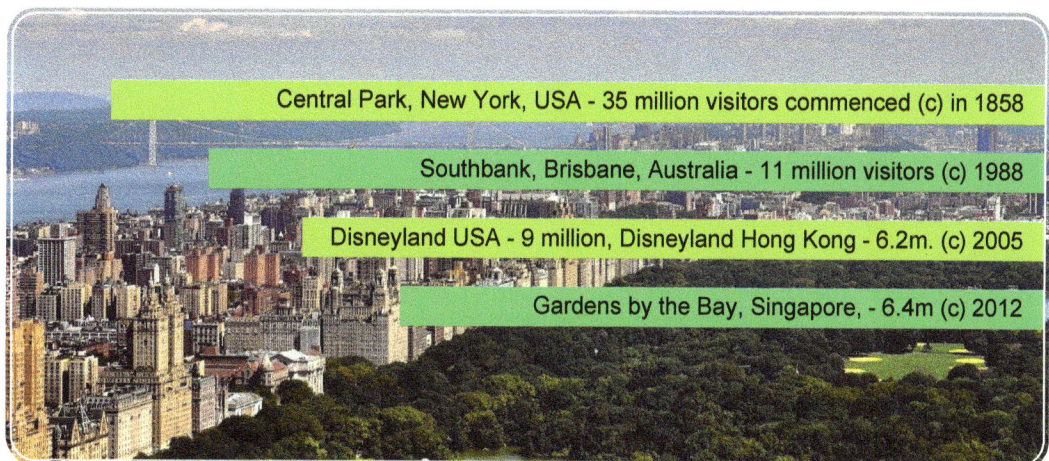

Image 15. *Visitor numbers*

Central Park, New York, USA - 35 million visitors commenced (c) in 1858

Southbank, Brisbane, Australia - 11 million visitors (c) 1988

Disneyland USA - 9 million, Disneyland Hong Kong - 6.2m. (c) 2005

Gardens by the Bay, Singapore, - 6.4m (c) 2012

Southbank

For many years Dr Catherin Bull has ably steered the vision and teamwork for Southbank in Brisbane:

"Our vision is underpinned by the precinct's core values of delivering a welcoming and inclusive place that everyone can enjoy – one that is supported by excellent design and infrastructure; uniquely Queensland; innovative, creative and bold; ecologically and financially stable; collaborative; and balances community and commercial needs." [439]

The inner city *Southbank* site has gradually evolved since 1988 when it began life as the *World Expo 88* site. Landscape Architects *Media Five*, (subsequently Desmond Brooks International), were appointed to design and oversee construction of the original Southbank project, which was completed in 1992. Since then the Southbank Corporation and several other Landscape Architects and design professionals have been involved in the progressive evolution of the site.

In contrast to Southbank, the Gardens by the Bay project in Singapore was developed as a purpose-built site. It is intended as a role model for others and was opened in 2012. The project aims to transform Singapore from a "Garden City" to a "City in a Garden." As indicated in the Image 14 map, Gardens by the Bay includes a diverse range of botanical and tourist attractions on the harbour front site.

Southbank has a different but coordinated mix of facilities that serve the needs of residents and visitors from city and regional catchments. These facilities include public entertainment venues, public transport interchanges and a riverbank promenade that is popular with joggers, walkers, ferry passengers and cyclists. There are gardens, lawns and picnic areas scattered through the site, plus a large, resort-style swimming pool fringed by palm trees. Located in this setting are public outdoor markets; heritage listed buildings and educational facilities; apartment and hotel buildings; plus approximately ninety restaurants, bars, cafes and boutiques. [440]

In comparison to the smaller numbers of visitors to Gardens by the Bay in Singapore and Southbank in Brisbane, there are 35 million visitors annually to Central Park in New York. [441] With a population of 8.6 million, New York has four times the number of residents as Brisbane. [442]

With annual visitor numbers around one to two million people, gardens such as the New York Botanic

Image 16. *Trees in Towns. Above and at left are examples of how the 50 percent tree cover is achieved on the Southbank site in Brisbane. On other sites, food trees are often incorporated into urban gardens, as the popularity of organic, home grown produce continues to grow.*

Gardens and Kew Gardens in London each receive a much lower annual visitation rate. These statistics illustrate the global trend towards public gardens such as Gardens by the Bay or Southbank being integrated with and managed as part of the larger urban landscape, rather than as separate gardens per se. This trend has been driven to a large extent by international recognition of the need to implement a sustainability agenda for cities. In conjunction with well-designed urban places where people can interact and enjoy exercising outdoors, this has been a popular and winning combination!

d) Urban: Managing trees, water and urban renewal

Moving to a more detailed scale of site planning, whether it is on the Southbank site or a derelict urban wasteland, planting trees that will harness the energy of light and use it to store carbon is part of the broader sustainability and *Light Garden* agenda. As described on page 41, although there are multiple ways of sequestering carbon, research has shown that planting millions of trees is currently the most effective means of doing this. Redesign of inhospitable urban environments and debilitating towns can proceed with the knowledge that people the world over are genetically predisposed to respond positively to the beauty of trees, as part of the normal *Light Garden* principle of *Perception and Measurement.*

For example, the multiple, synergistic benefits of the *Light Garden* experience are well illustrated in Image 16. A cyclist on his way to work in the nearby city CBD enjoys the beauty of flowers, the shade of trees and the space and time to use a safe, well-constructed cycleway. He is contributing towards a zero carbon economy through not using fossil fuels for transport. He is choosing to be part of a wave of public support to plan modest but satisfying urban lifestyles, that are within the carrying capacity of the planet's ecosystems to support them. In his spare time, he enjoys assisting to rejuvenate these ecosystems by socialising and campaigning with his friends for government subsidies to be redirected towards support for organic farming, and away from the fossil fuel industries.

Many cities today have legally enforceable codes that specify requirements for sustaining healthy trees. An example from the Brisbane City Council Landscape Code is given below. It highlights the importance of achieving minimum amounts of tree canopy cover. The Brisbane City Council

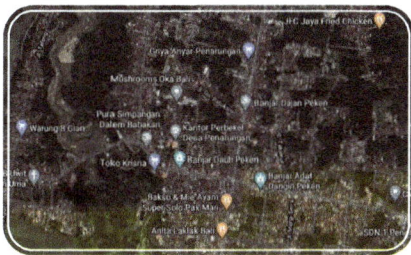

Image 17. *Urban expansion has proliferated in the Balinese rural landscape*

Landscaping Code requires that for all non-residential sites, trees be planted in agreed "landscaped areas" along the frontage of the sites.

This code demonstrates a commitment to detailed design and maintenance so that every site contributes towards quality outcomes for public open space, urban design and subtropical climate management. Here we see a correlation with several *Light Garden* principles such as work with context and environment; allow the space and time for natural systems to rejuvenate; plan for multiplier effects and act cooperatively like waves and particles.

The Landscaping Code does not just require developers to plant a certain number of trees in order to obtain planning and building approval for their projects. It goes a step further. As an example of the *Light Garden* principle *Perception and Measurement* in action, a fifty percent canopy spread of trees is required across the frontage of each site. This requirement is a means of working towards achieving the city's broader goals for climate management, stormwater management and other environmental metrics. Trees are required to be:

"large trees that achieve a canopy spread over a minimum of 50% of the frontage, within 10 years of planting." [443]

These concepts also translate into more detailed programs for towns and cities. In Brisbane, in order to reinstate an appropriate level of forest cover, 2.5 million trees were planted across 500 hectares of the city during the period 2007 to 2018. As announced by a City Councillor in 2018:

"Council is committed to ensuring our city is liveable and sustainable for many years to come, which is why we are investing $16 million this year to continue managing Brisbane's urban forest and to achieve 40% natural habitat cover by 2031." [444]

In Bali, there may not be the same landscaping codes for urban areas but for centuries the rainforests were traditionally managed as part

Image 18. *Forest regeneration*

of the essential water catchment within the Subak system of landscape management. There are approximately 1,200 subaks in Bali. Until recently, the whole landscape was managed in a way that reserved approximately one third of the total area as forest, one third as cultivated rice terraces and one third for other infrastructure such as villages, vegetable gardens, roads and water channels. This is consistent with *Light Garden* principles such as allowing ecosystems the space and time they need to rejuvenate and aiming for positive multiplier effects arising from particular actions.

As the climate becomes hotter, agricultural and forest management is becoming more complex. Debate rages about the best way for people to live in harmony with forests. For example, sadly, the excellent subak system has broken down in the 21st century due to corruption of the decision-making process. As illustrated in Image 17, urban expansion, as well as urban water use, has proliferated in Bali. Water has been diverted from villages and agriculture to tourist swimming pools and resorts. In the countryside, dry, brown, hillside rice terraces remain where once there were green, irrigated rice paddies.[445]

In seeking a solution to this dilemma, all the *Light Garden* decision making criteria are relevant, including number seven. This criterion acknowledges *nonlocality and aesthetics in human perception and measurement.* In this case, piping water all the way from the lakes in the mountains to the tourist resorts near the coast would quite foreseeably have "nonlocal" effects. The rice terraces between the lakes and the coast would be left without water and become dry and barren. Careful *measurement* of water and commitment to a comprehensive set of *Light Garden* decision making criteria could have aided planning to avoid this "nonlocal" effect.

A second foreseeable consequence of piping water in this way is that the *aesthetic perception* of tourists walking around the Balinese hillsides would not favourably match their expectations. The lush green terraces and waving palm fronds depicted in colourful travel brochures would not be there. Again the effect is "nonlocal." Word of disappointments such as this spreads quickly and the tourist dollar moves on, more rapidly than it arrived. The importance of having a comprehensive decision making process for management of water and other natural resources is highlighted here. The traditional Tri Hita Karana system of Bali should be reinstated, possibly with support from other processes such as *Light Garden* model. The *Light Garden* model might provide a bridge between cultures so that it is easier and more transparent for Balinese and non-Balinese stakeholders to communicate and develop strategies that support their long term goals.

Within the framework provided by the protection of water catchments and equitable distribution of water, care of particular trees and patches of forest requires skill and dedication all around the world. Depicted in Image 18 are the branches of the Australian native rainforest tree, *Araucaria cunninghamii,* (Hoop Pine). This tree can live to over 450 years of age.[446] As they inch their way forward, the branches claim the forest floor as their own, much as this genus has done for 200 million years. Imagine stepping outside the confines of one's own lifetime and becoming part of this ancient cycle. It is simple. By helping to keep alive an ancient forest tree species such as this, it can be done. As they grow, these trees drop small leaflets to the forest floor. In the shade of the trees, few weed species grow. Where the mulch accumulates, the rainforest regenerates, as it has been doing since the days of the dinosaurs. This is an example of *Light Garden* Principle Number Two: allow ecosystems the space and time they need to regenerate.

We can help this process by selectively removing weed species by hand and keeping the forest litter mulch intact. Working this way, not only the trees but also the soil microorganisms continue to sequester carbon, (or store it away), rather than release it to the atmosphere. Each person working in this manner is choosing to be part of the movement towards applying quantum biophysics *Light Garden* principles in the 21st century. For example, rainforest regeneration done in this way fosters quantum biophysics multiplier effects the soil and the ecosystem. The effects of this are far- reaching for millions of microorganisms.

This type of people-power weeding and rainforest regeneration also illustrates other *Light Garden* principles. For example, Principle 9 acknowledges that *Human Use* is part of an approach to natural resource management where use is carried out with intelligent, radical, restraint. It remains within the capacity of the planet's life systems for sustainable coexistence. When humbly and patiently focusing human use of resources on simple labour tasks such as removing weeds and keeping forest litter mulch and soil intact, Nature will soon step in and provide a diversity of trees and other vegetation.

Another example of how this type of forest regeneration activity is in accordance with managing the Earth's resources as a *Light Garden* is how it supports *Light Garden* Principle 1. This principle is concerned with consciously working with the energy flows of nature. In this case of the Hoop Pine, careful hand weeding allows the energy and carbon trapped within the soil and vegetation to remain there, rather than being released to the atmosphere. More invasive vegetation removal techniques such as bulldozing release much energy and carbon to the atmosphere. This process was described in more detail in Chapter 2. Many other examples in other chapters also indicate how trees are integrated into a diverse range of cultures.

Certainly in Australia and many other parts of the world, tree planting and forest regeneration must be considered in relation to fire management in the landscape. So much carbon sequestered in trees

9. Human Use
Manage human use with intelligent, radical restraint, within the capacity of the planet's life systems

Image 19. *Restraint in human use.*

can be released again to the atmosphere when a wildfire sweeps through the forest! As in the ancient practice of Feng Shui, a balance of the five elements of Fire, Water, Wood, Earth and Metal is needed. It is almost as though Feng Shui was designed with this issue in mind.

Forest management and water management go hand in hand. Water is not something that comes mindlessly out of a tap. It is managed as part of a living landscape - as part of the biosphere. Fire is managed hand in hand with the forests and the water and the land and the human settlements. That way, fire does not become a scorching dragon that consumes homes at every turn of its angry head. Human use of the landscape does not become a relentlessly growing dragon that consumes natural resources with every bite of its unrestrained head. *Light Garden* Principle Number Nine (Image 19) comes into play once again here: *Restrained Human Use* of natural resources.

12

Summary: Choose Life

We are creatures of domain.

The changing climate, society and economy of the 21st century have outpaced humanity's decision making capacity for effective action. We need to upgrade the ways in which we make decisions. The need for a new system is even more urgent now than it was last century at the end of the Second World War. At that time, the United Nations and the Bretton Woods financial systems were established. Since then, many opportunities for improving these systems and the economic and social frameworks that flowed from them have become evident. Moreover, the key questions that need addressing are different now.

How can we stabilise ecosystems and rejuvenate Life as a priority throughout the upcoming phenomena of the 21st century? The *Light Garden* model is framed to answer that question. *Light Gardens* place support for healthy living systems on planet Earth as the central motive for collective human activity. The economic and social background to why that is so was described in the first chapter.

In the 21st century, humanity's whole approach to the management of ecology, landscape, urban areas and oceans is predicated by a widely recognised need. That is to simultaneously address multiple global scale environmental, humanitarian and economic crises. These crises are interrelated, just like the quantum field, innerspring mattress analogy described in Chapter 2. Understanding the quantum field and how it underlies the growth, reproduction and repair of living organisms gives us a whole new springboard for action.

Humanity's decision making process for natural resource management and climate change can incorporate the boost that arises from understanding the quantum field and life processes. This supports what groups all around the planet are calling for: transformative change. As Geoge Monbiot noted in May 2020:

> *"A recent survey by Ipsos of 14 countries suggests that, on average, 65% of people want a green recovery. Everywhere, electorates must struggle to persuade governments to act in the interests of the people, rather than in the interests of the corporations and billionaires who fund and lobby them."* [447]

As we have seen in first two chapters of this book, by going back to basics and identifying the principles that underpin the growth of living organisms, we can then apply them to develop a new set of criteria for making decisions. These decisions are based on the laws of nature, not abstract concepts of economic growth. Making decisions on the probability that ecosystems will endure makes much sense!

Ironically, during the last century, humanity and scientists gained a far greater capacity to understand the laws of Nature at the galactic, global and sub-atomic scales. However, on a global scale, humanity is sadly remiss in applying this knowledge to maintain ecosystem and human health. That is why a large part of the first chapter of this book is devoted to discussing the underlying structural issues behind this dilemma and the opportunities for remedying it.

Fortunately, at the regional and local scales, there is a great diversity of excellent cultures that do work harmoniously with the laws of Nature. Examples of these cultures have been described throughout the book. The aim has been to deepen our understanding of cultural diversity and the different ways in which groups take inspiration from the natural resource of sunlight and use it for practical purposes. There are so many *Light Gardens* in action already! No doubt, each one is open to considering new and useful knowledge as well.

The *Light Garden* principles and associated decision making criteria are summarised in Image 1. The quantum biophysics principles that form the basis for these include Entanglement, (where particles cannot be perceived or measured separately); Non-locality, (where existence occurs in space or time without being attached to a particular place); Coherence, (where similar properties exist at the small and large scales); Probability (and uncertainty); Behaviour (as both a wave and particle); and Energy (in the quantum field).

The ten elements of the *Light Garden* model were explained in detail in Chapters 1 and 2. The manner in which these ten elements manifest in different cultures around the globe was reviewed in chapters three to ten. A summary of findings from each of those chapters is presented in Image 2 of this chapter. In the context of those findings, ten *Light Garden* decision making criteria was developed as a tool for use by all cultures, in conjunction with their traditional methods. These criteria apply at detailed, regional and global scales. Refer to Image 1 on the following page for a summary.

An example: How to save the Great Barrier Reef using Light Garden decision making criteria

For instance, if we start now to make decisions based on these criteria, we can make a huge difference to saving ecosystems such as the Great Barrier Reef. We will make jobs that defend and improve ecosystem health equivalent to the jobs that defend and improve human health through the defence forces and health care systems. All these jobs will be secure, long term, well paid, satisfying career jobs.

When the ocean chemistry, temperature and growing conditions return to what corals need, the reefs will regenerate. However, for that to happen, we need to utilise all ten of the *Light Garden* decision making criteria. The first of these is to manage human-induced energy flows to support living systems and stop carbon emissions. That is essential for the reef, so the acidity and temperature of the ocean stop increasing and corals stop being bleached and dying. A more acidic ocean means many sea creatures have problems maintaining the normal calcium in their skeletal structure. If they cannot, they become weaker and more vulnerable. In an interesting parallel, it is also the calcium component of human cells that is one of the significant vectors of disruption through which the covid virus is rendering the global human population weaker and more vulnerable.

The Ten Light Garden Decision Making Criteria

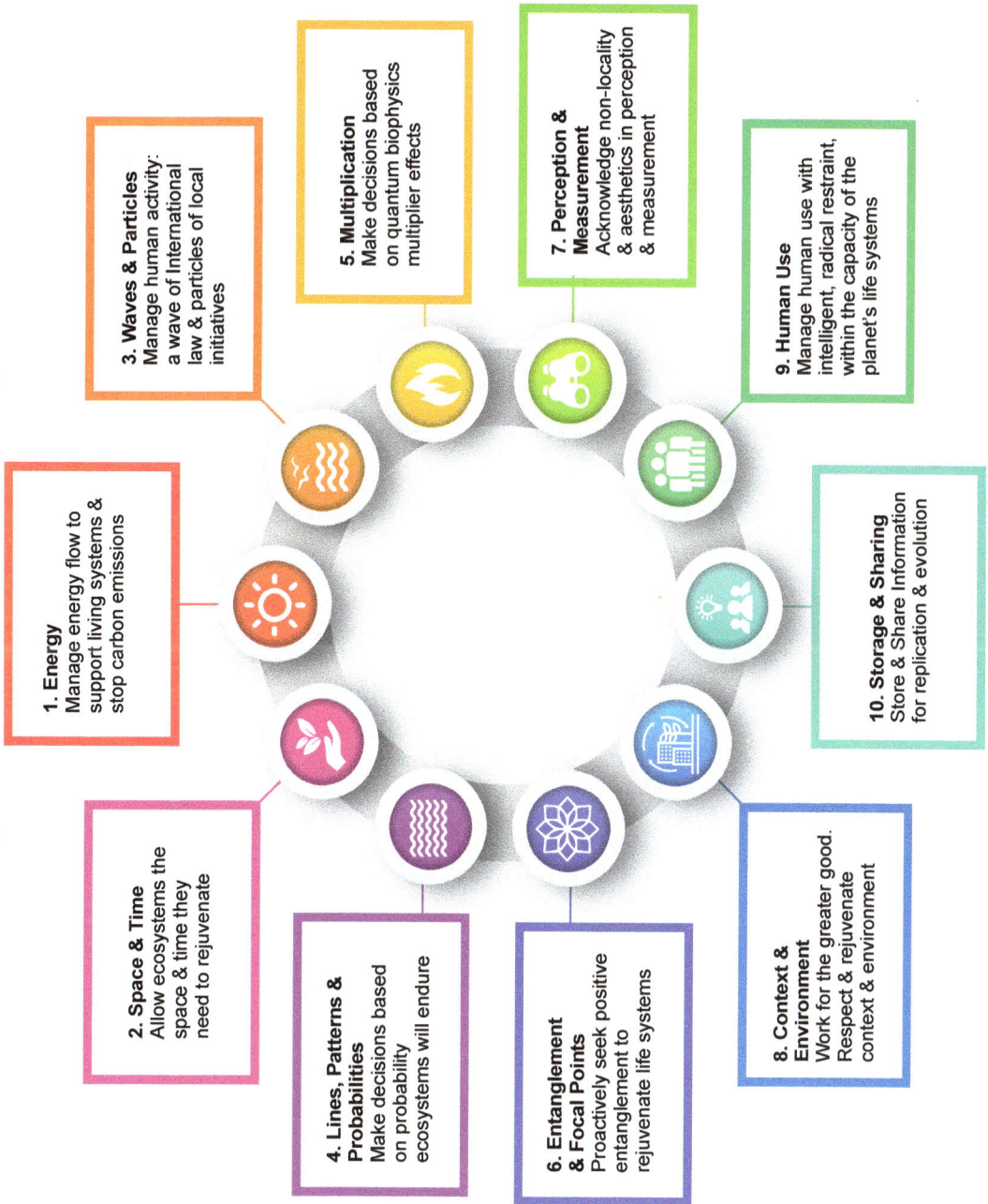

3. Waves & Particles
Manage human activity: a wave of International law & particles of local initiatives

5. Multiplication
Make decisions based on quantum biophysics multiplier effects

7. Perception & Measurement
Acknowledge non-locality & aesthetics in perception & measurement

9. Human Use
Manage human use with intelligent, radical restraint, within the capacity of the planet's life systems

1. Energy
Manage energy flow to support living systems & stop carbon emissions

10. Storage & Sharing
Store & Share Information for replication & evolution

2. Space & Time
Allow ecosystems the space & time they need to rejuvenate

4. Lines, Patterns & Probabilities
Make decisions based on probability ecosystems will endure

6. Entanglement & Focal Points
Proactively seek positive entanglement to rejuvenate life systems

8. Context & Environment
Work for the greater good. Respect & rejuvenate context & environment

Image 1. *The Ten Light Garden Decision Making Criteria*

Another of the *Light Garden* decision making criteria of relevance to ecosystems on the Great Barrier Reef, is to manage human use of resources with intelligent restraint, within the capacity of the planet's living systems. That means many things in terms of how we can save coral reefs. It includes limiting the harvesting of fish but it also means thousands of jobs applying intelligent restraint to how much of terrestrial environment that adjoins reefs is cleared or managed to maintain vegetative cover. By maintaining suitable vegetative cover on the land, the quality of water that flows onto the adjoining reefs can be managed. The goal is that the water quality supports the rejuvenation of life on the reef, rather than adding to the stresses that have caused the death of half the Great Barrier Reef during the first quarter of the 21st century.

We know how important it is to retain wetlands and forest ecosystems as the overall framework within which human uses such as agriculture, urban and industrial development occur. Water flows through this framework from the land out into the ocean reefs. Here is one challenge we face: will we be like frogs in an ever warming pot of acidic water, or can we decide to go with the flow and apply the knowledge of the modern quantum life sciences to save ourselves from the same fate as the frogs and the corals?

Throughout the world, not only are places like the Great Barrier Reef dying rapidly, there are also significant levels of underemployment as people have become disconnected from working in stewardship roles that aim to maintain the healthy functioning of such ecosystems. Artificial intelligence, robotics and the digital, financial and bio technologies are being used to restructure society and displace the former roles of people. However, they are not being used to identify useful ways to re-engage people in meaningful, much needed roles.

Re-engaging people is a significant challenge that we currently face and one that modern quantum and plasma science can help us to solve! Consistent with this approach is Gandhi's philosophy of Swaraj, which is described on pages 108 - 113. It includes the universal participation and empowerment of citizens, as well as proactive government policies for rejuvenation of society. The relevance of these concepts in 21st century society is only too apparent!

As part of an integrated approach to rejuvenating the economy, tourism, employment and environmental management, the *Light Garden* model may be used as a tool. With this approach, the Government will allocate funds to rejuvenate the economy through integrated financial planning that includes support for the nation's farmers. In the process, we will create thousands of new jobs that defend and improve ecosystem health in a carbon negative economy. This approach has already proved successful. For example, in 2020, Robyn Williams of the ABC's *The Science Show* interviewed Pia Winberg about her algae farming enterprise on the South Coast of New South Wales in Australia.[448] During that interview, he exclaimed how incredulous people would have been ten years earlier if it had been suggested that algae farming would lead the rejuvenation of a whole set of related industries in the region.

The government of the north Indian State of Sikkim has taken this type of integrated, organic planning a step further. They have legislated so that there is meaningful work for all local people. Their activities include to grow and market a wide variety of organic foods; rejuvenate the soils and forests; manage the water quality and supply; participate in local decision making forums; build homes; provide healthcare and support roles in the community, hospitality and education.

At the international scale, the *Light Garden* decision making criteria have many similarities to the recently released set of AgroEcology Principles developed by the FAO, (the Food and Agricultural Organisation of the United Nations). The FAO has a mission to ensure food security and nutrition for all people. In the past, the FAO has used techniques such as introducing new strains of genetically modified or "high yield" rice to farmers. Now their principles are more targeted to making decisions that will regenerate the ecosystems and biosphere, upon which we all depend for food security.

The benefits of the *Light Garden* model accrue when all the principles are applied in unison. This is similar to how a living creature needs to have all its life support systems operating in unison to maintain health: such as the circulation system, the nervous system and the waste disposal system. However, more than just maintaining ecosystems and human health, we need to rejuvenate them and adopt strategies for net positive action!

As discussed in the first chapter, in the 21st century we need to over-compensate for the net embodied waste, energy and resources that are consumed by human societies at large. Otherwise, our strategies for climate and natural resource management will be inadequate to address the ever burgeoning levels of resource depletion and inequitable wealth distribution. There is no doubt that current strategies leave a depleted inheritance for the countless generations of living creatures born this century. The *Light Garden* model is based on applying the positive *multiplier effects* and other phenomena that arise when quantum biophysics principles are understood and applied to the management of living systems, including human ones.

This final chapter includes a summary of how the ten components of the *Light Garden* concept can be applied to decision making in the 21st century. What is unique about the ten *Light Garden* criteria for decision-making is that they are based on quantum biophysics principles and lead to a cascade of multiple synergistic benefits. These benefits accrue in the economic, social, scientific, governance and environmental spheres. Through this cascade of benefits, humanity has some chance of managing climate change and natural resource management before disaster scenarios kick in more sharply.

The *Light Garden* model is not anthropocentric. Only one of the ten *Light Garden* principles specifically refers to *Human Use* of natural resources. All lives matter! Here we see one of the differences between the *Light Garden* model and many others. The *Light Garden* model was developed to test the hypothesis that a simplified set of quantum biophysics principles could be applied to the management of natural resources, including light. Doing so would help humanity act swiftly enough to avoid ongoing calamities that are accruing as we continue along our current path. Climate change and natural resource management in the 21st century need urgent attention now.

The current United Nations Food and Agricultural Organisation's, (FAO's), set of *Ten Elements for Agroecology* recognises this. However, it is more human-centred in its focus than the *Light Garden* model. More information about this was provided in Image 2 in Chapter 11. The FAO's charter is to ensure food security and nutrition for all people. The rationale behind how the FAO plans to deliver this human-centred charter has remarkable similarities to the *Light Garden* model. They both acknowledge the importance of ecosystem services. As noted on FAO's Agroecology website in 2020:

> *"By planning and managing diversity, agroecological approaches enhance the provision of ecosystem services, including pollination and soil health, upon which agricultural production depends."* [449]

The *Light Garden* model goes further than this concept by advocating for proactive management to *rejuvenate* self-regulating ecosystems. These ecosystems provide the essential, protective framework in which humans and all other species exist, as well as the particular *ecosystem services* to which the FAO refers. The *Light Garden* model also includes the tripartite concept that in the 21st

Summary of Light Garden Principles in Different Cultures

Chapter	What is an example from this chapter showing the application of Quantum biophysics?	How does this example fit with the concept of the Earth as a Light Garden?
3 North East Asia	The emphasis on Feng Shui and the energy of the Earth as vital design elements in these cultures is equivalent to the application of the quantum biophysics concept that energy fields influence movement, growth and patterns in life forms.	Human induced energy flows can be managed to support living systems, rather than degrade them. This is consistent with managing Light Garden Earth as a balanced, living energy system. For example, if too much heat energy is entering the garden to support stabilisation and rejuvenation of living systems, then the flow needs to be reversed to regain balance and reduce climate induced loss of life.
4 Islamic	Light is used as a symbol to help people gain an understanding of God in Islamic texts and Paradise Gardens. It predates quantum entanglement theory, where multiple objects are linked together because they have the same quantum state of energy and momentum.	The analogy here is the influence of religious beliefs upon human energy and actions. Managing the planet as a field for the making of Paradise Gardens parallels the Light Garden quantum entanglement concept that results of measurements made at a particular location can depend on the properties and influences of distant objects.
5 Africa	Quantum biophysics is concerned with a diverse range of inter- dependent life forms having access to the natural resources they need to survive. The smallholder farmers of Africa support such biodiversity through the diversity inherent in their farming practices, if human population restraint also can be practised.	Supporting traditional farming practices in Africa, (which are being ravaged due to warfare, corruption, land and water grabs by foreign entities and so on), is consistent with the aims of the Light Garden concept. This concept recognises the need for a legally enforceable, cooperative international program for equitable access to Light Garden resources.
6 India	The quantum biophysics principle of coherence between the macro and micro scales within organic matter has been applied by the people of the Indian state of Sikkim. The Government declared Sikkim as the world's first fully organic state in 2018.	This demonstrates the power of government to prioritise and achieve outcomes that support the organic life processes that are the focus of the Light Garden decision making criteria. As in Sikkim, all members of society contribute to this through giving labour and or resources to achieve the goal.

Chapter	What is an example from this chapter showing the application of Quantum biophysics?	How does this example fit with the concept of the Earth as a Light Garden?
7 Europe	After the unabashed display of power by monarchs such as Louis XIV of France, the people in many European countries rebelled and established cultures of restraint in the use of resources, with more equitable, participatory systems of governance. Restraint in human use is one of the quantum biophysics principles.	The Light Garden concept includes light energy as a valuable resource to be shared equitably and used consciously within a culture of restraint. Without this, the probability is high that systems will be unstable when changes ripple through them. With restraint in human use of resources, the quantum field can absorb ripples and remain intact.
8 South and Central America	The awareness of the role of light in the growth of crops and in the monitoring the calendar each year at sites such as Machu Pichu demonstrates application of the quantum concept that light travels in discrete packages of energy and arrives on Earth in repeatable patterns.	This is consistent with managing the Earth as a Light Garden, where decision making supports the equitable distribution of light energy and other natural resources, rather than allowing them to be controlled by small powerful groups. Millions of citizens in groups such as La Via Campesina are calling for this.
9 North America	The work of the Quakers is an example of applying quantum multiplier effects principles and of achieving outcomes that align with the quantum biophysics property of coherence between macro and micro scales.	Through working for abolition of slavery, although often relatively few in number, religious groups such as the Quakers have had a strong influence in shaping the current culture of the USA. Quakers believe the light of God exists within each person. The light of each person potentially affects the behaviour of larger groups of people.
10 South East Asia	Thousands of shrines dot the landscape and villages of Bali, so the probability of being in proximity to the influence of at least one shrine within this network is high. This is an example of application of quantum probability theory in society.	Multiple shrines throughout the land is consistent with managing the natural resources of Light Garden Earth as a network of many interconnected living systems, so the probability is high for the survival of biological and cultural diversity in any particular location within the network.

Image 2. *Summary of Light Garden principles in different cultures and locations 3 - 10.*

century, agriculture and agroecology are valued and funded under three equally important criteria. These are the provision of meaningful, place-based livelihoods; secondly, food production and thirdly the rejuvenation of living ecosystems. The global role of agriculture extends far beyond the production of human food!

This type of expansion of the role of agriculture is a significant step forward in terms of how agriculture is perceived in many 21st century communities around the globe. In some societies, such as the Amish, agriculture is highly valued and has remained so for centuries. In many other societies, where the influence of globalisation has taken hold, agriculture is not valued in this way.

Income support programs in the 21st century often assist people to live in cities, rather than move to where their work is needed and valued in rural areas. The *Light Garden* model highlights the absolute need and value of this work for human survival within a healthy biosphere and ecosystem rejuvenation in general. The changes needed to make this happen will not occur while financial resources, human services, wealth accumulation opportunities and quality of life are perceived to be more favourable in cities.

For example, in Australia, temporary work visas are granted to Pacific Island residents to work doing agricultural work because there is a lack of other willing workers in Australia. This is because agricultural work is perceived by many as insecure; vulnerable; lowly paid; uncomfortable; lacking in career prospects; lacking in city-based support services such as education and not well valued by society. Meanwhile, many Australian residents receive income support subsidies to live in towns and cities. There is a clear role for government here to redirect subsidies and funding support towards long term, well paid, highly valued, career employment for this type of rural agricultural lifestyle. Proactively informing the whole community of the value of this approach would be an early step towards success.

If we now look in the opposite direction towards the interior of living organisms, once again, we find a balance of millions of organisms that coexist. A healthy person of weight 70 kilograms will usually carry within their intestinal tract approximately 10 trillion microorganisms. These weigh a total of 200 grams.[447] The human skin does a marvellous job of keeping all those creatures within!

Just as the human skin is a wonderful membrane between the outer environment and the body's inner world, so too Earth's atmosphere provides a wonderful membrane between the incoming solar wind plasma and climatic conditions here on Earth. This was described in Chapter 2.

Review how the Light Garden model leads to better management of climate change

In the 21st century, we need the light energy from the sun to power the Earth's ecosystems, (which include human food production), but our atmosphere has changed. Too much heat and greenhouses gases are being retained to continue to support the planet's existing food chains. Species such as polar bears and corals on the Great Barrier Reef are suffering and dying. So the need for a decision has arisen: how to stabilise ecosystems and rejuvenate life in the context of climate change?

One response to the temperature rise that has occurred during the 21st century is that scientists in various countries are conducting large scale climate modelling and experiments. This work consists of trying to manipulate particles in the atmosphere and oceans to try to stop the sun's rays from overheating the Earth.

However, for example, the published results of a recent five billion pound study in the United Kingdom into climate geoengineering were so alarmingly dangerous for life on Earth that the project was abandoned. The study indicated that billions of people in various regions on the Earth would be adversely affected by droughts, floods and other effects of climate engineering.[450] There is a strong case that the billions of pounds budgeted for climate engineering should be diverted towards creating net positive local agroecology communities at the grassroots level of managing climate change. Refer to Chapter 11 for more discussion of this subject.

There have been reports in books and the mainstream media about the predicted impact of climate change since the 1960s. For example, in 1988, a NASA study modelled a climate scenario that has proved to be quite accurate thirty years later.[451] By the year 2020, the vast majority of citizens and scientists acknowledged that the evidence had become overwhelming that the concentration of carbon dioxide in the atmosphere is rising and that the effects of climate change are accelerating.

From now on, carbon *drawdown* must be an imperative principle for all human activities, as we seek to maximise sequestration of greenhouse gases in plants, in the soil and through an array of other technologies.

Although there are thousands of valuable technological advances and projects underway to address climate change, humanity's collective efforts have not yet produced results that are effective at the required scale. Action is not being achieved within the time frames necessary to avoid changes that will be catastrophic for human life on Earth. In my native country of Australia, this need for international action was cited for many years by business and the ruling political parties as a reason for *not* taking effective action at the national level. The alacrity with which this lack of action was promoted demonstrates the ongoing need for greater understanding and application of the quantum biophysics principle of coherence. The natural world includes coherence between the macro and micro scales within the quantum field – and that means appropriate action taken in one country will contribute towards the global whole. Some background data to the global context of this is provided overleaf in Image 3, then tested against the *Light Garden* model.

By the year 2018 – 19, with international business leaders solidly recognising the risks they were being held accountable for with regard to climate change,[452] the politics changed. For example, the Australian Federal Government announced: "An effective response to climate change requires collective action by all countries and sectors."[453]

As indicated by the climate data in Image 3, the level of carbon dioxide in the Earth's atmosphere reached 400 ppm in 2016. The last recorded time the level of CO_2 was that high was during the Pleistocene Epoch, which occurred from 5.3 to 2.6 million years ago. Antarctic Beech trees grew in Antarctica at that time and sea levels were 20 metres higher than in 2019. Scientists have recorded global temperatures as being 20 degrees C hotter during the Pleistocene Epoch than at the pre-industrial date of 1870.

We have a historical precedent that draws attention to the immediate need for rapid and effective action in response to climate.[454] Imagine surviving summer temperatures that are 20 degrees hotter than anything experienced before! Imagine moving from the lethargy-inducing heat of 40 degrees C to the death-inducing heat of 60 degrees C.

As summarised in Image 4, application of all but the tenth *Light Garden* principle leads to more effective action when making decisions about the management of climate change. For example, the application of the quantum biophysics concept of *probability* is relevant. It can be easily understood by the general public and politicians when it is presented as a policy to make major strategic decisions about natural resource management based on the *probability* that ecosystems and humanity will endure. *Do or die* is a reasonable catch cry.

Due to the accumulation of scientific data from multiple sources, the probability is staring us in the face that ecosystems and human settlements all around the globe will not endure for many decades under current policy.

The ringing bell of climate change warns that we are in a crisis of danger. Nevertheless, we are ringed by opportunity. In the abundant and wonderful world of nature and quantum biophysics, opportunity knocks not once but constantly. It resonates as music around the globe. Like the solar wind that flows past planet Earth, opportunity constantly bathes us in a fresh stream of life-giving energy. However, we need to choose to tap into this energy and realign our priorities. We need to realign our economic, social, governance and natural resource management systems to work together to support this goal. As Brutus said to Cassius on the eve before battle:

> *"There is a tide in the affairs of men.*
> *Which, taken at the flood, leads on to fortune;*
> *Omitted, all the voyage of their life*
> *Is bound in shallows and in miseries.*
> *On such a full sea are we now afloat"* [455]

The poor and disenfranchised of the world are afloat on this full sea. They are not alone. The rich and powerful are there too. There is no escaping this tide. It cannot be escaped by harnessing and corralling the whole of the world's natural resources. It cannot be escaped by gaining control over all the gold, all the sunlight and all the food that is produced in the whole world. Control over these resources is to no avail as climate change takes hold. As reported in July 2020:

> *"The Ministry of Water Resources said that a total of 443 rivers nationwide have been*
> *flooded, with 33 of them swelling to the highest levels ever recorded [in China]."* [456]

In many texts, opportunity is portrayed as a competitive battle, where one party is the victor at the expense of the other. Embedding this mindset into the general populace aligns with the interests of powerful forces. It implies that there is a limited bundle of resources that need to be corralled so that there will be enough to support a particular nation or group. Within the larger human population, some will suffer depredations. How this process has occurred, (or not occurred), in different cultures has been described with detailed examples throughout this book. Because it aligns with the naturally occurring phenomena of nature, the *Light Garden* model is inherently peaceful and cooperative, rather than competitive. It is not an abstract economic model constructed by the human mind for a particular purpose, such as garnering resources, power and control. As Mahatma Gandhi knew, power rests in the hands of those who find alternatives to unjust systems.

In the world of quantum biophysics, many things cannot be perceived or measured independently of each other. It is equally feasible to plan for a joyful, abundant world in which resources are fairly and equitably distributed, as it is to plan for one where scarcity, competition and death prevail.

In the first quarter of the 21st century, this situation is perceived by many groups as a problem, rather than as an opportunity. We have the knowledge of powerful physics but a problem with translating that into joy, abundance and fair management of natural resources.

Physicist Robert Oppenheimer wrestled with a similar and related dilemma in the mid-20th century. He searched outside his own culture to find words to help articulate his conscience and feelings. Oppenheimer led the team that developed the first atomic bomb. On the day the first bomb test explosion occurred in the Nevada Desert, Oppenheimer was moved to quote the words of Lord Krishna, who is recorded in the Bhagavad-Gita as saying:

> *"Now I am become Death, the destroyer of worlds."* [457]

On that day in 1945, it was not too late to turn back from further use of the atomic bomb. The world community now faces a similar opportunity to turn back from the current debilitating path of depletion of natural resources and climate devastation on planet Earth.

Speaking 75 years after Oppenheimer in July 2020, Dr William Perry, Professor (emeritus) at Stanford University and a former Secretary of Defence in the USA, described how a whole series of opportunities to turn back from the use of nuclear bombs was missed:

> *"There was an opportunity early on, firstly not to use the bomb, or to use it in a different way. There was an opportunity after we used it to stop using it and there was an opportunity to maybe bring it under international control but that opportunity and all subsequent opportunities to control the use of this weapon were simply lost by poor management, by poor decisions and somehow we drifted into the situation which we have today which we now consider normal but which was arrived at without any serious, deliberate thought."* [458]

Turning back from a course of action and taking up a new and better course of action requires energy, dedication and skill but it can be done. Fortunately, the supply of energy to planet Earth from the sun is limitless for all practical purposes. Scientists estimate that the Sun will eventually burn out four to five billion years from now. [459]

Although it may be likened to trying to turn around the '*Titanic*' in full steam across the ocean, changing the depletion of natural resources and the path of climate change on planet Earth can be done. It is not an easy task but with the will, and with the assistance of decision making criteria based on quantum biophysics principles, it can be done.

In the Hindu text, the *Bhagavad-Gita*, the concept of time is non-linear and the concept of death is woven inextricably into the cycle of life, death and rebirth. In 1947, Robert Oppenheimer was unable to reconcile the totality of his human life with the death and destruction that his team of physicists and his homeland culture of the USA had unleashed through the nuclear bomb. He died of cancer at the relatively young age of 62 years. Some years earlier, he had publicly lamented:

> *"The physicists have known sin."* [460]

Fortunately, in the 21st century, physicists have the opportunity to turn back from the death and destruction of the nuclear bomb and to work with the life-enhancing properties of the world of quantum biophysics.

Some Background Data for the Light Garden Decision Making Model about Climate Change

In order to inform how the *Light Garden* model can be applied to answering the question: How to stabilise ecosystems and rejuvenate life in the context of climage change, some basic comparitive data from multiple sources is summarized in the table below.

Note References for events (a) to (l) below are indicated in chapter references.[461]

Events and Milestones	CO2 in atmosphere (parts per million ppm)	Sea Level	Temperature change (degrees C compared to year 1870	Millions of years ago
Cretaceous period. The Gondwana land mass separating into continents of Antarctica, Africa, Australia, South American and Indian subcont't (a)	1,000	?	?	100
Mass dinosaur extinction event (b)	Not known	?	?	65
Pliocene Epoch (c) Antarctic beech trees alive in Antarctica.	400	20 metres higher	20 degrees hotter	5.3 - 2.6
Homo sapiens species emerges (current human species)	Similar to 280	?	?	0.8 - 0.3
Zero million years ago (dates below this line are in current era years)				
Pre-industrial revolution (e)	280	0 (baseline in mm)	0	1760
Mid 20th century (f)	310	90mm	?	1948
Paris Agreement signatories aim to limit global warming to 1.5 degrees C (g)	399	239mm	?	2015
Average annual global CO2 above 400 ppm (h)	400	?	?	2016
Average national summer temperature 2°C above 30 year previous long term average in Australia (i) and (j)	410	255mm	2 degrees	2019
Fossilised Antarctic beech tree Nothofagus beardmorensi leaves found in Antarctica: announcement made in the public media. (k) and (l)	410			2019

Image 3. *Data confirming climate change*

Testing the Light Garden Model: Climate Change

The *Light Garden* model can be applied to answering the question: How to stabilise ecosystems and rejuvenate life in the context of climate change? Using data from the previous page, the results of screen testing with the ten criteria are shown below.

A Scoring: How relevant is this to stabilising ecosystems and rejuvenation life? (rate 1 – 5 highest).
B Scoring: To what extent is this happening already, without the *Light Garden* model? (rate 1 - 5)

Does the Light Garden model prompt more rapid and effective action?	A	B
1. ENERGY. Yes. Managing energy flows to stop carbon emissions prioritises stabilisation of ecosystems and rejuvenation of life more rapidly and effectively than presently planned reductions.	5	2
2 SPACE and TIME. Yes. Allowing ecosystems the space and time they need to stabilise and rejuvenate entails a radical curtailment of human resource use through international restraint and equitable access to resources.	5	2
3. WAVES and PARTICLES. Yes. The model of a wave of international law and particles of local initiatives is sorely needed and greatly lacking at present, so these features would greatly assist stabilisation of life and climate.	5	1
4. LINES, PATTERNS and PROBABILITIES. Yes. Making decisions based on the probability that ecosystems will endure implies a reordering of priorities away from exploitation of resources and towards rejuvenation of living systems.	5	1
5. MULTIPLICATION. Yes. Making decisions based on quantum biophysics multiplier effects has the potential to rapidly lead to a radical reordering of priorities away from exploitation of natural resources and towards rejuvenation of living systems.	5	1
6. ENTANGLEMENT and FOCAL POINTS. Yes. Proactively seeking positive entanglement to rejuvenate life systems has the potential to rapidly improve the effectiveness of action towards rejuvenation of living systems.	5	1
7. PERCEPTION and MEASUREMENT. Acknowledging non-locality in perception and measurement implies adopting existing systems such as quadruple bottom line accounting. With this type of accounting, social, environmental, economic and governance issues are all more comprehensively factored into measurements and decision making, thus greatly increasing opportunities for taking effective climate change action.	5	1
8. CONTEXT and ENVIRONMENT. Yes. Working for the greater good, plus respecting and rejuvenating context and environment set the framework for an equitable and just society: one that is capable of taking rapid and effective climate change action.	5	1
9. HUMAN USE. Yes. Adopting intelligent, radical restraint in human use of resources, (so that it occurs within the capacity of the planet's living systems), is a goal that is sorely lacking but that could be rapidly achieved, as history has shown in cases of rationing.	5	1
10. STORAGE and SHARING. No. Information Storage and sharing may not lead to effective action. More detailed plans are required here.	2	1

Image 4. *Testing the Light Garden model for managing climate change*

Biological and Cultural Diversity

Not only the physicists and other scientists can take inspiration from this approach. As described in the first chapter of this book, movements such as the International Alliance for Localisation (IAL), are building powerful alternatives to the destructive economic and social structures that have led to the depletion of the Earth's natural resources and climate stability. This process of building better alternatives is critical because all life forms need the protective umbrella of cultural and natural biodiversity to survive. This is a simple concept with complex implications. That is why in this book, it has been explored in relation to a diverse range of global cultures, as well as our economic and social systems. In the process, a deeper understanding of the significance of the protective umbrella of diversity is revealed.

For example, in Chapter Seven, the world renowned site of Machu Pichu in South America is reviewed. It proved to be a short lived venture and one that was not consistent with many of the *Light Garden* principles. In comparison, the traditional Tri Hita Karana culture for management of the rice terraces and forests of Bali is consistent with many *Light Garden* principles and it did preserve the protective umbrella of diversity. This culture flourished for centuries. Like many other valuable cultures in the 21st century, this system is now under threat. It requires urgent redress, as water from the forests is piped to urban areas, leaving rural rice terrace hillsides dry and barren.

This concept of a protective umbrella of diversity includes the principle that preservation of particular species requires preservation of their habitat. In degraded habitats with low biodiversity, individual native species often exist under stressful conditions. Stress makes them less able to contribute to a stable, self-regulating ecosystem and more likely to carry viruses. The human body behaves similarly. As described in more detail in Chapters Two and Eleven, humans and other species living in degraded habitats lose the protective framework that comes from living in healthy, self-regulating ecosystems.

At the smaller scale of the human microbiome, (or intestinal tract), if the balance of microorganisms that live there becomes unhealthy, then the health of the whole person will also suffer.

Summary

Harking to the principles of quantum biophysics which inspired the *Light Garden* model, we recall that every part of the biological field interacts with the whole field. 99% of the universe is thought to exist in the plasma state. Here on Earth, once the plasma energy of the Sun is filtered by our atmosphere, it travels on to land on the leaves of plants. The same quantum biophysics processes occur from the global scale to the microscopic scale. How plasma is converted to matter by plants and the relevance of quantum biophysics to that process was described in Chapter Two.

Building upon the principles of quantum biophysics, a set of *Light Garden* principles was developed. The hypothesis of this book was then tested in relation to a diverse range of cultures. The hypothesis is that making decisions based on the *Light Garden* model will assist humanity to effectively manage climate change and natural resources in the 21st century.

Structured by life-supporting gravitational and magnetic fields, a diverse, healthy, self-regulating ecosystem can absorb a shock passing through it without falling apart. It can provide refuge for newborns, for ailing creatures and for struggling populations while they rejuvenate. It can provide challenge, adventure and livelihoods for young and old as they act as stewards of it. Surely these are some of the most important characteristics of healthy societies and ecosystems.

Here too, we see the transformative qualities of the *Light Garden* model in the 21st century. What role do *Light Gardens* have in the daily lives of the tens of millions of refugees, where survival on a day to day basis is the chief concern? There is a strong case for refugee settlements to be internationally funded with no interest, long term loans. Refer to the Rohingya example in Chapter 6 for more detail of this concept. The goal is to co-create *Light Garden*, self-contained, zero carbon, net positive, local economies that contribute to implementing a new vision for global climate change management.

In one of the ironies of the 21st century, we now have the technology to plan this type of low carbon economy in accordance with *Light Garden* principles. Rather than costing the international community money, such communities and economies would save money by not generating greenhouse gases and thus not exacerbating the costs of international climate change management.

The low ecological footprint of these communities will be a net positive contribution to the management of climate change and provide a visionary framework for local cultures to flourish. These communities will grow their own food; create their own employment; grow trees to establish the framework for rejuvenation of local biodiversity; collect and store their water requirements; largely self-organise; respect cultural diversity and generate their fuel energy through a suite of renewable sources such as solar power, gas from waste composting and wind power. International respect for cultural and biological diversity is a vital component for the success of these ventures, but that is another story unto itself.

Biophysics offers us a holistic understanding of how Life happens. Life grows, repairs and reproduces to produce the myriad of diverse forms in the plants, animals and microorganisms that are all around us. By applying the principles of the life sciences, a sustainable future is possible. This is a future dedicated to the young and future generations. It is a future where the lives of small farmers who save seeds and grow organic food are championed, not locked into silos. It is a future where there is role for everyone who lives in the cities and everyone who lives in the country - tending their *Light Gardens* and rejuvenating the life that is all around and within us.

Fields such as human settlements, medicine, ecology, natural resource management and climate change have lagged some one hundred years behind in implementing the principles of quantum physics and our understanding of the nature of light, as both a particle and a wave. The *Light Garden* model provides one way of quickly stepping forward to redress that lag.

Quantum biophysics has been found to be better than earlier schools of thought in explaining the behaviour of light, energy fields, waves, electromagnetism and the way in which living organisms regulate their growth, repair, reproduction and collaborative existence on planet Earth. In this context, the need for this book - and the "Earth as *Light Garden*" model that it proposes - has arisen.

One could say that life on Earth has evolved in a great diversity of forms which align with electromagnetic and gravitational fields, harvest light plasma, and transform light into living matter. Quantum biophysics places emphasis on understanding the discrete parcels of energy found in living creatures, in the atomic structure of crystals and in the plasma of light.

The behaviour of light, when described in terms of quantum principles, underpins the set of *Light Garden* principles. When acting in unison, these principles generate positive multiplication effects and operate with synchronicity across the boundaries between biophysics, plasma science and living organisms. By articulating, supporting and applying these principles at the local and at the global scales, the *Light Garden* model is inherently focused on supporting living systems, rather than on mechanised, or non-living systems. Application of the synchronistic quantum principles embedded in the *Light Garden* principles allows multiple benefits to accrue simultaneously. This gives humanity opportunities to make changes at a scale and pace that can effectively regenerate the planet's living systems.

One of the great beauties of this approach is that it is peaceful and does not require the competitive consumption of resources or warfare. It is also compatible with strategies to reduce global resource use and avoid waste.

Dr Liz Elliott notes that 50 – 70% of global resource use occurs because of waste, corruption and "needless profit." In her book *"New Way Now"*[462] Liz explains how this undue level of profit accrues mainly in the form of unnecessarily high interest charges, other rentier charges, financial transaction fees and profits, tax evasion and similar means that lead to accumulation of funds for a relatively small number of already wealthy entities.

The *Light Garden* principles provide some common ground between the individual citizen and the huge global corporations and elite entities of the global financial system. This is because the *Light Garden* principles encompass both the local and the global scales. In addition, because the *Light Garden* principles are derived from the principles of quantum biophysics that order life processes, they are inherently supportive of people living in harmony with natural resources.

Image 5. *We are creatures of domain*

Regardless of this, in the year 2020, although climate change was upon us, corona virus overtook us. Vulnerability to viruses has occurred within this context of needing to live in harmony with natural systems and it is another example of the scale of radical change needed.

In this context, we may recall that the same *Light Garden* principles apply, regardless of whether they are used at the local or the global scale. The connections between people's lives, diverse cultures and diverse ecosystems are valued in the *Light Garden* model. Life is not to be devalued, separated from place and context, then herded as fodder for profit and power. This is a destructive process.

It overlooks an immutable fact. The genes of humanity have evolved over millennia with input from the DNA of the far more numerous microorganisms that surround us in the soil, air and water of this planet, as well as from the universal field that permeates our galaxies.

We are creatures of domain. Within that domain, the DNA and bodily systems of living creatures continuously emit biophotons of light, acting in unison as part of the rare and wonderful process of Life on Earth.

Image 6.

Image References

Chapter 1: An expanded consciousness of light.

Chapter 2: Light, Biophysics and Growth.

Chapter 5: Africa

Chapter 6 India

Chapter 7: Europe

Chapter 8: South America

Chapter 9: North America

Chapter 10 South East Asia

Chapter 11: The Light Garden in the 21st Century

Chapter 12: Choose Life

Index Subject

References

1   https://www.asiaglobalonline.hku.hk/anthropoceneclimatechange/

2   https://www.twinrocks.com/legends/

3   Atwood, Lara, Ancient Religion of the Sun: The Wisdom Bringers and The Lost Civilization of the Sun, Mystical Life Publications Ltd, 2018, https://www.amazon.com/Ancient-Religion-Sun-Bringers-Civilization/dp/0992381541

4   http://www.chemistry.wustl.edu/~edudev/LabTutorials/Vision/Vision.html

5   https://www.britannica.com/science/Anthropocene-Epoch

6   Vandana Shiva, speaking on 14 March 2019 at the United Nations Office in Geneva. https://www.youtube.com/watch?v=Ek2M-obq9LE

7   Dr Tony Bartone, Australian Medical Association (AMA) President, and GP; Professor Ian Hickie AM, Co-Director, Health and Policy, The University of Sydney Central Clinical School, Brain and Mind Centre; and Professor Patrick McGorry AO, Executive Director, Orygen, Centre for Youth Mental Health, University of Melbourne, "Covid-19 impact likely to lead to increased rates of suicides and mental illness", published 7 May 2020 at

    https://ama.com.au/media/joint-statement-covid-19-impact-likely-lead-increased-rates-suicide-and-mental-illness

8   https://www.britannica.com/science/biophysics

9   https://en.wikipedia.org/wiki/Globalization

10 https://www.ethicalmarkets.com/voices-of-hope-launch-of-the-international-alliance-for-localization/

11 https://www.localfutures.org/

12 https://www.localfutures.org/

13 https://medium.com/@clayspace/knocking-down-the-fence-globalization-anti-culture-and-the-death-of-tradition-bdde7d551ec3

14 https://medium.com/@clayspace/knocking-down-the-fence-globalization-anti-culture-and-the-death-of-tradition-bdde7d551ec3

15 Seshan, Suprabha, "Locking Down Leviathon", post on 1 May 2020 at https://www.localfutures.org/locking-down-leviathan/

16 Op. Cit.

17 Elliott, Liz, "New Way Now", self-published, Australia, 2017.

18 https://www.newindianexpress.com/nation/2018/oct/14/sikkim-indias-first-fully-organic-state-bags-un-award-1885380.html

19 https://transitionnetwork.org/wp-content/uploads/2018/08/The-Essential-Guide-to-Doing-Transition-English-V1.2.pdf

20 Op. Cit.

21 Elliott, Liz, "New Way Now," self-published in hard copy, Australia, 2017. Alos available as an ebookat https://www.nationofchange.org/

22 Tyman, John, http://www.johntyman.com/africa/, photographs reproduced with written permission.

23 https://regenerationinternational.org/

24 Birkeland, Janis, Net-Positive Design and Sustainable Urban Development, Routledge, Australia, 2020, p29.

25 Op. Cit.

26 Klein, Naomi, "This Changes Everything: Capitalism vs. The Climate", (2014), p233.

27 Raworth, Kate, Doughnut Economics: How to think like a 21st Century Economist", Random House Publishers, 2018.

28 Elliott, Liz, Op. Cit.

29 https://vscoronatimes.blogspot.com/2020/08/vikalp-varta-13-north-east-network.html

30 https://vscoronatimes.blogspot.com/2020/08/vikalp-varta-13-north-east-network.html

31

32 United Nations Intergovernmental Science-Policy Platform on Bidiversity and Ecosystem Servcies, media release in 2020 on https://ipbes.net/news/Media-Release-Global-Assessment

33 Birkeland, Janis, "Net-Positive Design and Sustainable Urban Development", Routledge, Australia, 2020.

34 https://www.wordnik.com/words/meta-organism

35 https://www.smh.com.au/politics/federal/distrustful-nation-australians-lose-faith-in-politics-media-and-business-20170118-gttmpd.html

36 https://www.nationalgeographic.com/news/2016/03/160327-wilson-half-planet-conservation-climate-change-extinction-ngbooktalk/

37 Attenborough, Sir David, originally recorded in 2011 at https://www.bbc.co.uk/programmes/b018kymr. This weblink is no longer functioning but the same reference is included in Jack Stiglow's "Experiment Earth" book published by Routledge in 2015 and at https://experimentearth.files.wordpress.com/2015/02/experiment-earth-chapter-1.pdf

38 http://en.Wikipedia.org/wiki/Atomism

39 https://www.bbc.co.uk/bitesize/guides/zq8s2nb/revision/4

40 Bordoni, Bruno, PhD DO, Marelli, Fabiola, PhD, and Sacconi, Beatrice, MD, "Emission of Biophotons and Adjustable Sounds by the Fascial System: Review and Reflections for Manual Therapy", Journal of Evidence Based Integrative Medicine, 2018; 23: 2515690X17750750. Published online 2018 Feb 1.

41 Bordoni, Op. Cit.

42 Bordoni, Op. Cit.

43 Cifra M, Pospíšil P. Ultra-weak photon emission from biological samples: definition, mechanisms, properties, detection and applications. Journal of Photochemisty and Photobiology, B. 2014;139:2–10. [PubMed]

44 https://en.wikipedia.org/wiki/Biophotonics

45 Russell, Bertrand, A History of Western Philosophy, 1945, Simon & Schuster (US) and George Allen & Unwin (UK), 1945, retrieved from https://www.famousscientists.org/Democritus/ (page 22 quote by Bertrand Russell)

46 https://fractalfoundation.org/resources/what-are-fractals/

47 https://mathshistory.st-andrews.ac.uk/Biographies/Mandelbrot/

48 Richardella A, et al. Visualizing critical correlations near the metal-insulator transition in Ga1-XMnXAs. Science. 2010; 327:665–669. [PubMed] [Google Scholar]

49 Bercioux, Dario & Ainhoa Iñiguez, "Electrons with fractional dimension have been observed in an artificial Sierpiński triangle, demonstrating their quantum fractal nature." In Nature Physics volume 15, pages111–112, (2019).

50 Captur, Gabriella, Audrey L. Karperien, Alun D. Hughes, Darrel P. Francis, and James C. Moon', "The fractal heart — embracing mathematics in the cardiology clinic", Nat Rev Cardiol. 2017 Jan; 14(1): 56–64, Published online 2016 Oct 6. doi: 10.1038/nrcardio.2016.161

51 Keshe, Mehran, "The Structure of Light: Book #2, second edition", published by Stichting The Keshe Foundation, 2012.

52 Mc Kusick, Eileen, PhD, "Electric You, Electric Universe: the New Cosmology", 2013, https://www/slideshare.net/emckusick/electric-you-electric-universe

53 Hubacher J. "The phantom leaf effect: a replication, part 1," J Alternative Complement Med. 2015;21(2):83–90. [PubMed]

54 https://www.jain108.com/

55 Kafatos, Menas, C., PhD, Gaétan Chevalier, PhD, Deepak Chopra, MD, John Hubacher, MA, Subhash Kak, PhD, and Neil D. Theise, "Biofield Science: Current Physics Perspectives, " MDGlob Adv Health Med. 2015 Nov; 4(Suppl): 25–34, Published online 2015 Nov 1. doi: 10.7453/gahmj.2015.011.suppl

56 Kafatos, Op. Cit.

57 Kafatos, Op. Cit.

58 https://en.wikipedia.org/wiki/Complementarity_(physics)

59 Jain, S, et. al. "Biofield Science and Healing: An Emerging Frontier in Medicine" article in Global Advances in Health and Medicine, Nov 2015, DOI: 10.7453/gahmj.2015.106.supp, https://www.researchgate.net/publication/284216836 _Biofield_Science_and_Healing_An_Emerging_Frontier_in_Medicine/link/56ab877608aed5a0135c1e62/download

60 https://blogs.scientificamerican.com/observations/we-have-no-reason-to-believe-5g-is-safe/

61 Bawdon-Smith, Jason, "In the Dark", Major Street Publishing Pty Ltd, Australia, 201.

62 https://www.plasma-universe.com/aurora/

63 https://www.plasma-universe.com/aurora/

64 https://www.plasma-universe.com/aurora/

65 https://en.wikipedia.org/wiki/Plasma_display

66 https://www.diffen.com/difference/LED_TV_vs_Plasma_TV

67 https://www.diffen.com/difference/LCD_TV_vs_LED_TV

68 https://www.ncbi.nlm.nih.gov/pmc/articles/PMC4016545/

69 https://www.space.com/17137-how-hot-is-the-sun.html

70 https://en.wikipedia.org/wiki/Plasma_Surgical

71 https://www.engadget.com/university-of-michigan-plasma-disinfectant-224810558.html

72 ps://keshe.foundation/about/wpt

73 https://en.kfwiki.org/wiki/World_Peace_Treaty

74 https://keshe.foundation/media/attachments/2017/07/20/template_of_letter_to_world_leaders_excellency.pdf

75 https://en.wikipedia.org/wiki/Plasma_Surgical

76 https://www.stanfordchildrens.org/en/topic/default?id=what-is-plasma-160-37

77 https://www.sciencelearn.org.nz/resources/243-space-plasma, https://www.britannica.com/science/plasma-state-of-matter

78 Keshe, Mehran, "The Structure of Light: Book #2, second edition", published by Stichting The Keshe Foundation, 2012.

79 Keshe, Op. Cit.

80 https://medium.com/starts-with-a-bang/nasas-maven-discovers-how-mars-lost-its-atmosphere-f8fbfee7a92d

81 https://www.theguardian.com/environment/2019/jul/04/planting-billions-trees-best-tackle-climate-crisis-scientists-canopy-emissions

82 https://www.britannica.com/science/quantum

83 https://www.britannica.com/science/quantum

84 Kafatos, Menas, C., PhD, Gaétan Chevalier, PhD, Deepak Chopra, MD, John Hubacher, MA, Subhash Kak, PhD, and Neil D. Theise, "Biofield Science: Current Physics Perspectives, " MDGlob Adv Health Med. 2015 Nov; 4(Suppl): 25–34, Published online 2015 Nov 1. doi: 10.7453/gahmj.2015.011.suppl

85 Crofts, Anthony R., "Disentangling entanglement," Department of Biochemistry and Center for Biophysics and Computational Biology University of Illinois at Urbana-Champaign, Urbana IL 61801 http://www.life.illinois.edu/crofts/papers/Epistemology_and_QM.pdf

86 Akihiro Ogawa, Professor of Japanese Studies at the Asia Institute, University of Melbourne, quoted in "Japan's awakening protest movement", by Akihiro Ogawa   http://asaa.asn.au/japans-awakening-protest-movement/

87 Mr Okuda quoted in "Japan's awakening protest movement", by Akihiro Ogawa, at http://asaa.asn.au/japans-awakening-protest-movement/senanglement

88 Reynolds, Garr, "Presentation Zen", Pearson Education (US), 2011.

89 Curran, Giorel, "21st Century Dissent: Anarchism, Anti-Globalization and Environmentalism", Springer, 200, Page 54 in https://www.researchgate.net/publication/29462125_21st_Century_Dissent_Anarchism_Anti-Globalization_and_Environmentalism

90 https://en.wikipedia.org/wiki/Coherence_(physics)

91 https://en.wikiquote.org/wiki/Greta_Thunberg

92 https://en.wikipedia.org/wiki/Guo_Pu

93 http://www.fengshuigate.com/zangshu.html

94 Loc. Cit.

95 Li, Min (2009). 30 Talks on the Chinese Classical Gardens. China Architecture & Building Press. Quoted in: https://stud.epsilon.slu.se/3875/7/pang at Swedish University of Agricultural Sciences Faculty of Landscape Planning, Horticulture and Agricultural Science Department of Landscape Architecture "Ideas and Tradition behind Chinese and Western Landscape Design - similarities and differences". Junying Pang quotes Min Li in a Degree project in landscape planning, 30 hp Masterprogramme Urban Landscape Dynamics Independent project at the LTJ Faculty, SLU Alnarp 2012

96 Li, Min, Loc. Cit.

97 Pang, Junying, in a Degree project in landscape planning, 30 hp Masterprogramme Urban Landscape Dynamics Independent project at the LTJ Faculty, SLU Alnarp 2012.

98 Bagua compiled by Anne Whittingham from multiple non copyright references about Feng Shui.

99 http://www.fengshuigate.com/zangshu.html

100 https://en.wikipedia.org/wiki/West_Lake

101 Loc. Cit.

102 https://en.wikipedia.org/wiki/West_Lake

103 http://whc.unesco.org/en/list/1

104 Loc. Cit.

105 Loc. Cit.

106 Loc. Cit.

107 https://en.Wikipedia.org/wiki/Central_Park

108 Report on the public use of Central Park assets.centralparknyc.org/pdfs/. . . /3.002 Report+on+the+Public+Use+of+Central+Park.pdf

109 https://en.wikipedia.org/wiki/Doseon

110 https://www.360cities.net/image/ongnyucheon-stream-changdeokgung-palace

111 https://en.Wikipedia.org/wiki/Changdeokgung

112 Loc. Cit.

113 Loc. Cit.

114 Loc. Cit.

115 http://www.cdg.go.kr/eng/cms_for_cdg/contents/c3_1.jsp

116 http://www.cdg.go.kr/eng/cms_for_cdg/contents/c3_1.jsp

117 https://www.theguardian. com/cities/2017/may/19/seoul-skygarden-south-korea-london- garden-bridge

118 Hong, Sun-Kee, Song, In-Ju and Wu, Jianguo, "Fengshui theory in urban landscape planning", in Urban Ecosystems, Vol 10, 2006/08/08, p221 – 237, DO - 10.1007/s11252-006-3263-2

119 Loc. Cit.

120 Loc. Cit.

121 Loc. Cit.

122 Reynolds, Garr "Presentation Zen" Pearson Education, USA 2020.

123 Yanagi, Soetsu, The Unknown Craftsman: A Japanese Insight Into Beauty, adapted by Bernard Leach, Kodansha International, Tokyo, New York, London, revised edition 1989.

124 attributed to The Buddha (Gautama Buddha), "Muryoju-kyo" ("Sutra of Eternal Life), cited in "The Unknown Craftsman: a Japanese Insight into Beauty", by Yanagi, Soetsu, adapted by Leach, B., Kodansha International, Tokyo, New York, London. revised edition 1989, p130.

125 Op. Cit.

126 Multiple sources are available for this, for example https://worldloveflowers.com/events/taj- mahal-garden

127 The Qu'ran 24: 35-6 which was translated to English by Andul Haleem at http://www.vam.ac.uk/content/articles/festivals-of-light-islam

128 Multiple sources, for example http://www.vam.ac.uk/content/articles/festivals-of-light- islam

129 The Qu'ran 24: 35-6 which was translated to English by Andul Haleem at http://www.vam.ac.uk/content/articles//festivals-of-light-islam

130 https://www.dw.com/en/the-worlds-top-10-must-see-landmarks/a-19266178

131 https://whc.unesco.org/en/list

132 http://www.bbc.co.uk/religion/religions/islam/practices/salat.shtml

133 https://en.wikipedia.org/wiki/Shalimar_Bagh,_Sringar

134 https://en.wikipedia.org/wiki/Nur_(Islam)

135 https://whc.unesco.org/en/list

136 https://www.thecitizen.in/index.php/en/NewsDetail/index/3/12243/Gar-firdaus-bar-rue-zamin-ast-hami-asto-hamin-asto-hamin-ast

137 https://whc.unesco.org/en/list

138 https://en.wikipedia.org/wiki/Shalimar_Bagh,_Sringar

139 https://en.wikipedia.org/wiki/Shalimar_Bagh,_Sringar

140 http://en.Wikipedia.org/wiki/Gardens of Versailles

141 https://en.wikipedia.org/wiki/God_in_Islam

142 http://en.Wikipedia.org/wiki/Gardens of Versailles

143 Nash, Elizabeth, at https://www.independent.co.uk/news/world/europe/after-650- years-the-wisdom-of-the-alhambra-is-revealed-1658050.html

144 Loc. Cit.

145 https://www.piccavey.com/granada-alhambra-walls/

146 Loc. Cit.

147 http://www.traveller.com.au/burhanpur

148 Loc. Cit

149 https://worldloveflowers.com/events/taj-mahal-garden/

150 Loc. Cit.

151 https://whc.unesco.org/en/list

152 https://www.tripadvisor.com.au/Attraction_Review-g187441-d191078-Reviews- The_Alhambra-Granada_Province_of_Granada_Andalucia.html

153 https://whc.unesco.org/en/list/

154 https://www.thecitizen.in/index.php/en/NewsDetail/index/3/12243/Gar-firdaus-bar-rue-zamin-ast-hami-asto-hamin-asto-hamin-ast

155 https://en.Wikipedia.org/wiki/Tetracty special-about-the-golden-ratio

156 Abdullahi, Yahya and Emb, Mohamed Rashid Bin, "Evolution of Islamic geometric patterns" in Frontiers of Architectural Research, Vol 2, Issue 2, June 2013, Pages 243-25 and at https://www.sciencedirect.com/science/article/pii/S2095263513000216

157 https://www.nationalgeographic.com/environment/urban-expeditions/green-buildings/dubai-ecological-footprint-sustainable-urban-city/

158 Leet, Leonora, "The Secret Doctrine of the Kabbalah: Recovering the Key to Hebraic Sacred Science", Inner Traditions, Rochester, Vermont, 1999, page 85.

159 Petruccioli Attilio, "Rethinking the Islamic Garden", page 3, Islamic Environmental Design Research Centre, Como, Italy, and at https://environment.yale.edu/publication- series/documents/downloads/0-9/103petruccioli.pdf

160 Loc. Cit.

161 Emirates News Agency, 2018. http://wam.ae/en/details/1395302665808

162 Emirates News Agency, 2018. http://wam.ae/en/details/1395302665808

163 Emirates News Agency, 2018. http://wam.ae/en/details/1395302665808

164 https://diamond-developers.ae/

165 https://www.nationalgeographic.com/environment/urban-expeditions/green- buildings/dubai-ecological-footprint-sustainable-urban-city

166 https://www.insydo.com/things-to-do/sustainable-city-dubai-sustainable-development/

167 Damluji, Salma Samar, The Architecture of the U.A.E., Reading, UK, 2006.

168 Loc. Cit.

169 http://www.treehugger.com/"www.treehugger.com /corporate-responsibility/fracking-water-rights-how-foreign-interests-are- cleaning-out-africa.html

170 Attributed to Milton Friedman at https://quoteinvestigator.com/2014/12/09/sand/   This quote is commonly attributed to Tacitus, who lived in period approximately 55 AD – 120 AD. He was a Roman Lawyer and Senator. Historical controversy exists around the source of this quote.

171 https://phys.org/news/2018-03-sahara-expandingworld-largest-grew-percent.html Deserts are typically defined as land where the annual rainfall is less than four inches.

172 Tyman, J. at http://www.johntyman. com/africa/37 - 45.html

173 Tyman, J. at http://www.johntyman. com/africa/37 - 45.html

174 Tyman, J. at http://www.johntyman. com/africa

175 John Tyman at http://www.johntyman.com/africa/07.html

176 Dr John Tyman, at http://www.johntyman.com/africa/07.html

177 https://www.one.org/us/2015/05/13/how-the-artisan-sector-can-change-the-world/

178 http://www.unhcr.org/en-au/africa.html

179 http://www.johntyman.com/africa/37.html

180 Connie Nielsen, http://www.nation.co.ke/lifestyle/buzz/Connie-Nielsen-in-"www.nation.co.ke/lifestyle/buzz/Connie-Nielsen-in-Kenya/441235-2413788-2ygxty/index.html

181 http://www.johntyman.com/africa

182 https://iglus.org/nairobi-another-urban-city-in-prepration/

183 http://www.kibera.org.uk/facts-info"www.kibera.org.uk/facts-info

184 http://www.treehugger.com/corporate-responsibility/fracking-water-rights-how- "http://www.treehugger.com/corporate-responsibility/fracking-water-rights-how-"w.treehugger.com/corporate-responsibility/fracking-water-rights-how- foreign-interests-are-cleaning-out-africa.html

185 https://en.wikipedia.org/wiki/Ancient_Egyptian_creation_myths

186 https://www.sanbi.org/wp-content/uploads/2018/03/sanbi-annual-report-2016-17.pdf

187 http://www.bsienvis.nic.in/Database/Status_of_Plant_Diversity_in_India_17566.aspx#

188 http://www.fao.org/docrep/008/ae537e/ae537e0k.htm

189 https://www.venerabletrees.org/how-many-tree-species/

190 https://www.bbc.com/news/science-environment-39492977

191 https://www.dovepress.com/plant-wealth-of-a-sacred-grove-mallur-gutta-telangana- state-india-peer-reviewed-fulltext-article-IJGM

192 https://en.wikipedia.org/wiki/Rigveda

193 https://www.researchgate.net/publication/289032426_The_Shankaracharya_sacred_grove_of_Srinagar_ Kashmir_India. An alternative reference for the work of Kewal Kumar is also available but this requires a payment in order to read it: https://www.sciencedirect.com/science/article/abs/pii/S0378874115003463

194 dovepress.com/plant-wealth-of-a-sacred-grove-mallur-gutta-telangana-state-india-peer-reviewed-fulltext-article-IJGM

195 https://www.dovepress.com/plant-wealth-of-a-sacred-grove-mallur-gutta-telangana- state-india-peer-reviewed-fulltext-article-IJGM

196 Loc. Cit.

197 https://en.wikipedia.org/wiki/Sacred_groves_of_India

198 https://www.daytranslations.com/blog/2016/09/closer-look-indias-languages-7831/

199 https://www.thehindu.com/sci-tech/energy-and-environment/sacred-groves-of-the- western-ghats-are-shrinking-and-their-deities-being-sanskritised/article22260107.ece

200 Loc. Cit.

201 Loc. Cit.

202 https://en.wikipedia.org/wiki/Vasudhaiva_Kutumbakam

203 http://www.navdanya.org/site

204 Loc. Cit.

205 Loc. Cit.

206 https://www.mkgandhi.org/articles/swaraj.htm

207 Loc. Cit.

208 Loc. Cit.

209 Loc. Cit.

210 http://www.navdanya.org/site

211 Loc. Cit.

212 http://www.navdanya.org/site

213 https://www.localfutures.org/programs/the-economics-of-happiness/film/

214 https://www.ancient.eu/Surya/

215 https://www.onthegotours.com/au/India/guide-to-diwali-festival-of-lights

216 http://www.navdanya.org/site

217 Loc. Cit.

218 Loc. Cit.

219 Loc. Cit.

220 Loc. Cit.

221 https://www.localfutures.org/planet-local-bhaskar-save-the-gandhi-of-natural-farming/

222 https://sites.google.com/site/cdgggg000002/professional-relationships. Author's note: Reference 222 is a quote that can be found in several locations. The origin of the quote was not attributed in any sources that can be found, so it appears to have passed into general use.

223 https://en.Wikipedia.org/wiki/Yarlung Tsangpo

224 https://en.Wikipedia.org/wiki/Donyi-Polo

225 Mibang, Tamo and Chaudhuri, Sarit Kumar, "Understanding Tribal Religion". Mittal Publications, 2004. Sourced via https://en.Wikipedia.org/wiki/Donyi-Polo

226 Chaudhuri, Sarit Kumar, "The Institutionalization of Tribal Religion. Recasting the Donyi- Polo Movement in Arunachal Pradesh", in: Asian Ethnology, Volume 72, Number 2, Nanzan Institute for Religion and Culture • 2013, 259–277. Sourced from https://en.wikipedia.org/wiki/Donyi-Polo

227 https://whc.unesco.org/en/tentativelists/5893/

228 https://whc.unesco.org/en/tentativelists/5893/

229 https://whc.unesco.org/en/tentativelists/5893/

230 https://www.researchgate.net/publication/242335346_A_sustainable_mountain_paddy- fish_farming_of_the_ Apatani_tribes_of_Arunachal_Pradesh_India

231 https://www.researchgate.net/publication/242335346_A_sustainable_mountain_paddy- fish_farming_of_the_ Apatani_tribes_of_Arunachal_Pradesh_India

232 https://whc.unesco.org/en/tentativelists/5893/ and https://www.soas.ac.uk/tribaltransitions/publications/ file32488.pdf

233 Loc. Cit.

234 https://whc.unesco.org/en/tentativelists/5893

235 https://www.thehindu.com/news/national/other-states/causes-behind-brahmaputra- turning-black-could-be-natural-union-minister/article21258572.ece

236 https://timesofindia.indiatimes.com/city/ itanagar/arunachal-river-turns-black-officials- blame-china/article

237 https://commons.wikimedia.org.wiki/File:Taj_site_plan.png

238 https://en.wikipedia.org/wiki/List_of_World_Heritage_Sites_in_Indiahttps://worldlovefl owers.com/events/taj-mahal-garden/

239 https://en.wikipedia.org/wiki/india

240 https://www.worldheritagesite.org/connection/Chahar+Bagh+Gardens

241 https://worldloveflowers.com/events/taj-mahal-garden/.

242 https://en.wikipedia.org/wiki/Vastu_shastra

243 https://www.vaastu-shastra.com/taj-mahal-vastu-analysis.html

244 Op. Cit.

245 Kumar, Rewar, (PhD in Vastua Shatra), at http://www.rewakumar.org/meet-rewa- kumar.html

246 Translation by Sri Aurobindo from Book 1, Canto 1 (The symbol Dawn), in the Rigveda, quoted in http://savitri.in/1/1/1 . The Rigveda is a collection of over 1,000 Hindu Sanskrit hymns. It is the oldest of the Hindu Scriptures, dating back some thousands of years.

247 https://en.wikipedia.org/wiki/Vastu_shastra

248 https://pdfs.semanticscholar.org/e19d/d80dae67f0f6bdeb32a4a96eac1cef53d342.pdf

249 https://www.nativeplanet.com/travel-guide/all-about-kandariya-mahadev-temple-in- khajuraho-002269.html

250 https://www.onthegotours.com/au/India/guide-to-Diwali-festival-of-lights

251 Loc, Cit.

252 https://asiasociety.org/education/origins-buddhism https://www.tripadvisor.com.au/Attraction Review-g424922-d3619160-Reviews-Bodhi Tree-Bodh Gaya Gaya District Bihar.html

253 ttps://indiaheritagesites.wordpress.com/tag/Bodhi-tree/

254 Lewandowski, Susan J. (1977). "Changing Form and Function in the Ceremonial and the Colonial Port City in India: An Historical Analysis of Madurai and Madras". Modern Asian Studies. Cambridge University Press. 11 (02): 183–212.

255 King, Anthony D. (2005), Buildings and Society: Essays on the Social Development of the Built Environment, Taylor & Francis e-library, ISBN 0-203-48075-9.

256 Bayly, Susan Saints, Goddesses and Kings: Muslims and Christians in South Indian Society, 1700-1900, 1989. Cambridge University Press. pp. 29–30. ISBN 978-0-521-89103-5.

257 G. Venkatramana (2013). Alayam - The Hindu temple - An epitome of Hindu Culture. Mylapore, Chennai: Sri Ramakrishna Math. p. 31. ISBN 978-81-7823-542-4. quoted in https://www.revolvy.com/page/Meenakshi-Temple

258 Bayly, Op. Cit.

259 Harman, Op. Cit.

260 Harman, Op. Cit.

261 Harman, Op. Cit.

262 https://en.Wikipedia.org/wiki/Meenakshi Temple

263 https://en.Wikipedia.org/wiki/Meenakshi Temple

264 Google Earth imagery copyright 2018

265 https://en.wikipedia.org/wiki/List_of_ cities_by_population_density

266 https://www.statista.com/statistics/ 279040/population-density-in-urban-areas-of-china- by-region/

267 United Nations High Commission for Refugees

268 https://news.mongabay.com/2018/01/bangladeshi-forests-stripped-bare-as-rohingya- refugees-battle-to-survive/

269 United Nations High Commission for Refugees

270 httpswww.rfa.orgenglishnewsmyanmarrefugees-jobs-11012017172548.htm

271 Loc. Cit.

272 http://worldpopulationreview.com/countries/india-population/

273 https://en.wikipedia.org/wiki/Islam_in_Bangladesh

274 IOM, the UN Migration Agency at https://www.iom.int/news/micro-gardening-scheme- help-feed-rohingya-refugees-bangladeshi-local-communities

275 United Nations Food and Agricultural Organisation's website: Floating Garden Agricultural Practices in Bangladesh, Ministry of Agriculture, People's Republic of Bangladesh. http://www.fao.org/3/a-bp777e.pdf

276 Loc. Cit.

277 United Nations Food and Agricultural Organisation's website: Floating Garden Agricultural Practices in Bangladesh, Ministry of Agriculture, People's Republic of Bangladesh. http://www.fao.org/3/a-bp777e.pdf

278 https://www.downtoearth.org.in/news/agriculture/resort-to-heritage-53346

279 http://thelivinggreens.com

280 Loc. Cit.

281 Loc. Cit.

282 http://www.navdanya.org/site

283 Loc. Cit.

284 https://wttc.org/Portals/0/Documents/Reports/2020/Global%20Economic%20Impact%20Trends%202020.pdf?ver=2021-02-25-183118-360

285 https://ec.Europa.eu/Eurostat/statistics

286 https://newhavenurbanism.org/european-urbanism/paris/

287 https://en.wikipedia.org/wiki/Eiffel Tower

288 https://newhavenurbanism.org/european-urbanism/paris/

289 https://nca2009.globalchange.gov/corn-and-soybean-temperature-response/index.html

290 http://www.massey.ac.nz/massey/learning/colleges.colleye-of-sciences/clinics-and- services/weeds-database/wild-turnip.cfm

291 https://www.statista.com/statistics/264065/global-production-of-vegetables-by-type/

292 The weight of tulip bulb production was estimated by the author using the following technique. Statistics about how many tons of tulip bulbs are produced annually at the global scale are not available. The average weight of a tulip bulb varies with size, quality, variety, etc and no average statistics are available. Tulip sales on www. Amazon.com, indicate that a packet of 10 tulip bulbs produced in China weighed 7 ounces. So the weight of one tulip bulb from that packet was less than one ounce. I assumed a weight of one ounce per bulb for the calculation that was used for the weight of annual tulip bulb production in tons.

293 https://www.hollandtradeandinvest.com/key-sectors/horticulture-and-starting- materials/horticulture-facts-and-figures

294 https://earthobservatory.nasa.gov/images/92148/flower-power-in-the-Netherlands

295 https://psmag.com/news/stories-you-might-have-missed-this-week-October-19-2018

296 https://www.abc.net.au/news/2018-10-11/can-we-quit-coal-in-time/10361552

297 https://www.ipcc.ch/2018/10/08/summary-for-policymakers-of-ipcc-special-report- on-global-warming-of-1-5c-approved-by-governments/

298 http://www.bom.gov.au/climate/updates/articles/a032.shtml

299 https://en.Wikipedia.org/wiki/Keukenhof

300 https://en.wikipedia.org/wiki/Daylight

301 http://www.rsc.org/learn- chemistry/content/filerepository/CMP/00/001/068/Rate%20of%20photosynthesis%20limi ting%20factors.pdf

302 https://www.abc.net.au/news/2017-03-02/short-sightedness-epidemic-as-people- spend-less-time-outside/8318882

303 https://en.wikipedia.org/wiki/Vaux-le-Vicomte

304 Op. cit.

305 viacampesina.org/en/struggles-la-via-campesina-agrarian-reform-defense-life-land- territories/

306 https://en.wikipedia.org/wiki/Via_Campesina

307 https://www.theguardian.com/environment/2014/may/28/farmland-food-security-small- farmers

308 www.fao.org/fileadmin/templates/nr/sustainability pathways/docs/Coping with food and agriculture challenge Smallholders agenda Final.pdf

309 https://www.bbc.com/news/world-latin-america-49460022

310 https://en.wikipedia.org/wiki/Illuminance

311 https://en.wikipedia.org/wiki/Illuminance

312 https://www.smithsonianmag.com/history/farming-like-the-incas-70263217/

313 https://www.smithsonianmag.com/history/farming-like-the-incas-70263217/

314 https://www.ancient.eu/article/792/inca-food--agriculture/

315 ttp: en.wikipedia.org wiki Brazilian cuisine

316 http://www.fao.org/3/a-i5251e.pdf

317 https://en.wikipedia.org/wiki/Solidaridad

318 ttps://whc.unesco.org/en/list/274

319 http://www.bbc.com/ travel/story/20120606-

320 https://www.poetsofmodernity.xyz/POMBR/Spanish/Neruda.htm

321 https://en.wikipedia.org wiki Land of poets

322 https://ourworld.unu.edu/en/growing-corporate-hold-on-farmland-risky-for- world-food-security

323 Loc. Cit.

324 https://sustainablefoodtrust.org/articles/viva-la-produccion-urban-farming-in- cuba/

325 324 https://www.smithsonianmag.com/smart-news/chile-adding-11-million-acres- national-parks-180962592/

326 Loc. Cit.

327 https://medium.com/thrive-global/how-amish-people-live-a-sustainable-life- 53e977d24abd http://hournalofethnicfoods.net/"http://hournalofethnicfoods.net (an open access article under CC BY-NC-ND license)

328 http://www.bbc.co.uk/religion/religions/christianity/subdivisions/amish_1.shtml

329 Park, S., Hongu, N., Daily, J.W. III, Native American foods: History, culture, and influence on modern diets, in Journal of Ethnic Foods,

330 http://factsheets.okstate.edu/documents/fapc-194-growing-north- american-indigenous-corn/

331 http://www.brainyquote.com/"www.brainyquote.com/ authors/geronimo

332 Geronimo's Story of his Life, taken down and edited by S. M Barrett, published by Duffield & Company , New York, 2006 and available at https://www.ibiblio.org/ebooks/Geronimo/GerStory.htm

333 Op. Cit.

334 https://healingdelight.bandcamp.com/track/infinite-sun-kuate

335 https://www.businessinsider.com.au/money-secrets-of-the-amish-2013- 4?r=US&IR=T#they-eat-like-kings-but-they-grow-most-of-their-meals-themselves-12

336 Op. Cit.

337 http://amishamerica.com/what-happens-at-an-amish-barn-raising

338 FLO to Mariana Griswold Van Rensselaer (draft, [June 1893]), Frederick Law Olmsted Papers, Library of Congress, quoted in an article by Charles Beveridge in the Twenty-fifth Anniversary issue of Nineteenth Century, the journal of the Victorian Society in America (Volume 20, no. 2, pp. 32–37, Fall 2000) and included at http://www.olmsted.org/the- olmsted-legacy/olmsted-theory-and-design-principles/olmsted-his-essential-theory

339 Op. Cit.

340 legacy/olmsted-theory-and-design- principles/olmsted-his-essential-theory

341 http://www.thoughtco.com/frank-lloyd-wright-famous-american-architect-177881

342 https://theculturetrip.com/north-America/articles/the-10-oldest-national-parks-in- the-world

343 http://www.yosemite.ca.us/library/origin_of_word_yosemite.html

344 Op. Cit.

345 https://en.Wikipedia.org/wiki/Mariposa Battalion and https://www.myyosemitepark.com/park/miners-and-mariposa-battalion

346 Op. Cit.

347 Op. Cit.

348 Op. Cit.

349 youtube – top ten most beautiful gardens in the world

350 Whysall, S., https://vancouversun.com/news/staff-blogs/2011-04-04/beautiful-Butchart- gardens

351 http://www.olmsted.org/the-olmsted-legacy/olmsted-theory-and-design- principles/olmsted-his-essental-theory

352 https://en.wikipedia.org/wiki/Longwood_Gardens

353 Rockwell, J., Heslop, T., 'Cultures of Beauty', https://longwoodgardens.org/blog/2015-11- 16/cultures-beauty

354 https://www.energy.gov/articles/history-air-conditioning

355 https://www.bloomberg.com/ opinion/articles/2018-01-02/the-first-atrium-wasn-t-in-a- hyatt

356 https://en.wikipedia.org/wiki/Patrick_ Blanc#/media/File:Patrick_Blanc_Puteaux.jpg

357 https://www.thoughtco.com/frank-lloyd-wright-famous-american-architect-177881

358 Essay by Charles Wiebe on https://www.khanacademy.org/humanities/ap-art- history/later-europe-and-americas/modernity-ap/a/frank-lloyd-wright-fallingwater

359 https://mcharg.upenn.edu/book

References

360 https://www.localfutures.org/a-tale-of-two-cities-Beijing-and-detroit

361 https://jvtf.org/

362 www.okofarms.com/

363 https://en.m.Wikipedia.org/wiki/Decline of Detroit

364 https://theculturetrip.com/north-America/usa/Michigan/articles/the-best-urban-farms- in-Detroit-mi/

365 https://www.usda.gov/media/blog/2018/08/14/vertical-farming-future

366 https://www.usda.gov/media/blog/2018/08/14/vertical-farming-future

367 https://www.space.com/38723-astronauts-farm-plants-install-garden-instrument.html

368 http://www.qivc.org/faq-qivc

369 http://www.pewresearch.org/fact-tank/2015/12/23/americans-are-in-the-middle-of-the- pack-globally-when-it-comes-to-importance-of-religion/

370 https://www.gfk.com/insights/press-release/us-ranks-among-top-three-countries-for- gardening-every-day-or-most-days/

371 https://en.wikipedia.org/wiki/Arcosanti

372 v Estoque, R. C., Ooba, M., Avitabile, V., Hijioka, Y., DasGupta, Rajarshi, Togawa, T., Murayama, Y., [Nature Communications 10, Article number: 1829 (2019). "The future of Southeast Asia's forests."

373 Estoque et al, Op. Cit.

374 Wilson, E. O., "Half Earth: Our Planet's Fight for Life," Liveright; 1 edition (April 4, 2017).

375 Estoque et al, Op. Cit.

376 Teske, Sven (Ed.) "Achieving the Paris Climate Agreement Goals, Global and Regional 100% Renewable Energy Scenarios with Non-energy GHG Pathways for +1.5°C and +2°C", Open Access publishing, 2019 at https://www.springer.com/gp/book/9783030058425, and quoted on https://www.leonardodicaprio.org/the-global-deal-for-nature

377 Estoque et al, Op. Cit.

378 Estoque et al, Op. Cit.

379 Schneider, A., C M Mertes1, A J Tatem2,3, B Tan4, D Sulla-Menashe5, S J Graves6, N N Patel7, J A Horton1, A E Gaughan8, J T Rollo,, "New urban landscape in East–Southeast Asia, 2000– 2010", Published 3 March 2015 • © 2015 IOP Publishing Ltd, Environmental Research Letters, Volume 10, Number 3

380 Estoque et al, Op. Cit.

381 Estoque et al, Op. Cit.

382 Estoque et al, Op. Cit.

383 Estoque et al, Op. Cit.

384 Estoque et al, Op. Cit.

385 Zeng, Z., Estes, L., Ziegler, A. D., Chen, A., Searchinger, T., Hua, F., … & Wood, E. F. (2018).Highland cropland expansion and forest loss in Southeast Asia in the twenty-first century. Nature Geoscience, https://news.mongabay .com/2018/07/southeast-asian-deforestation-more-extensive-than- thought-study-finds/

386 Salamanca, A.M., A. Nugroho, M. Osbeck, S. Bharwani and N. Dwisasanti (2015), "Managing a living cultural landscape: Bali's subaks and the UNESCO World Heritage Site", SEI Project Report 2015-05. https://www.sei.org/publications/managing-a-living- cultural-landscape-balis-subaks-and-the- unesco-world-heritage-site/

387 Keys, Patrick & Wang-Erlandsson, Lan & Gordon, Line & Galaz, Victor & Ebbesson, Jonas. (2017). Approaching moisture recycling governance. Global Environmental Change. 45. 15-23. 10.1016/j.gloenvcha.2017.04.007.

388 Loc. Cit.

389 https://www.usc.edu.au/research-and-innovation/forests-for-the-future/tropical-forests- and-people-research-centre/research-projects/16-years-of-research-in-the-philippines-and- still-going#background , Enhancing Livelihoods through Forest and Landscape Restoration, 2017-2022, funded through Australian Centre for International Agricultural Research (ACIAR), Leaders: Professor John Herbohn and Dr Nestor Gregorio

390 Tyman J. www.johntyman.com bali

391 https://whc.unesco.org/en/list/1194 Cultural Landscape of Bali Province: the Subak System as a Manifestation of the Tri Hita Karana Philosophy

392 https://whc.unesco.org/en/list/1194 Cultural Landscape of Bali Province: the Subak System as a Manifestation of the Tri Hita Karana Philosophy   https://whc.unesco.org/en/list/1194

393 Loc. Cit.

394 http://lokhabalitours.com/Lempuyang-temple-sacred-bali-tour

395 https://whc.unesco.org/en/list/1194 Cultural Landscape of Bali Province: the Subak System as a Manifestation of the Tri Hita Karana Philosophy

396 http://lokhabalitours.com/Lempuyang-temple-sacred-bali-tour

397 Loc. Cit.

398 Cole, S., Browne, M. Tourism and Water Inequity in Bali: A Social-Ecological Systems Analysis. Hum Ecol 43, 439–450 (2015). https://doi.org/10.1007/s10745-015-9739-z , accessed via https://link.springer.com/article/10.1007/s10745-015-9739-z?shared-article-renderer

399 Tyman J. www.johntyman.com bali

400 Tyman J. www.johntyman.com bali

401 Loc. Cit.

402 Loc. Cit.

403 Loc. Cit.

404 Loc. Cit

405 Winberg, Pia, when interviewed by Robyn Williams, on The Science Show program Microalgae the basis for fuels, food and more. Radio National, Australian Broadcasting Corporations, 1 Aug 2020. https://www.abc.net.au/radionational/programs/scienceshow/the-seaweed-revolution-and-keeping-brains-fit/12512404

406 FAO (2018) The state of world fisheries and aquaculture 2018 - meeting the sustainable development goals. Food and Agriculture Organisation of United Nations, Rome. Quoted by Campbell, I., Kambey, C.S.B., Mateo, J.P. et al. Biosecurity policy and legislation for the global seaweed aquaculture industry. J Appl Phycol (2019). https://doi.org/10.1007/s10811-019-02010-5, and accessed via https://link.springer.com/article/10.1007/s10811-019-02010-5, 23rd International Seaweed Symposium

407 Winberg, Loc. Cit.

408 https://ensia.com/features/kelp-carbon-sequestration-climate-mitigation/

409 Winberg, Loc. Cit.

410 Pages, Mark, Loc. Cit.

411 Hanish, Quentin, Associate Professor at the University of Wollongong, speaking about his recent report "Dark Fleets, Ghost Ships & Flying Squid" when interviewed by Phillip Adams, on the Late Night Live program, Radio National, Australian Broadcasting Corporation, 27 July, 2020. https://www.abc.net.au/radionational/programs/latenightlive/dark-fleets,-ghost-ships-&-flying-squids/12496912

412 Hanish, Loc. Cit.

413 Hanish, Loc. Cit.

414 https://ceres.org.au/what-do-wetlands-and-seaweed-farming-have-in-common/

415 https://climatechange.lta.org/case-study/marin-sequestration/

416 https://animals.howstuffworks.com/mammals/methane-cow.htm

417 https://animals.howstuffworks.com/mammals/methane-cow.htm

418 https://geneticliteracyproject.org/2017/03/02/1-percent-us-farmland-certified-organic-arent-american-farmers-making-switch/

419 https://climatechange.lta.org/case-study/marin-sequestration/

420 https://climatechange.lta.org/case-study/marin-sequestration/

421 https://climatechange.lta.org/case-study/marin-sequestration/

422 https://ellenbrown.com/2019/07/25/the-cheapest-way-to-save-the-planet-grows-like-a-weed/

423 www.polyfacefarms.com

424 https://meta.eeb.org/2020/03/24/agroecology-farming-for-a-better-future/

425 https://meta.eeb.org/2020/03/24/agroecology-farming-for-a-better-future/

426 https://meta.eeb.org/2020/03/24/agroecology-farming-for-a-better-future/

427 http://www.fao.org/agroecology/home/en/

428 Noble, Andrew, former director of the Water, Land and Ecosystems project in Sri Lanka, quoted in the article by Jeff Smith, " Sunshine: India's new cash crop", at https://wle.cgiar.org/sunshine-india-new-cash-crop

429 https://theconversation.com/why-is-everyone-talking-about-natural-sequence-farming-106232

430 Elbein, Saul, April 26, 2019 at https://www.nationalgeographic.com/environment/2019/04/how-to-regrow-forest-right-way-minimize-fire-water-use/ This story was produced in partnership with the Pulitzer Center on Crisis Reporting and the National Geographic Society.

431 Burley Griffin, Walter, quoted in the New York Times, 2 June 1912, and sourced from https://en.wikipedia.org/wiki/Walter_Burley_Griffin

432 Utzon, Jorn, "Sydney Opera House Design Principles", 2002.

433 https://en.wikipedia.org/wiki/Gardens_by_the_Bay

434 https://www.localfutures.org/a-tale-of-two-cities-beijing-and-detroit/

435 Loc. Cit.

436 Loc. Cit.

437 https://en.wikipedia.org/wiki/World_population

438 https://www.un.org/development/desa/en/news/population/2018-revision-of-world- urbanization-prospects.html

439 Bull, Catherin, Southbank Corporation, annual report 2016 – 17.

440 Loc. Cit.

441 https://en.Wikipedia.org/wiki/Central Park

442 worldpopulationreview.com/us-cities/new-York-city-population

443 https://www.Brisbane.qld.gov.au/sites/dehault/files/ chapte5_landscaping code.pdf

444 https://www.ausleisure.com.au/news/brisbane-city-council-plants-2.5-million-trees-since-200

445 https://www.aljazeera.com/news/2019/12/bali-tropical-indonesian-island-running-water-191201051219231.html

446 https://www.anbg.gov.au/gnp/interns-2014/araucaria-cunninghamii.html

447 https://www.monbiot.com/2020/05/01/bail-out-the-planet/

448 https://www.abc.net.au/radionational/programs/scienceshow/abc-illawarra.jpg/12511916

449 http://www.fao.org/agroecology/home/en/

450 https://www.bbc.com/news/science-environment-30197085

451 https://www.theguardian.com/environment/climate-consensus-97-per- cent/2018/jun/25/30-years-later-deniers-are-still-lying-about-hansens-amazing-global-warming- prediction

452 https://aicd.companydirectors.com.au/advocacy/governance-leadership-centre/external- environment/climate-change-a-growing-focus-for-boards

453 Australian Government Department of Foreign Affairs and Trade, "Climate Change" website post downloaded April 2019

454 https:// www.theguardian.com/science/2019/apr/03/south-pole-tree-fossils-indicate- impact-of-climate-change

455 Shakespeare, William, Julius Caesar, Act-IV, Scene-III, Lines 218-224.

456 Nectar, Gan (14 July 2020). "China has just contained the coronavirus. Now it's battling some of the worst floods in decades". CNN. Retrieved 16 July 2020. This source was obtained via the publicly available website https://en.wikipedia.org/wiki/2020_China_floods.

457 https://en.wikipedia.org/wiki/J._Robert_Oppenheimer

458 Perry, Dr William J. (professor emeritus at Stanford University), interviewed in 2020 at https://www.abc.net.au/radionational/programs/latenightlive/75-years-of-nuclear-threat,-and-a-new-nuclear-arms-race/12440080

459 https://www.sciencealert.com/watch-here-s-how-the-sun-will-eventually-destroy-earth

460 https://en.wikipedia.org/wiki/J._Robert_Oppenheimer

461 References in table (a) to (l)
(a) https://thebulletin.org/2019/04/a-climate-change-preview-trees-at-the-south-pole-60- feet-of-sea-level-rise/
(b) https://www.nationalgeographic.com/science/prehistoric-world/mass-extinction/
(c) https://www.sciencealert.com/there-were-trees-at-the-south-pole-the-last-time-there- was-this-much-co2-in-the-air
(d) https://en.m.Wikipedia.org/wiki/Timeline of human
(e) https://climate.nasa.gov/vital-signs/sea-level/
(f) https://www.climate.gov/news-features/featured-images/2015-state-climate-carbon- dioxide
(g) https://www.climate.gov/news-features/featured-images/2015-state-climate- carbondioxide
(h) https://www.climate.gov/news-features/featured-images/2015-state-climate-carbon- dioxide
(i) https://climate.nasa.gov/vital-signs/sea-level/
(j) http://www.bom.gov.au/climate/updates/articles/a032.shtml
(k) https://abcmedia.akamaized.net/rn/podcast/2019/04/ssw_20190413_1229.mp3
(l) https:// www.theguardian.com/science/2019/apr/03/south-pole-tree-fossils-indicate- impact-of-climate-change

462 Elliott, Liz, Op. Cit.

www.ingramcontent.com/pod-product-compliance
Lightning Source LLC
Chambersburg PA
CBHW051616030426
42334CB00030B/3219